Developments in Aquaculture and Fisheries Science, 2

FARMING THE CUPPED OYSTERS OF THE GENUS CRASSOSTREA

Developments in Aquaculture and Fisheries Science, 2

FARMING THE CUPPED OYSTERS OF THE GENUS CRASSOSTREA

A Multidisciplinary Treatise

P. KORRINGA
Rijksinstituut voor Visserijonderzoek, IJmuiden (The Netherlands)

ELSEVIER SCIENTIFIC PUBLISHING COMPANY
Amsterdam – Oxford – New York 1976

ELSEVIER SCIENTIFIC PUBLISHING COMPANY
335 Jan van Galenstraat
P.O. Box 211, Amsterdam, The Netherlands

Distributors for the United States and Canada:

ELSEVIER/NORTH–HOLLAND INC.
52, Vanderbilt Avenue
New York, N.Y. 10017

ISBN 0444-41333-2

Printed in The Netherlands

PREFACE

This second volume dealing with the farming of marine organisms is exclusively about the cultivation of the 'cupped' oysters belonging to the genus *Crassostrea.* Cultivation of these oysters, popularly known as the Pacific oyster, the American Atlantic oyster, the Australian rock oyster, etc., produces a noteworthy tonnage of oyster meat at a price similar to that of low grade mammalian meat. They contribute materially to the provision of animal protein, within reach of the purse of the average consumer. Like mussels, dealt with in the previous volume, cupped oysters are predominantly served in main dishes. They are stewed or fried and sometimes used in soups or chowders. They are a basic food, rich in animal protein, rather than a luxury item. Still, some Australian and American Atlantic oysters — always those of top quality — are served raw on the half shell as an appetizer.

The so-called Portuguese oyster, *Crassostrea angulata,* is a special case. This oyster is so closely related to the Pacific oyster that some authors claim them to be identical. There have been rich beds of this oyster in Europe for centuries; in Portugal, for instance, in the Sado and Tagus Estuaries. Peculiarly enough, this natural resource was hardly exploited in Portugal at all, before French oyster farmers arrived in the second half of the nineteenth century to buy the oysters for use in their newly established parks when they were short of flat oysters. This eventually led to large-scale farming of the Portuguese oyster in France, ousting the flat oyster. The Portuguese oysters are not eaten as the main course, but are eaten as an appetizer from the half shell. They are cheaper than the flat oyster, and are therefore available to a wider range of the population. The numbers produced by far exceed the numbers of flat oysters grown in France, and thousands of farmers make a living in this field.

To enable comparison of the various cases described in this volume with each other and with the cultivation of mussels, flat oysters and fishes, I decided to adopt the standard division of each chapter used in the volume dealing with mussel farming. Again, the section dealing with the work involved in farming forms the body of the descriptions:

- A. Background
  - A.1. General principles
  - A.2. Biology of the species
  - A.3. Geographical situation
  - A.4. Hydrographic pattern
  - A.5. Legal aspects

B. Sequence of operations
B.1.—B.x.: This section forms the body of the descriptions giving step-by-step all the required operations from the early developmental phases to marketing, with indications of techniques used and labour involved.

C. Farming risks
C.1. Hydrographic conditions
C.2. Predators
C.3. Parasites and diseases
C.4. Competitors

D. Economic aspects
D.1. Rents
D.2. Inventory items
D.3. Expendable items
D.4. Purchase of seed stock
D.5. Labour
D.6. Sales

E. Governmental assistance

F. General impression

G. Bibliography

In some cases notes on technical details are to be found at the end of the relevant chapter.

Again, the economic aspects are as far as possible expressed in quantitative units, such as the number of the personnel, gallons of diesel oil used per year, tonnages sold, etc., rather than in monetary units. This will prevent the material presented in this book from becoming outdated. However, some information is expressed in monetary units, always in the currency of the country concerned. A conversion table may serve to compare the local units with the American dollar. The figures given are for November 6th, 1972, a date representing more or less the middle of the period in which the data were collected, but to show how rapidly these figures can change, a list of more recent conversion rates (viz. March 20th, 1975) is added.

Name	Abbreviation	Conversion rate 6-11-1972	Conversion rate 3-3-1975
Australian Dollar	$(A)	0.482	0.73
American Dollar	US $	1.00	1.00
French Franc	Ffr	5.035	4.15
Japanese Yen	Y	301.00	285.23

P. Korringa

ACKNOWLEDGEMENTS

First of all I feel impelled to express my gratitude to the leaders of the enterprises chosen as examples for enabling me to make use of their experience of many years' standing and for giving me such a detailed insight to the work and economics involved in farming oysters. Without this kind and frank cooperation it would not have been possible to make such a useful comparison of the various systems used in different parts of the world. Their names, noted in the heading of each chapter, need not be repeated here.

Further, I wish to thank my colleagues who so kindly provided me with additional scientific information on the local hydrographic and biological conditions. Mr D.R. Rochford of CSIRO and Mr D.D. Francois, Director of Fisheries, assisted me by providing hydrographic and biological information for oyster farming in Australia. For oyster farming in Long Island Sound, I am greatly indebted to Mr C.L. MacKenzie, at the time working as shellfish biologist at the Biological Laboratory at Milford, for his detailed information, the elaborate replies to my questionnaire, and for allowing me to use his photos of the oyster industry. For oyster farming in Louisiana, I received valuable assistance from the staff of the Louisiana Wildlife and Fisheries Commission in New Orleans, in particular from Mr Lyle S. St Amant, both in conversation and writing. Valuable assistance in collecting information on the farming of Portuguese oysters in the Charente Maritime was given by my old friend Pierre Vaurigaud at Chaillevette, and Dr J. le Dantec was kind enough to supplement my scientific information on oyster farming in the Bay of Arcachon.

Mr P. Businger, Agricultural Attaché of the Royal Netherlands Embassy in Tokyo, kindly visited a representative oyster farm in the Hiroshima area and collected detailed information for me on that enterprise. He was assisted by his secretary Mr Y. Akimoto and they provided pictures to elucidate this case. I would like to cordially thank them both for their valuable assistance.

I wish to thank my friend and colleague Clyde Sayce, Director of the Willapa Shellfish Laboratory of the Washington Department of Fisheries, for his help with oyster farming in Willapa Bay.

Again, I wish to express my gratitude to my diligent secretary Miss E.L. van der Weele for all the work she has done in preparing this volume, and to Mr B.L. Verboom for the excellent job he has made of the charts and drawings elucidating the various chapters.

P.K.

CONTENTS

INTRODUCTION

The "cupped" oysters of the genus *Crassostrea* contribute a far greater tonnage of animal protein to the market than the flat oysters of the genus *Ostrea*. However, this was not the case in time gone by. Farming techniques, such as offering suitable collectors and growing oysters in hanging culture in well-sheltered and duly protected sites, date back to the time of the ancient Romans. The crucial period of switching from exploitation of natural beds to true cultivation, occurred in the middle of the nineteenth century in Europe, following the research of Professor Coste at the request of Emperor Napoleon III; they worked exclusively with the flat oyster *Ostrea edulis*.

Farming of "cupped" oysters of the genus *Crassostrea* started in Japan as far back as the 17th century and it was only much later that farming techniques for these oysters were applied in America, Australia and Europe. Initially, they exploited natural beds of cupped oysters where those were found in the areas occupied by European settlers. Such beds had been used as a source of food by the original population since time immemorial, but the white settlers began exploitation on truly commercial scale which in some areas led to virtual destruction of the natural resources, sometimes accelerated by outbreaks of parasites or competitors. Chesapeake Bay, once famous for its tremendous oyster production, was soon only a shadow of its former glory, and the prolific beds in Australia virtually collapsed after a vigorous attack of *Polydora*.

Where man switched from fishing to farming, the former productivity could not only be regained but was often surpassed. Oyster larvae settle, by preference, in sites with low current velocities and in these conditions they later run short of food, since the tidal currents transport the planktonic food to these sedentary creatures. Oyster larvae can settle over quite a wide vertical range, but under natural conditions survival is often best in the intertidal zone where starfish, boring sponges and several other enemies can do little harm. Oyster farming involves not only offering of a suitable substratum (collectors), to improve settling conditions, but also transferring the young oysters to sites where they will not settle naturally, but where growth and fattening are much better, due to a good food supply. It is also necessary for the oyster farmer to protect his crop against a variety of predators, parasites and competitors. Since the ecological range of cupped oysters is definitely greater than that of the flat oysters of the genus *Ostrea*, the farmers often achieve excellent results by transferring their young oysters to areas of reduced salinity where many predators and parasites cannot reach them. In a highly evolved farming system, the following phases can be distinguished:

"captage" (seed production), "élevage" (the growing phase) and "affinage" (fattening to marketable quality). It is not surprising that these terms are in French; oyster farming is probably most advanced in France. Initially for flat oysters, the techniques were later applied to Portuguese oysters in the Charente Maritime with its famous "claires" producing choice quality for the epicuristic consumer.

Cupped oysters differ in many respects from flat oysters. They are intrinsically creatures adapted to subtropical conditions, since they require high water temperatures during the larval and settling stages. This does not mean, however, that they are very sensitive to low water temperatures for they can often stand freezing weather much better than flat oysters, and the larvae will even survive when placed in a refrigerator, but normal larval development is only possible at water temperatures well above the 20°C level.

It so happens that the water is usually richer in planktonic food at higher latitudes than in truly subtropical or tropical areas. Therefore, one finds the best grounds for growth and fattening in regions where spatfall is often deficient. Where the oyster farmers experience difficulties in producing enough seed each year they either import seed stock from warmer areas (e.g. directly from Japan in the farming of Pacific oysters in the State of Washington) or take their collectors to various special sites, often far from their headquarters in an effort to ensure a regular supply of seed. Special sites such as Dabob Bay (Washington) and Pendrell Sound (British Columbia) can be mentioned, where very special hydrographical conditions provide the required high water temperatures.

The further south, the better the larval development and settling, but the greater the impact of predators, parasites and competitors, and hence survival is poorer. This is the main reason why oyster farming rarely thrived in truly tropical waters, despite the excellent conditions for reproduction, since farming requires an investment in money and labour which makes it unacceptable to have too high and too irregular a mortality rate.

Not all countries where cupped oysters are grown are mentioned in this volume. Oysters are grown on quite a large scale in the Philippines and in Korea using methods comparable to those developed in Japan. In India *Crassostrea gryphoides* are grown on some scale, and in South Africa in Knysna Lagoon, *Crassostrea margaritacea* are farmed. This is a young industry in the development of which the author of this book has played a part.

Chapter 1

FARMING THE ROCK OYSTER (*CRASSOSTREA COMMERCIALIS*) IN AUSTRALIA

Example
J. Padmos and A. Salm, oyster farmers, Tanilba Bay, New South Wales 2301.
Period of observation: 1970—1971.

A. BACKGROUND

A.1. General principles

Oyster farming, Australian style, is a semi-culture in which both larval development and the provision of food for both juvenile and adult oysters is fully left to nature. The Government leases suitable areas to oyster farmers, where the latter can either put out collectors in an attempt to catch oyster seed, or place their young oysters for further growth and fattening. As is usual with oysters, the best sites for settlement do not always provide optimal conditions for growth and fattening. The collectors, made of locally available wood, are placed on racks so that they do not touch the sea bottom, and the young oysters are transferred to areas where good growth and fattening are to be expected on the basis of the natural food supply, also fastened on racks and kept off the bottom. When the oysters have reached marketable size, they are harvested by removing them from the collectors on which they have settled. They are graded into two categories, and sold wholesale, in the shell, at the fish markets in the cities.

A.2. Biology of the species

The oyster farmed in Australia is the rock oyster, *Crassostrea commercialis* (Iredale and Roughley). It is a bivalve mollusc of which the two shells are of different shapes; one shell is, more or less, saucer-shaped, the other is almost flat. The latter is covered with horny scales of prismatic structure, whereas the former is devoid of a prismatic layer. The two shells are connected by an elastic ligament and by one large, centrally-placed, adductor muscle. In the larval state the oyster can swim with the aid of a ciliated velum, and can later also crawl onto solid objects, velum retracted, with the aid of an extensible foot. For settling the larvae seek a suitable substratum, which should be both hard and clean, exploring it carefully and attaching themselves with a kind of glue produced by the byssus gland. The left (cupped)

valve is then cemented to the substratum chosen. Velum and foot soon disappear and the gills, which are used to filter sea water in search of food and oxygen, develop rapidly. Once settled, the oyster cannot move from the spot and has to content itself with the quality of the water passing by and the food contained therein. Oysters of the genus *Crassostrea*, provided with a promyal chamber, have a greater filtering capacity than the flat oysters of the genus *Ostrea*, and can moreover stand low salinities and silt-laden water considerably better than the latter. Oysters are obligatory herbivores, feeding on small and very small varieties of phytoplankton. Large spiny diatoms are not ingested and some of the smaller and smoother diatoms may pass through the intestinal tract alive.

Settling of oyster larvae is favoured in water having prolonged spells of very low current velocities. Thus areas where there are eddies are the best sites for profuse settling. Unfortunately, oysters later realize that it is the tidal currents which bring the food. Too low current velocities and too limited a degree of flushing, therefore, hamper their growth and fattening. Many oysters settle in the intertidal zone. When the water retreats on the ebb tide, they close their valves hermetically and can survive thus for many hours in succession, even in hot sunshine. They switch over from the usual aerobic life to an anaerobic metabolism during their sojourn in the air. Such hours are, of course, lost so far as feeding and growth are concerned. The calcareous material required for construction of the shell is taken from the sea water in dissolved ionic form. The digested food is partly used for various metabolic activities, including shell movements and water filtration, and partly for growth and fattening. Fattening means storage of glycogen in special cells of the connective tissue. The glycogen is mobilized again when the oyster is preparing itself for spawning; the gonads then become rapidly filled with eggs or sperm. Oysters of the *Crassostrea* type require quite a high water temperature for spawning (over 20° C), and eject eggs and sperm freely and often simultaneously in the ambient sea water. There fertilization takes place and, within a remarkably short time, the eggs develop into veliger larvae, equipped with two tiny shells and a ciliated velum enabling them to swim. They are, of course, at the mercy of the tidal currents as far as their horizontal displacement goes. Only comparatively few manage to find a suitable piece of substratum on which to settle after a period of pelagic life.

A.3. Geographical situation

The company under consideration carries out its oyster farming operations in Port Stephens, a bay on the east coast of New South Wales, Australia situated 20 miles northeast of the city of Newcastle, and some 130 miles north-northeast of Sydney. The exact geographical position is 32° 42′ S and 151° 58′ to 152° 11′ E. The bay penetrates deep inland and consists of two sections divided by ‘The Narrows’ at Soldiers Point, where the bay is less

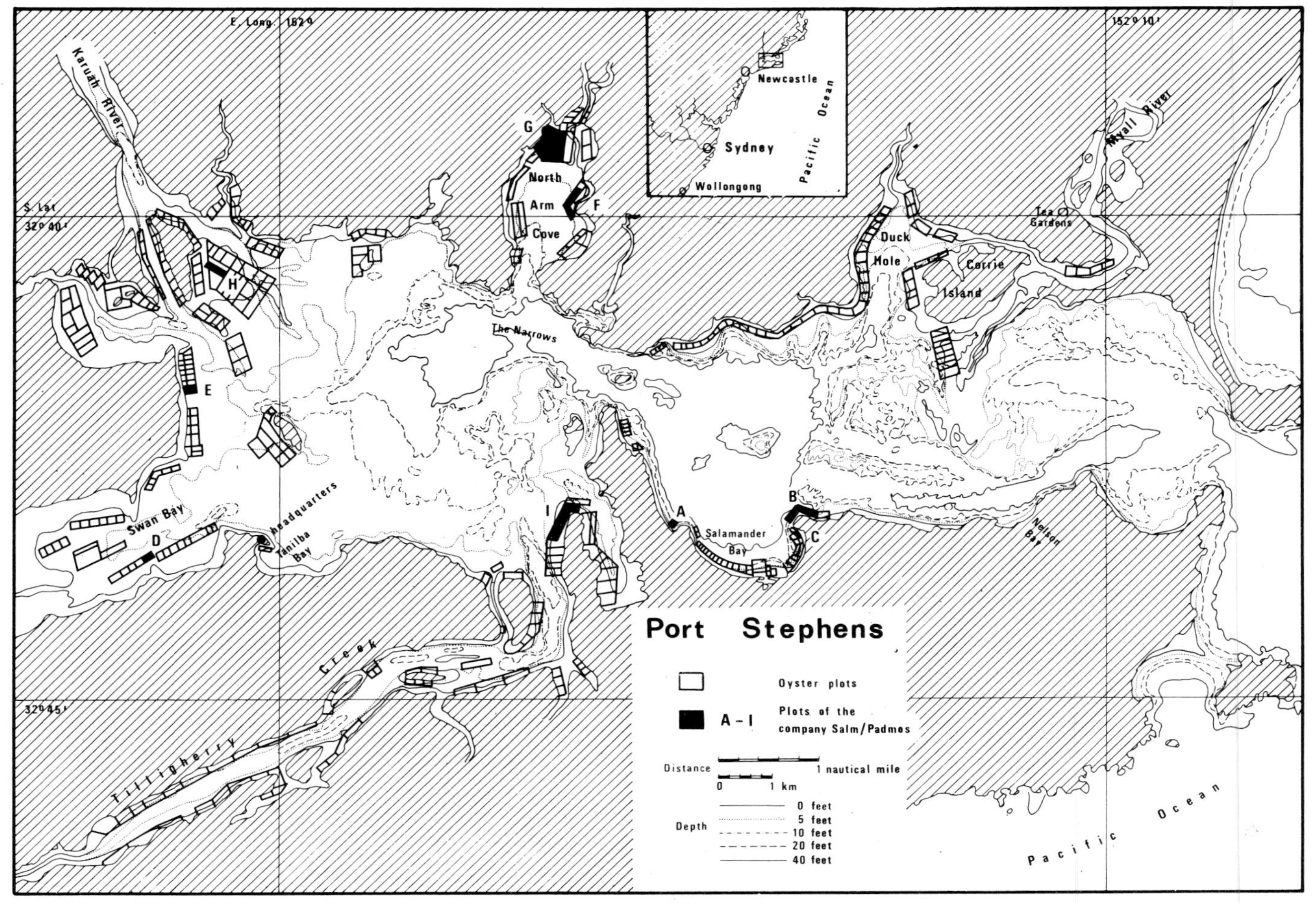

Port Stephens
Oyster plots
A – I
Plots of the company Salm/Padmos
Distance
0
1 km
1 nautical mile
Depth
0 feet
5 feet
10 feet
20 feet
40 feet
Newcastle
Sydney
Wollongong
Pacific Ocean
Myall River
Tea Gardens
Corrie Island
Duck Hole
Nelson Bay
Salamander Bay
The Narrows
North Arm Cove
Karuah River
Swan Bay
Tanilba Bay
headquarters
Tilligherry Creek
E. Long. 152°
152° 10'
S. lat 32° 40'
32° 45'

than half a sea mile wide. The eastern section, continuous with the Pacific Ocean, measures roughly 6.4 × 2 sea miles, the section west of The Narrows, roughly 4.5 × 3 sea miles. The area surrounding the bay is predominantly rather flat on the southern shore, but there are some hills, some of which are over 300 feet high, on the northern shore. The best shelter is found in North Arm Cove. Tanilba Bay, where the Company has its headquarters, is to be found on the southern shore of the western basin at 32° 43′ 40″ S and 151° 59′ 90″ E, northeast of the town of Salt Ash.

A.4. Hydrographic pattern

Depth. The eastern basin of the bay has a depth ranging from 15—60 feet, the southern shore being much steeper than the northern. In the central section of the northern shore is "Duck Hole", a cove which has a depth of 10—25 feet. In The Narrows the depth reaches 100 feet in places, but the western basin is mainly rather shallow, with depths ranging from 6 to 15 feet, although somewhat deeper due west of The Narrows. Steep shores are not found here. The North Arm Cove, situated in the northeastern section of the western basin, has a depth of 10—15 feet. Rivers of some importance debouching into the bay are the Karuah River, the Myall River and the Tilligherry Creek; some creeks of lesser importance enter North Arm Cove, Duck Hole, and Swan Bay.

Tides. The tidal range is about 5 feet 5 inches at spring tide, and about 2 feet at neap tide. In one of the deeper channels of the eastern basin current velocities up to 2.8 knots have been measured at spring tide, and up to 1.7 knots at neap tide. In the shallower parts and in the western basin lower current velocities prevail, but faster currents run in The Narrows.

Waves. The weather is only rarely calm here. Usually the wind blows quite hard and the bay offers little shelter from southern winds. The waves may then reach a height of well over 3 feet. The wind often also blows hard from the west, but in this case the area where most of the oysters are placed for growth and fattening, near the western shore of the west basin, is on the lee side.

Water temperature. There are no regularly kept records of water temperatures at Port Stephens, but the data published in the Oceanographic Station Lists of the Australian Commonwealth Scientific and Industrial Research Organization (CSIRO) indicate that, in the bulk of the Port Stephens water, the winter minimum will be about 12°C, whereas the summer maximum amounts to some 25°C. In shallow places the annual range can be somewhat greater than this.

Salinity. There are no daily records of water salinity kept at Port Stephens, but the information available in CSIRO's Oceanographic Station Lists indicates that the salinity is approximately the same as that of the ocean off the coast of New South Wales, especially in the eastern section of the bay. Occasionally the salinity drops, however, due to the influx of river water. The upper layers of water in the bay, especially, have a lower salinity during periods of heavy rain. It is usually in the months of February and March when there is most rain here — in the order of 10 inches per month. The salinity in the bulk of the Port Stephens water may then fall to about 25‰, although in the vicinity of the rivers discharging into the bay, much lower salinities may prevail. Since the river water carries a brownish coloured silt, a brown discolouration of the water in Stephens Bay will be seen during periods of great freshwater influx. The discolouration usually makes its first appearance near the mouth of the Karuah River, in North Arm Cove and Swan Bay, but sometimes the whole bay will show a brownish tinge which may even extend into the ocean. Occasionally this phenomenon is localized, for instance when fresh water from the Myall Lake comes down the Myall River following a local downpour. The lower salinities lead to a less salty taste of the oysters, but only in extreme cases to their death; for instance, to mortality among the spat near Tea Gardens and Corrie Island when the Myall River floods.

Plankton. No regular observations are made at Port Stephens on the quality and quantity of the phytoplankton, the food for the oysters and their larvae. The water in the bay is always somewhat greener than the water of the adjacent Pacific Ocean, which indicates a richer phytoplankton content. The western basin is generally greener than the eastern, which could be attributed to the fertilizing effect of the inflowing river water. The degree of transparency of the water is, as usual, related to both the silt and the phytoplankton content. Near the southern shore of the eastern basin one can usually see the bottom up to a depth of 30 feet, in the western basin, on the other hand, it can only be seen up to a depth of 10 feet. In periods of excessive rain, the visibility diminishes a great deal, whereas the water is unusually clear during periods of prolonged drought.

Pollution. Among the oyster areas in Australia, Port Stephens counts as one of those with the least polluted waters. Investigations carried out by the Australian Health Department revealed that the Port Stephens oysters can meet the highest standards of bacteriological purity as virtually no domestic sewage is discharged into the bay. Some concern has been expressed regarding the Nelson Bay area in the southeastern section of the eastern basin, where large numbers of tourists often congregate, but efforts are already being made to keep the bay clean at this site as well.

Sea bed conditions. Since in the Australian system of farming the oysters are always kept off the bottom, the nature of the subsoil is not of crucial importance. In Salamander Bay, the area in the eastern basin where the company collects its seed oysters, the bottom consists of a yellowish white sand. In the area in the western basin where growth and fattening take place, the bottom consists of mud or of a blackish, muddy sand.

A.5. Legal aspects

The oyster company under consideration is a partnership between Mr A. Salm and Mr J. Padmos, both of them Dutch emigrants and sons of shellfish farmers. Oyster farmers require suitable grounds for catching oyster seed and for the growth and fattening of their oysters. All the grounds at Port Stephens belong to the State of New South Wales. Oyster farmers can approach the Fisheries Department if they wish to lease certain grounds. This application is made public and if no one raises any objection, the ground selected can be used. There are two Fisheries Inspectors for Port Stephens, one for the western and one for the eastern basin, stationed in Karuah and Tea Gardens, respectively. The Inspector measures the plot to be leased on the spot and stakes it out by placing numbered hardwood poles at each corner (the indication 'O.L.54.71.' means oyster lease applied for in 1954, listed as number 71). The Inspector then hands the deed to the lessee, which means that the latter can use the plot under consideration for a period of 15 years, after which he can apply for a renewal of the lease. The rent to be paid differs according to the quality of the ground and is a matter of negotiation between the inspector and the lessee. Current rents vary between \$(A)2.50 and \$(A)5.00 per acre. Since 1968 the lessee has also had to pay a form of local tax known as Council Rates, amounting to \$(A)3.00—4.00 per acre. For these, completed questionnaire forms are sent, via the Fisheries Department, to the "Value General Department" which then decides the rate to be paid during the following 3 years. The Council Rates are reassessed for each 3-year period.

That the rents paid to the State do not reflect the real value of the ground, can be deduced from the price paid when an oysterman sells his lease to another. Since good ground is scarce and much in demand, sums ranging from \$(A)400.00 to \$(A)600.00 per acre are paid for the transfer of a lease. Such a private transfer agreement is then officially inscribed and the new lessee henceforth pays the rent, currently in force, to the State.

One of the conditions for leasing a plot is that it should not be worked between the hours of sunset and sunrise, although police supervision is not intensive. The oyster farmers inspect the area themselves with their speedboats to prevent theft of oysters. In reality theft occurs only rarely in the western basin, and virtually never in the eastern basin where only young oysters are grown.

The company under consideration has three plots in the eastern basin with a total surface area of some 3 acres at its disposal for catching seed (see chart): lease A is the smallest (about 1 600 square yards), but by far the best for spat collection so that more than half of the firm's collectors (22 500 "sticks") are placed there; lease B, which is much greater, is only partly suitable for spat collection (15 300 "sticks"); whereas lease C is of lesser quality, as it is situated in the lee of other catching leases, which is the reason why only 5 500 "sticks" are placed there.

In the western basin, where growth and fattening of the oysters take place, the firm has six plots at its disposal, indicated on the chart by D—I, of which four (D, E, F, G), covering a total of 32 acres, are in actual use, whereas plots H and I, measuring 2 and 8 acres respectively, are at present not in use because of their poorer quality for oyster farming.

B. SEQUENCE OF OPERATIONS

B.1. Procuring the seed

Nature takes care of the first phase of the oyster's development: spawning, fertilization of the eggs, and the ensuing development of the pelagic oyster larvae into full-grown larvae ready to settle on a piece of substratum. Though the rock oyster was formerly extremely abundant on the eastern and southern coasts of Australia, and is still locally found in great numbers attached to rocks in the intertidal zone, including at Port Stephens, there are reasons to surmise that it is the cultivated oysters on the leases of the oystermen which produce most of the larvae: these oysters are known to spawn profusely and they produce far more eggs per individual than the small wild oysters of the intertidal zone. The spawning season here is of much longer duration than in the centres of oyster farming in Europe. Not all the oysters in the bay spawn simultaneously. Observations on the leases indicate that the time of spawning differs somewhat from place to place. Though there are no regular observations on the number of oyster larvae occurring in a given volume of water, the oystermen have reason to assume that larvae are abundant throughout the summer season, from September to April. Spat collectors put out by the company late in November 1970, in mid-December 1970, and early in January 1971 all caught good numbers of spat. Spat collectors are usually offered from November till March, and since spatfall is evidently not restricted to 1 or 2 weeks per year, there seems to be no need here for spatfall prediction based on plankton investigations.

The company uses one type of collector only: hardwood sticks, nailed together in the form of lattices which, after having received a coating of tar, are put out on racks constructed on the catching plots in the eastern basin.

The first action to take at a catching lease is to place some extra sea marks of hardwood between the official corner poles. Next, long racks [1]* have to be built there as supports for the collectors. For this, double rows of poles, 3 feet apart, are planted in such a way that their tops just emerge at low water neap tide. For driving poles into the rather hard bottom of the catching lease use is made of a motor pump with rubber hose to which an

* The reference numbers refer to paragraphs giving more detailed description in the section "Technical details" in this and following chapters.

iron pipe is attached. Holding the pipe at the position for a pole, water is used to blow a hole into the hard bottom. This allows the poles to be inserted without effort. Once the poles are placed in perfectly straight rows, a series of battens is nailed horizontally on the inside of the poles, just at their heads. Both poles and battens are made of first quality, coal-tarred hardwood such as "brush-box" (*Tristania conferta* R. Br.) or "turpentine" (*Syncarpia procera* Salisb.). Such racks will withstand attacks of shipworms (*Banksia australis*) for at least 6 to 8 years. Shipworms should be especially feared in those parts of the racks which are rarely or never exposed to the air and sun.

Meanwhile collectors are constructed at the headquarters of the company at Tanilba Bay. For these, various types of Australian hardwood ("brush-box", "turpentine", "blue-gum" (*Eucalyptus saligna* Sm.), "blackbutt" (*Eucalyptus pilularis* Sm.)), which can be supplied by the saw mills as waste wood, are used. Sticks of such wood, 6 feet long and 0.75 inch square, can be purchased by the 1 000 and delivered to Tanilba Bay. The company buys some 44 000 such sticks each year, some (28 000) for the use in the ultimate production of marketable oysters, the remainder for producing seed oysters to be sold to oyster farmers in Bateman's Bay, 300 miles further south.

Specially constructed lattices are then made [2] (Fig. 1). At first sight, it appears that these have 21 sticks nailed to two runners with two more runners

Fig. 1. Constructing lattices of hardwood at the headquarters. In the background, an "oyster punt" and a "tray" for storage of oysters. (Photo A. Salm.)

nailed on top, but in reality the construction is such that two lattices fit into each other and are held together by four nails (Fig. 2). The interspacing between the sticks in the combined lattices is 2.75 inches, in each individual lattice, 6.25 inches. The next step is to dip the layers in thin coal tar (purchased from the steel works) for which a shallow masonry hod, measuring roughly 10 × 7 feet, is used. Then the layers are lifted up with the aid of a hand winch and left for about 20 min in an inclined position to drain off the excess tar (Fig. 3). The collectors are piled up on sloping wooden rails leading to the water to dry and are ready the following day to be transported to the racks on the catching leases.

For transportation of the collectors to the site, the layers are pushed down the rails and loaded by hand into so-called oyster punts, flat-bottomed open rectangular boats of sturdy but simple construction [3] (Fig. 5). Three piles of layers are placed to fill the punt to the top of the hold, and further layers are built up over the sides. Thus up to 4 500 sticks can be loaded onto one punt. The oyster punts are towed by a motor vessel [4] equipped with a 30 h.p. diesel engine. On arrival at the catching lease, the collectors are placed on the racks, six layers on top of each other, the sticks parallel to the racks, and attached to the racks with No. 10 gauge galvanized iron wire. The wire

Fig. 2. Two lattices fitted into each other, fastened together with four nails, two of which are clearly visible in the runner in the foreground. (Photo A. Salm.)

Fig. 3. Draining off excess tar from the lattices which have been dipped in the tar hod. Later they will be put on the "race" leading to the water. (Photo A. Salm.)

is wound by hand around both battens and collectors and fastened securely with a "twister", a tapering piece of iron about 1 foot long. When the sticks are placed this way they form a rather compact mass on the racks. This is not a disadvantage, however, as the water bearing the oyster larvae, coming in with the tide, can penetrate freely all the interspaces of the sticks, and the latter break the tidal current to such a considerable extent that the larvae can easily find a well-sheltered place in which to settle. Therefore, this system usually leads to a greater number of spat per stick than when the layers are less closely spaced.

Since it is nature which takes care of the spatfall, all the oystermen have to do during this phase is to inspect their collectors from time to time.

Fig. 4. The lattice collectors emerge at low tide on the catching leases in Salamander Bay. (Photo A. Salm.)

B.2. Transfer to the western basin

During the last quarter of the year, from September to December, the oystermen transfer [5] the collectors from the catching leases in the eastern basin to the leases in the western basin where faster growth can be expected. The oyster spat on the sticks is by then about 10 months old. Racks of a similar pattern to those on the catching leases have already been constructed here and the collectors, now covered with young oysters, are again fastened, with galvanized iron wire, six layers on top of each other, the sticks parallel to the racks (Fig. 6). Keeping the sticks so close together may to some extent hamper the influx of water, bearing the planktonic food, but on the other hand, the most notorious oyster enemy, the porcupine fish (*Dicotylichthys mysersi*), is thus kept out, and moreover, most of the young oysters are better protected against the hot sun at low tide than is the case when the sticks are more dispersed.

B.3. Thinning out

When the oysters are about 18 months old, in the June of their second year, it is time to offer them more space and food. The layers are therefore

Fig. 5. The oyster "punt" is used for transport of lattices with young oysters. Note the hook used to hoist bundles of lattices when they are destined for Bateman's Bay.

detached from the sturdy racks of the "depots" in the western basin by cutting the iron wires; use is made of the hand winch to lift them. They are transported to the racks in the growing leases in the western basin to which they are fastened in single layers (Fig. 7). This time the layers are placed with the sticks square to the direction of the racks, with the runners of the lattice outside the battens. Now each layer is attached to its rack with four nails, a procedure which requires considerably less time than attaching each single layer to the rack with iron wire. The layers are now all nailed with the oysters facing upwards. For all this work the farmer is usually working from the "flatty", a small flat-bottomed boat, of the same type as the oyster punt, but only 12 feet long [6].

Nailing out is a delicate operation, for hammering causes vibration, especially when, occasionally, a nail is missed. Many oysters can fall off the sticks because of this, and can be considered lost, for it is not thought to be eco-

Fig. 6. The collectors with oyster spat are fastened six layers deep to the racks on the growing leases, with the sticks parallel to the racks. (Photo A. Salm.)

nomic to glue these young oysters onto the sticks again with a type of cement. The introduction of the nail gun [7], some 4 years ago, was a great improvement. This instrument reduces vibration to such an extent that the losses formerly suffered in this phase of the operations are virtually reduced to nil. Since the oysters now have more space and receive a faster flowing current of water, they grow well in their new position. They are left to grow until the May of their third year. Then, when they are about 29 months old, the oyster farmer will decide whether or not it is wise to thin them out once again. This will usually be necessary when the sticks are very well covered with oysters. The individual sticks still have interspaces of only 2.75 inches, which may hamper the oysters in their growth. To remedy this it is sufficient to lift off the top lattice with the aid of an iron bar. This is easy, since the two lattices forming one layer are kept together by only four nails. The top lattice can be taken off (Fig. 8) to be fastened again on an empty section of a rack, for which use is once more made of the nail gun. The individual sticks now have interspaces of 6.25 inches, which leaves enough room for even the biggest oysters. When transporting the layers with oysters to other racks, great caution is required to stack the layers in such a way in the oyster punts that they fit into each other and no oysters are crushed. Any oysters falling off in this phase of the operations are taken back to the company's head-

Fig. 7. The lattices with young oysters are nailed out in a single layer to the racks on the growing leases. The sticks are now perpendicular to the battens of the racks. (Photo A. Salm.)

quarters, as they are, by then, large enough to be sold for consumption as small oysters ("bottle oysters").

B.4. Harvesting of marketable oysters

Unlike most other countries, the sale of oysters knows no close season in Australia. However oysters full of spawn, 'ripe and running' as they are colloquially described, are considered as being at the height of their flavour and, therefore, the summer season brings the greatest demand, with peaks on special days such as Melbourne Cup Day, Christmas and New Year. In many Australian oyster areas the quality is often rather poor in winter, but the oysters of Port Stephens are usually of good quality throughout the winter season, so there is great demand for them then. The oyster farmer has to decide when is the best time to take up his oysters for the market. In making this decision he has to consider not only the actual demand, but also the size and quality of his oysters. The oysters, as a rule, are big enough when they are 3 to 4 years old. When they are actually spawning or have just spawned they are left alone for a while until their quality has improved again. The Australian oyster has a pleasant sweet flavour, especially when full of spawn, a condi-

Fig. 8. In their third year, the oysters are thinned out again, this time by splitting the double lattice so that there are 6.25-inch spaces between the sticks. (Photo A. Salm.)

tion which in many other types of oyster gives them an unpleasant oily tang. Also, they do not have the cucumber-like flavour so characteristic of that other *Crassostrea* species, the Portuguese oyster (*Crassostrea angulata*).

In harvesting the oysters from the racks, the lattices, now very heavy with oysters, are sawn in two on the spot using a simple hand saw and loaded by hand onto the punt. Loads of some 400 oyster carrying sticks are then brought to the sorting shed at the headquarters for detaching and grading. This shed, measuring 40 × 15 feet, stands over the water and has both a roof and lattice side-walls. The shed is open at one end so that the loaded punt can be manoeuvred into it. It is here that the oysters are detached from the sticks and graded into three categories. This work is carried out on the punt, but the shed roof protects workers and oysters from both rain and sun. The oysters are detached from the stick by vibration. This means hitting the sticks hard with either a small axe or a piece of hardwood. Oysters from 250 to 300 sticks can be detached in 1 h. After this the sticks are of no further use and are burned. An old file is useful for separating oysters which have grown together in clusters. However, small clusters of two or three oysters of similar size are often left together to avoid loss of oysters through breakage. The detached oysters are now graded, roughly according to size, into three categories: "plate oysters", "bottle oysters", and "spat". The "plate oysters" are the

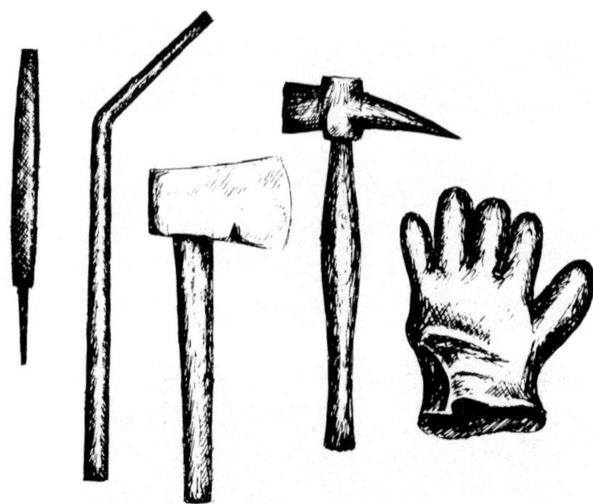

Fig. 9. Some utensils of the Australian oyster farmer.

large oysters — weighing about 70 kg per 1 000 — to be served on the half shell in restaurants; the "bottle oysters" are somewhat smaller — weighing about 40 kg per 1 000 — and will be used to fill glass bottles when shucked, whereas the "spat", too small for direct consumption, is sold to oystermen in areas where trays are in use for growth and fattening, especially in Botany Bay. No oysters are taken back to the growing leases in Stephens Bay after having been harvested and graded.

B.5. Storage

Not all the oysters detached from the sticks can be immediately packed and shipped after grading. Therefore, alongside the shed a so-called "tray" has been constructed for storage. This is a lattice of 3 × 1 inch battens raised about 1 foot above the sea bottom, covering an area of 35 × 7 feet (Fig. 10). The "tray" is on a solid foundation of impregnated timber, covered with a roof and provided with three simple lattice walls as protection against the sun, but is open towards the shed. In this tray the oysters can be spread out for temporary storage. At low tide the oysters on the lattice bottom are exposed, but at high tide they are immersed in water.

B.6. Shipment and marketing

The oysters are packed in standard oyster bags — burlap sacks measuring 37.5 × 22.5 inches — without prior scrubbing or washing, the shells often being covered with mud. A bag contains 80 to 110 dozen plate oysters or 150 to 180 dozen bottle oysters, and when filled, weighs about 70 kg. When the oysters are very "fat" they are graded to a somewhat smaller size than is

Fig. 10. Sorting shed and "tray" built offshore of headquarters. The tray is used for temporary storage of marketable oysters.

the case when the quality of their edible parts is less good, hence the difference in the number of dozens per bag. A small truck is used to carry the sacks containing the oysters to the nearby main road, where, on a given day, trucks of professional fish transporters pick them up to take them to market (for instance in Sydney). During the height of the season, oysters are shipped to Sydney every Monday, Tuesday, Wednesday and Thursday, with a peak shipment on Wednesday. Shipments are less frequent in the cooler season. Oysters packed in sacks can stand transportation and storage for a remarkably long time and can keep their valves tightly closed for many days in succession. However, when shipped in the summer to a city with high temperatures, such as Brisbane, they should be placed in cool storage on arrival.

In the cities the oysters are sold to wholesalers. The plate oysters usually find their way to special shucking houses where they are cleaned, separated where necessary, and the flat valves cut away. The opened oysters are carefully packed by the dozen in boxes, often in two or three layers separated by a sheet of paper, for delivery to restaurants and private buyers. Most of the oysters are eaten raw from the half shell, the remainder undergo preparation in the kitchen prior to being served either as stewed oysters, curried oysters, oysters Mornay or oysters Kilpatrick.

The "seconds", the smaller "bottle oysters", are shucked by hand and put in slender cylindrical glass bottles, about 8 inches long and some 2 inches diameter. Each bottle contains one dozen oysters, and is filled with normal tap water. These bottled dozens sell readily for \$(A)0.40 to 0.50, usually to be used in oyster soups or stews, although sometimes they too are eaten raw, after salt has been added. The fresh tap water causes the oysters to lose their natural salty taste and makes them swell up, giving them a plump appearance. Such bottled oysters can be stored without deterioration for periods of up to 2 weeks in a refrigerator.

The "spat" category of oysters, those too small for consumption, which are often found on the sticks when a late settling has taken place on top of the initial spatfall, are also packed in burlap bags and sold to oyster farmers in Botany Bay. There they are placed on trays for further growth.

As has been said before, the company under consideration does not keep all its collectors at Port Stephens until the oysters have reached a size suitable for consumption. Some of the sticks, once covered with spat, are not brought to the western basin like the rest, but are sold as such to an oyster farmer working in Bateman's Bay, 175 miles south of Sydney, where spatfall is poor. About 10 000 sticks with spat are sold annually by the company at a price of \$(A)180.00 per 1 000 sticks. They are shipped 5 000 to a truck and the freight charges (\$(A)25.00 per 1 000) are paid by the buyer.

C. FARMING RISKS

Everywhere in the world shellfish farmers occasionally have to contend with adverse conditions of a hydrographic and biological nature; the impact of predators, parasites, diseases, and the activities of competing organisms.

C.1. Hydrographic conditions

It is only exceptionally that hydrographical conditions in Stephens Bay are to blame for losses among the oysters. Excessive downpours of rain may lead to localized losses of spat from the sticks, but the catching leases used by the company under consideration are too far from the areas affected by the influx of fresh water to suffer from it. Wind forces are often considerable here, but never lead to noteworthy losses among the oysters of the company. Occasionally, layers of sticks have been torn loose from the racks by a gale, but when recovered and fastened to the racks again, the damage appeared to have been limited.

C.2. Biological conditions

In all the oyster areas of the world larval development in the open water is entirely in the hands of nature. Water temperature, weather conditions, quality and quantity of the minute organisms on which the larvae feed and also of the organisms which prey on the oyster larvae may lead to considerable variation in the numbers of spat settling on the collectors from year to year, even when the parent stock and the total number of larvae produced remains of the same order of magnitude. In Australia, spatfall shows some fluctuations, but in Stephens Bay a disappointing settlement of spat is said to occur only about once in every 6 years.

C.3. Predators

The only notorious oyster predator in Stephens Bay is the Porcupine fish (*Dicotylichthys mysersi*) (Fig. 11) which can destroy large numbers of oys-

Fig. 11. The Porcupine fish is the most notorious oyster predator in Stephens Bay. (Photo A. Salm.)

ters, especially during the warmer months of the year. Other fish species such as the bream (*Mylio australis*), the toad fish (*Sphaeroides hamiltoni*) and the sting ray may cause havoc among oysters in other Australian waters. Since oysters living on the sea bottom, as is normal in natural beds, are very easy victims of such fish, rack farming as developed in Australia is a very efficient way of avoiding such losses. But in rack farming itself there are various ways of limiting the losses caused by these voracious fish. The company under consideration packs the sticks so tightly together that the Porcupine fish cannot penetrate between them and at the most can only destroy some oysters on the extreme outsides of the collectors. Other oyster farmers prefer to make a fence around their collectors in the catching lease. These are either of galvanized gauze or of synthetic fibre netting stretched between poles connected by battens. However, the life of such materials and the costs of such measures raises the question as to whether it is not more economic to loose some oysters.

In the literature on Australian oyster fishing and farming mention is often made of damage caused by a predatory flatworm, named *Stylochus*, locally called a "wafer". Oyster farmers in Port Stephens have not complained about any impact from this predator.

C.4. Parasites and diseases

By far the greatest risk for the Australian oyster farmer is the so-called "opening disease", also named "winter mortality". In winter, especially during prolonged spells of high salinity, oysters may suddenly start to die for no obvious reason. This often begins in August and may continue until October. The larger oysters, apparently in good condition, die off, sometimes leading to the loss of 50 to 80% of the stock. Juvenile oysters do not succumb so easily to the disease but their growth may be seriously interrupted and retarded. Later they resume their growth and a whole oyster population in Port Stephens has not yet been wiped out. It is said that such has occasionally occurred in Botany Bay and that oysters kept on trays there for longer than one season should be transferred to higher grounds in time to avoid mass mortality in the winter.

The exact cause of the disease is not known, but the symptoms closely resemble those of infectious oyster diseases observed among oysters of other *Crassostrea* species, for example those on the Atlantic coast of the United States and Canada, and in France. Yellowish pustules on the gills are common to all these cases. The impression is given that some form of micro-organism is active, recurring in various degrees of virulence and hitting hardest when the oysters offer a lower degree of resistance. Whether high salinity makes the oysters less resistant, or renders the causative organism more active, is not yet clear. When the disease is raging, a sudden drop in salinity will not immediately arrest it. In a recent publication, P.H. Wolf (1972) describes a haplosporidan parasite from diseased Australian rock oysters, which apparently closely resembles the Haplosporidan *Minchinia* found in American oysters. It seems most probable that it is this organism which is responsible for the Australian opening disease.

The company under consideration sustained serious damage in the period August—October 1970, particularly among the oysters which had already sojourned for quite a long time on the growing leases. This was reflected in their sales: August, 82 sacks of plate oysters; September, 84; October, 33, and November, 20, instead of the expected increasing trend in sales figures. The following generation of oysters showed a seriously retarded growth, but resumed their former rate of growth once the water of the bay became brownish again after the rains of January and February 1971.

The Australian opening disease is a matter of serious concern, especially because its impact is apparently greater, the larger the number of oysters grown in a given area. However, there is certainly no reason for despair, since really catastrophic mortalities have not yet occurred.

C.5. Competitors

Several organisms may be reckoned among the competitors of the oysters due to the fact that they cause damage without being a direct cause of death. For instance, from what has been said earlier it will be clear that the shipworm *Banksia australis* is abundant here and that all wooden structures should be made of hard *Banksia*-resistant wood and/or be duly protected by a layer of coal tar. The sticks, though made of hardwood and coated with tar, may in due course become so honeycombed by shipworms that they break during handling, and this usually leads to loss of the oysters growing on them. This menace is observed to a much lesser degree in the topmost layers of collectors, since *Banksia* dislikes exposure to air and hot sunshine. For the same reason, shipworms thrive considerably better in sticks carrying a large number of oysters than in sticks which received only a scanty settling, as in the former sticks, the surface of the wood is less exposed and remains more moist at low tide.

The older literature on the Australian oyster industry mentions the havoc played among the oysters by *Polydora*, a polychaete worm which makes mud-blisters in the shell. This was especially true for the oysters growing in natural beds on the sea floor. In Stephens Bay, *Polydora* presents no problem to the oyster farmers, presumably because the oysters are grown well above the sea bottom.

Ascidians, sponges, bryozoa, polychaete worms and barnacles, epibionts on the oyster shell which in many places compete with the oysters for space and food, have so far caused no nuisance to speak of in Port Stephens. Serious competition may, however, result from mussel seed settling on the sticks. The appearance of great numbers of mussels on the collectors can lead to serious losses among the oysters which settled on them earlier. The oyster farmers say that the mussels "push off" the oysters. This is often a matter for serious concern on leases at the upper ends of the bay, for example in the mouth of the Karuah River and in Tilligherry Creek, but not on the leases used by the company under consideration.

D. ECONOMY OF OYSTER FARMING IN AUSTRALIA

D.1. Rents

As described above, the company uses three catching leases, covering a total of 3 acres, and six growing leases, covering 42 acres in total, for which the appropriate rents plus Council Rates have to be paid (see section A.5: Legal aspects).

D.2. Inventory items

The most expensive single inventory item is the 26-foot company ship, which is equipped with a 30 h.p. diesel engine. This ship was built by a local shipbuilder and cost, at the time of purchase, approximately \$(A)1 000.00. It is expected that the boat will have a useful life of some 30 years and the engine of some 15 years. The engine uses about 5 barrels of diesel oil per year plus 20 l of lubricating oil at a price of \$(A)47.50 and \$(A)5.00 per unit, respectively. A fresh coat of polyester paint every year for the boat costs about \$(A)20.00 for paint.

The 28-foot oyster punts, two of which are in use by the company, with a third under construction, cost about \$(A)600.00 each. They require very limited maintenance (one coating of tar per year) and are expected to have a useful life of over 30 years.

The small boats ("flatties") from which the farmers do their work on the racks, are not purchased from outside but built locally. It takes two men 1 day to build one for which about \$(A)50.00 in material is required. The company has two such boats in permanent use.

The plant located at the headquarters, that is the "shed", the "tray", the equipment for tarring the wood and the hand winch for loading the oyster-covered sticks onto the truck which takes them to Bateman's Bay, is of simple construction and requires only limited sums of money annually to cover the costs of depreciation. The van used for taking the sacks of oysters to the main road is a second-hand one, purchased for \$(A)350.00.

D.3. Materials

The purchase of wood is an ever-recurring item on the budget of the oyster farmer. He has, for instance, to buy poles and battens to build the racks for the catching and growing leases; racks which will withstand the attacks of shipworm from 6 to 8 years. The poles are of 2 × 3 inch hardwood and the battens of 1 × 3 inch hardwood. For every 1 000 sticks on racks on the catching leases 18 poles are required, placed 4 feet apart and of lengths varying from 4 to 10 feet, depending upon the nature of the subsoil. These 18 poles cost in total $(A)7.20 ($(A)0.40 each). The battens cost an additional $(A) 3.00. On the growing leases, where the subsoil is softer, poles 6—12 feet long, costing $(A)0.70 each, are required. These poles, however, are placed 6—7 feet apart. As the layers are placed six on top of each other on the catching leases and are eventually nailed out individually on the growing leases, far more poles and battens per 1 000 sticks are required on the growing leases. This amounts to 200 poles, costing $(A)140.00, plus battens, costing $(A)35.00. The company buys some 3 000 superfeet of battens annually, costing about $(A)400.00 delivered to headquarters. It takes two men about 6 h to dip all these battens in coal tar. The company uses about 4 barrels of tar each year, at $(A)12.00 per barrel, for tarring the poles and battens.

Sticks, which serve for one generation of oysters only, also have to be bought every year. The company buys 44 000 of these sticks annually for a price of about $(A)33.00 per 1 000, delivered to headquarters.

D.4. Labour

One man can convert 1 500 to 2 000 sticks into layers daily, the number depending on the degree of dryness of the wood. This means $(A)8.00 per 1 000 sticks in labour costs, plus $(A)1.25 for the 3 kg of 1.75-inch galvanized iron nails. Dipping 1 000 sticks in tar (250 at a time) is about one hour's work for two men. The company uses some 8 barrels of tar annually for dipping the sticks, at a price of $(A)12.00 per barrel.

The building of racks is not so time-consuming as these last from 6 to 8 years. One man can erect some 250 poles per day and a similar time is required to nail out sufficient battens to support 3 000 sticks. For this purpose galvanized iron nails, 2.5 inches long are used. The quantity of nails used for the racks is insignificant in comparison with that required for nailing the lattices. The only further material required is the galvanized steel wire used for attaching the collectors to the racks (150—200 kg per year) and the 2-inch nails required for nailing out the single layers with the nail gun.

At harvest time two men with an oyster punt require about 4 h to saw off 400 sticks carrying oysters ready for consumption and to detach these oysters from the sticks. When the sticks are well covered it takes three men about 2 days to sort out these oysters. The 400 sticks may then yield 12 sacks of plate oysters, three sacks bottle oysters plus three sacks of spat. When the sticks are less well covered it may take two men 1 day to sort the oysters and the result may then be perhaps eight sacks of plate oysters, two sacks of seconds and one sack of spat.

D.5. Sales

The oyster farmer is satisfied when a stick yields $(A)1.00—1.20 in oysters, which is the equivalent of about two and a half dozen plates plus half a dozen seconds per stick. The prices reached in Sydney at the time of writing (transportation and packing substracted) are $(A)41.00 for a 70-kg sack (80—110 dozen) of plates and $(A)24.00 for a sack (100—180 dozen) of bottle oysters or seconds. For spat for sale to other farmers in Botany Bay the current price is $(A)13.00 per sack. The sacks cost about $(A)0.52 each and the cost of their freight by truck to Sydney is about $(A)1.00 per sack.

In recent years the company produced the following quantities of oysters (the "oyster year" is counted from July 1st to June 30th):

1968 — 609 sacks
1969 — 524 sacks
1970 — 588 sacks
1971 — 640 sacks

These figures are recorded in the statistical archives of the Australian Fisheries Department. About 75% of these were plate oysters and 25% bottle oysters. Spat are not included in the table. The quantity of spat varies somewhat from year to year according to the spatfall pattern; an average yield is 5 sacks per week. Occasionally, sacks of what are called "all-ins", oysters that are over 3 years old but have not grown very well, are sold. However, if $(A) 1.00 cannot be made per stick of these it is preferable to leave such oysters on the growing leases to await further growth.

As previously mentioned, the company annually sells 10 000 sticks of young oysters to farmers in Bateman's Bay, for a price of $(A)180.00 per 1 000 sticks.

D.6. Losses

According to the farmers, losses from poaching amount to less than 1% of their production.

D.7. Personnel

All the work previously described is, for the greater part, carried out by the two partners themselves as, in Australia, it is very difficult to attract and keep labour. During the past few years, the company has been assisted by one hired hand, whose wages amount to $(A)70.00 per week.

D.8. Further development

The latter situation may now make it possible to expand production somewhat. The present aim is to place 34 000 sticks and to keep them until the oysters on them have reached consumption size. The main bottle-neck limiting the production of an oyster company is usually labour. In addition, the available acreage of high quality leases is a limiting factor, and in some years, "opening disease" may also reduce production.

E. GOVERNMENTAL ASSISTANCE

The Australian Government is the owner of the Port Stephens grounds and thus government fishery inspectors are responsible for the correct application of the leasing rules. Police patrolling is, in principle, carried out but is not, in fact, intensive here. The Australian Health Department keeps an eye on the sanitary conditions in Stephens Bay and now and then takes samples of oysters to check their bacteriological condition and to measure the content of heavy metals, such as mercury, in the oysters. There is no full-time biological research programme for the Australian oyster industry. Studies on parasites and diseases of the oyster, such as that by Wolf (1972), mentioned above, are only carried out occasionally. Experience gained elsewhere in the world shows that oyster diseases caused by microscopic parasites are very difficult to control. Although, in principle, it should be possible to produce disease-resistant strains of oysters by selective breeding, rearing larvae under laboratory conditions, such a venture has not, as yet, been undertaken.

F. GENERAL IMPRESSION

Oyster farming as carried out in Port Stephens is an excellent example of the remunerative exploitation of natural resources. Noteworthy quantities of high quality marketable oysters are produced by farming where nature, left to itself, would produce virtually nothing at all. The hydrographical qualities of the water of Port Stephens are almost ideal for oyster farming: spatfall is satisfactory year after year in the eastern basin, and in the western basin, where salinities are lower due to influx of river water, the oysters find so much food that growth and fattening leave little to be desired. Adverse conditions leading to serious losses among the cultivated oysters are a rare occurrence, but the "opening disease" gives reason for concern. It has, however, so far only led to economically bearable fluctuations in production. Port Stephens is characterized by its unpolluted water yielding oysters of a high bacteriological standard, so that the installation of a purification plant through which all the oysters should pass is unnecessary and unrealistic.

In some other Australian oyster areas (e.g. in Botany Bay) contamination by sewage does occur, and this means that passage through a purification plant for some oysters, at least during part of the year, is desirable. However, as the enforcement of such a measure would inevitably lead to unfair competition between the various Australian oyster areas, the Australian Government has, so far, not taken a decision on this matter. For the time being, the Health Department keeps an eye on danger spots and occasionally has had to suspend sales from these areas.

The material used for oyster farming, Australian style, is readily available. Labour is often the only limiting factor. Partnerships, such as that described here, give a sound economical basis to such ventures.

The Australian market can absorb large quantities of high quality oysters, at least as long as labour can be found to open the oysters to be served in the restaurants.

The total Australian production of cultivated oysters amounts to some 7 200 tons (weight in the shell) per year at a value of about $\$(A)3.4 \times 10^6$. Production is predominantly in New South Wales.

G. TECHNICAL DETAILS

G.1. Rack building

On the catching leases in the eastern basin the racks are, as a rule, constructed square to the coastline, "in and out" as the oystermen say. Deviations from this rule are, however, sometimes imposed due to the shape of the lease. Experience has taught the farmers which are the best sites for spat collection. To build racks, double rows of poles are placed in the sea bed. The nature of the bottom, which is usually quite hard here, determines how long the poles should be. On catching lease A the poles used are 4—7 feet long, on lease B 7—10 feet and on lease C 6—7 feet long. The poles are sunk with the aid of a motor pump using a hose and an iron pipe. The two rows for each rack are placed 3 feet apart, with a 10—12-foot space left between racks to enable the oyster punts to be manoeuvred between them. The heads of the poles should all be at the same height, at a level just above low water neap tide. Battens are nailed to the inside of the poles, flush with the heads. Poles and battens are made of first quality hardwood 3 × 2 inch and 3 × 1 inch respectively, duly tarred before use in the field. For tarring this wood, use is made of a long iron tar container, located at headquarters, which is covered with a sheet of corrugated iron when not in use. On the catching leases, the individual poles are placed 4 feet apart from each other. To make neat straight rows the line is marked by stretching a rope between the two terminal poles.

On the growing leases, rack building is slightly different. The softer bottom makes it necessary to use poles of greater length, 6—12 feet; these can be pushed into the bottom by hand, the finishing touch being given with a maul. The two rows are again 3 feet apart from each other, but the individual poles in each row are, in this case 6—7 feet apart from each other. On these growing leases 20 feet of water is left between the racks (Fig. 12). The racks are often very long. On the growing leases of the company under consideration, they are up to 300 yards in length. The size and shape of the catching leases, together with the more or less sloping bottom, enforces the occasional construction of much shorter racks than this.

G.2. Construction of layers of sticks

At the headquarters, a low frame has been erected which facilitates the construction of lattices of sticks, by giving the exact measurements and a good support. Two sticks of good quality are selected and put in place on the frame. Next, 21 sticks are distributed crosswise on these runners with interspaces of 2.75 inches. Then two more runners are placed on top parallel to the first two. In nailing the sticks to the runners (with 1.75-inch galvanized iron nails) nails are driven alternately, first through a stick in the undermost runner and then through the topmost runner in the next stick. Thus one creates in reality two lattices, fitting into each other, one kept together by the undermost runners, the other by the topmost runners. Next four nails are driven through the top runners, each at the crossing of the third stick which

Fig. 12. Building racks on the growing leases, leaving some 20 feet free in between. (Photo A. Salm.)

is already nailed to the undermost runner. Thus the two lattices are made into one single layer using these four nails. Such a layer can easily be split apart when the growth of the oysters makes this necessary. The outcome is two lattices with interspaces of 6.25 inches.

The construction of layers proceeds more quickly when the wood is not too dry, but, on the other hand, effective tarring requires the wood to be rather dry. Thus a sunny day is chosen for dipping the layers into the tar hod.

G.3. Oyster punt

Oyster punts are sturdy open boats, of a rectangular shape, 28 feet long, 8 feet broad and 4 feet high, constructed of 1.5-inch Oregon pine. To protect the wood against shipworm it is first tarred, next sheathed with bitumen paper, then tarred once again and finally sheathed with tinned iron or aluminium. The ledgers of the punts are made of hardwood, and the stern and aft are strengthened. A mast, to serve as a support for the hand winch used to hoist bundled layers, can also be erected. The mast has to be taken out before the punt enters the sorting shed.

G.4. Motor boat

The motor boat in use by the company is 26 feet long, 8 feet broad and draws 6—8 inches of water. It was built locally of 0.75-inch Oregon pine coated with polyester paint. Its engine is a 30 h.p. Fordson ship diesel. Part of the boat is covered to give its users protection against the weather. The boat is used to carry those working at the leases and also to tug the oyster punts loaded with equipment. The oystermen do not stay on board overnight.

G.5. Transfer to the "depots"

The layers are detached from the racks in the catching leases by cutting the restraining wires. The layers are then taken up by hand, one by one, and put in the punts with great care to avoid damaging the young oysters. Putting the layers vertically in the punts ensures a minimum of such damage. About 2 300 sticks with spat can be accommodated in one punt. Usually two punts are operated simultaneously.

On arrival in the western basin the layers are once more secured, again six on top of each other, to racks called "depots". First, two layers with the young oysters facing upwards, so that predatory fishes cannot reach them, the next four layers with the oysters facing downwards, to protect them from the hot sun.

In those cases where it is planned to pick up layers with spat destined for

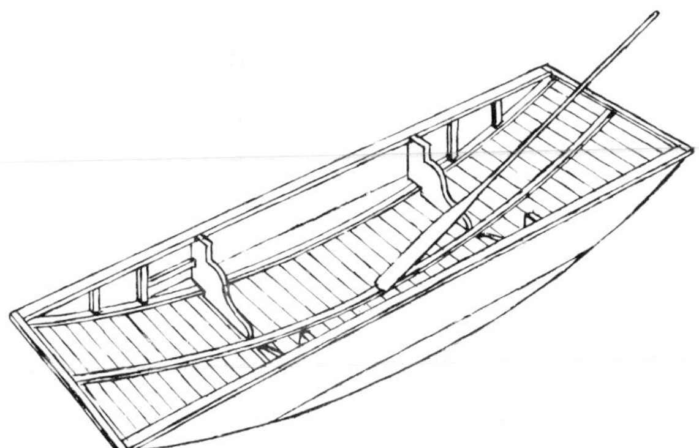

Fig. 13. The "flatty", the small home-made boat used by Australian oyster farmers.

transportation to Bateman's Bay six layers are bound together with steel wire. As an assembly of six layers is too heavy to lift by hand, use is made of a hand winch with a special type of metal hook, for insertion between the sticks of the layers, attached to the end of the steel cable.

G.6. The "flatty"

The small boats called "flatties" from which the oystermen do their work on the racks, are of a rectangular shape and of simple construction with a sloping stern and aft (Fig. 12). They measure 12 feet in length by 3 feet broad.

G.7. Nail gun

The nail gun, costing \$(A)120.00, carries 45 2-inch nails of special construction (flat rectangular heads) in its magazine. It operates by means of compressed air, contained in small metal bottles weighing about 20 pounds. A rubber hose connects the bottle with the gun and a trigger is used to drive the nails into the wood. The company uses about \$(A)6.00 for compressed air per year to nail out the sticks.

H. BIBLIOGRAPHY

Blackburn, M., 1947. Biology and cultivation of oysters in Australia. Fish. Newsl., June: 4—5, 16.

Cox, J.C., 1883. On edible oysters found on Australian and neighbouring coasts. Proc. Linn. Soc. N.S.W., 7: 122—134.

Haswell, W.A., 1885. Parasite of the rock oyster. Proc. Linn. Soc. N.S.W., 10: 273—275.

Humphrey, G.F., 1943. The biology and cultivation of oysters in Australia. Proc. Linn. Soc. N.S.W., 68: 13—16.

Kesteven, G.L., 1941. The biology and cultivation of oysters in Australia. I. Some economic aspects. Aust. Counc. Sci. Ind. Res. Pamphl., 105: 1—32.

Malcolm, W.B., 1971. The Sydney rock oyster. Aust. Nat. Hist., June: 46—50.

Rochford, D.J., 1952. The application of studies on estuarine hydrology to certain problems in Australian oyster biology. Rapp. P.V. Reun. Cons. Int. Explor. Mer, 131: 35—37.

Roughley, T.C., 1922. Oyster culture on the George's River, New South Wales, Tech. Educ. Ser. Tech. Mus. Sydney, 25: 1—69.

Roughley, T.C., 1925. The story of the oyster. Aus. Mus. Mag., 2: 1—32.

Roughley, T.C., 1925. The birth and growth of an oyster. Aust. Mus. Mag., 2: 163—168.

Roughley, T.C., 1925. The cultivation of the oyster. Aust. Mus. Mag., 2: 187—194.

Roughley, T.C., 1925. The pests of the oyster. Aust. Mus. Mag., 2: 235—242.

Roughley, T.C., 1925. The perils of an oyster. Mid-Pac. Mag., 1925: 117—122.

Roughley, T.C., 1926. An investigation of the cause of an oyster mortality on the George's River, New South Wales, 1924—5. Proc. Linn. Soc. N.S.W., 51: 446—491.

Roughley, T.C., 1933. The life history of the Australian oyster, *Ostrea commercialis*. Proc. Linn. Soc. N.S.W., 58: 279—333.

Thomson, J.M., 1948. Stick cultivation of oysters. Fish. Newsl., 7 (5): 12—13.

Thomson, J.M., 1950. The effects of the orientation of cultch material on the setting of the Sydney Rock Oyster. Aust. J. Mar. Freshwater Res., 1 (1): 139—154.

Thomson, J.M., 1954. Handbook for oyster farmers. Circ. 3 Div. Fish. CSIRO, 21 pp.

Thomson, J.M., 1954. The genera of oysters and the Australian species. Aust. J. Mar. Freshwater Res. 5 (1): 132—168.

Whitelegge, Th., 1890. Report on the worm disease affecting the oysters on the coast of New South Wales. Rec. Aust. Mus., 1 (2): 41—54.

Whitelegge, Th., 1891. On the recent discoloration of the waters of Port Jackson. Rec. Aust. Mus., 1: 179—192.

Wolf, P.H., 1972. Occurrence of a Haplosporidian in Sydney Rock Oysters (*Crassostrea commercialis*) from Moreton Bay, Queensland, Australia. J. Invertebr. Pathol., 19: 416—417.

Chapter 2

FARMING THE AMERICAN ATLANTIC OYSTER (*CRASSOSTREA VIRGINICA*) IN LONG ISLAND SOUND, U.S.A.

Example
Bloom Brothers Oyster Company, 132 Water Street, Norwalk, Connecticut.
Owners: Mr Hillard Bloom, 38 Cove Avenue, East Norwalk, Connecticut, and his brother Mr Norman Bloom.
Period of observation: 1971—1972.

A. BACKGROUND

A.1. General principles

Long Island Sound, on the Atlantic Coast of North America, sheltered to the south by Long Island (State of New York) and bordered on the north by the coastline of the State of Connecticut, has long been famous for producing large quantities of high quality oysters. During the early part of this century, the annual oyster production soared to between 3×10^6 and 4×10^6 bushels per year, but gradually the production in the Sound declined. Bit by bit the situation worsened and from the mid 1950's to the mid 1960's the production had fallen below 50 000 bushels per year. (1 bushel = 8 gallons = 36.4 litres, equivalent to 200 to 250 marketable sized oysters.)

Many oyster farmers, faced with repeated poor spatfalls and recurring high mortality rates, lost all faith in the future and decided to quit. However, the introduction of modernized farming techniques, under the guidance of scientists led to a spectacular resurgence. An estimate of the total Long Island Sound oyster population in the mid 1960's would be somewhere in the neighbourhood of 150 000 bushels, whereas it had risen to 2×10^6 or perhaps even 3×10^6 bushels by the year 1972, a more than tenfold increase! The annual production of marketable oysters from the Sound is now about 200 000 bushels and every bushel contains some 200 to 250 oysters.

There are now only six active oyster companies in Connecticut and New York. By far the largest are the *Long Island Oyster Farms* of New Haven, in reality a combination of four companies, controlling 17 000 acres of ground, employing over 150 men in the field and ashore and producing at least some 150 000 bushels of oysters per year.

The second largest is the *Bloom Brothers Oyster Company* at Norwalk, who produce 25 000 bushels of oysters per season, using a staff of ten full-time employees. This is the company selected as an example.

There is also the *Radel Oyster Company* which produces some 25 000 bushels of oysters per year, using about ten employees and 3 000 acres of oyster ground. This company operates from Bridgeport and from Oyster Bay, Long Island. There is a certain amount of co-operation between the Bloom Brothers Company and the Radel Oyster Company. The two companies often purchase their seed oysters jointly, putting them on the Radel Company's growing grounds, with the Bloom Company being responsible for cultivation and marketing. The costs of seed purchase and the profits are then shared equally. In addition, there are the *F. Flower and Sons Oyster Company*, *Shellfish Incorporated*, and the *Bluepoints Company*. The latter company has a larger labour force but now only works on a very limited scale with oysters (500 bushels in 1971) and is practically exclusively concerned with clams.

All the oyster companies in Long Island Sound now work partially with the hard-shelled clam or quahog, *Mercenaria mercenaria* which is much in demand on the market. Estimates of the percentages of income earned from sales of hard clams are as follows: 5% for Long Island Oyster Farms, 66% for the Bloom Oyster Company, 25% for the Radel Oyster Company, 50% for F. Flower and Sons Oyster Company, 90% for Shellfish Incorporated and 99% for the Bluepoints Company.

Oyster farming in Long Island Sound is a typical example of a semi-culture. Larval development is entirely left to nature, but when the settling period approaches, shells are planted as collectors. The shells used are old oyster shells, produced as the result of the work of the oyster companies themselves, as most of the oysters are sold shucked, leaving large quantities of the shells. Seed oysters are produced on both public and private grounds, most of which are situated in inshore water. The inshore waters are, however, affected by domestic pollution. Therefore it is not permitted to market oysters which have been grown there. This is one of the reasons why seed oysters are transplanted to other beds for growth and fattening, out of reach of pollution. The oysters grow on the food provided by nature.

If an oyster farmer restricted his activities solely to planting shells and transplanting seed oysters, his harvest would be poor, because various predators and competing organisms inflict serious losses at all stages. Pest control is therefore a prerequisite in modern oyster farming. By the application of modern methods the survival percentage can be raised considerably. Production is now increasing rapidly and, as a result, marketing can hardly keep pace with development.

A.2. Biology of the species

Little needs to be said here concerning the biology of the American Atlantic oyster, *Crassostrea virginica.* This is not only because of the wealth of biological information in Galtsoff's book "The American Oyster, *Crassostrea virginica*, Gmelin" (Fishery Bulletin, Fish and Wildlife Service 64, 1964), but also because of the general remarks on the biology of this species which are made in the chapter dealing with oyster farming in Louisiana.

Long Island Sound is situated at a much higher latitude than the Delta of the Mississippi river. The oysters living in Long Island Sound have adapted to the local hydrographical situation. They can, for instance, stand low temperatures during freezing weather for quite a long time. Growth of the oyster is, however, interrupted in the colder season. Hence, it takes the Long Island Sound oysters much longer to reach marketable size than the oysters in the Mississippi Delta, on an average from 4 to 5 years.

It has been demonstrated that the Long Island Sound population of *Crassostrea virginica* shows normal gonad maturation at water temperatures as low as 15—18°C, whereas oysters from more southern populations are not able to do so. Once the oysters are ready to spawn they need a certain temperature stimulus to expel their gametes.

While the pelagic larvae are developing, they can stand quite a wide range of water temperatures, but the time required to reach the settling phase decreases with increasing water temperature. At 30°C it takes the larvae only 10 days to reach the settling stage. Thus larval survival and the intensity of settling are best at water temperatures of 20°C and higher. As the water temperature does not generally rise much above the 20°C level in the bulk of the Long Island Sound water, good settling years may alternate with years of poor or moderate settling. This is a normal phenomenon in areas approaching the northern limits of the range of a species with pelagic larvae. It is assumed that the inshore parts of the Sound and the estuaries debouching there produce most of the settling larvae because of higher water temperatures occurring there.

A.3. Geographical situation

Long Island Sound is located between latitudes of 41° and 41° 15′ N and longitudes 72° and 73° 50′ W, due east-northeast of the city of New York on the Atlantic Coast of the United States of America. Norwalk, where the headquarters of the company under consideration are located, is situated at 41° 07′ N, and 73° 25′ W.

A.4. Hydrographic pattern

Long Island Sound is a rather shallow body of water, some 150 km long and with a maximum width of 30 km, covering an area of about 900 nautical square miles. To the east, it is continuous with the Atlantic Ocean whereas, to the west, there is only a rather narrow passage to the sea via the East River, passing New York city.

Long Island offers good shelter against southern winds, the Connecticut coast against winds from the north and west.

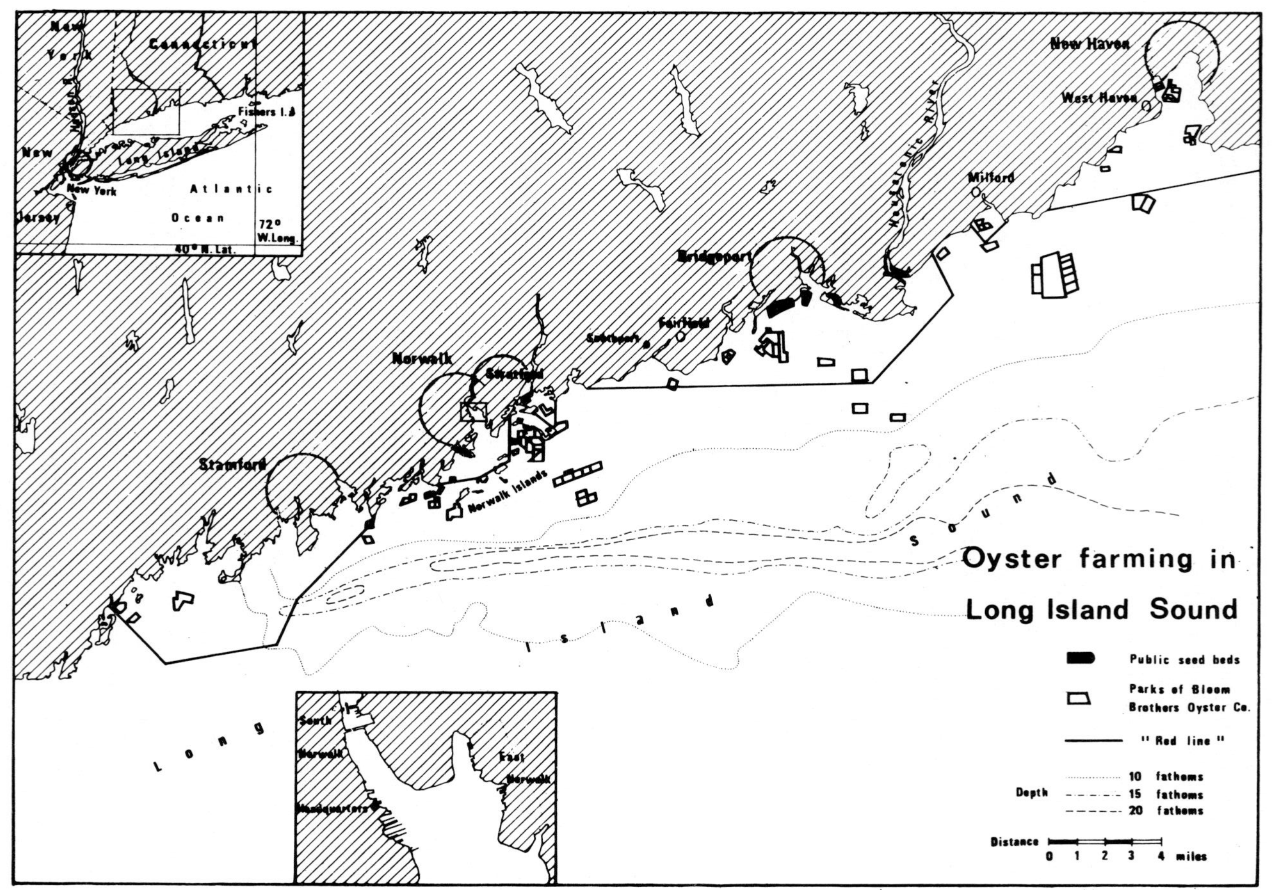
New York
Connecticut
Fishers I.
Long Island
New York
New Jersey
Atlantic
Ocean
72°
W.Long.
40° N.Lat.
New Haven
West Haven
Milford
Housatonic River
Bridgeport
Fairfield
Norwalk
Stamford
Norwalk Islands
L o n g I s l a n d S o u n d
South Norwalk
Headquarters
East Norwalk
Oyster farming in
Long Island Sound
Public seed beds
Parks of Bloom Brothers Oyster Co.
" Red line "
Depth
10 fathoms
15 fathoms
20 fathoms
Distance
0 1 2 3 4 miles

Depth. Over most of its area the depth of the Sound is less than 35 m, the average depth being about 20 m. Most of the oyster leases are laid out at a depth of 3—10 m.

Tides. The tidal range is on an average 2 m, leading to current velocities of 2—3 knots and a tidal interchange of 8.6% of the volume of the Sound below mean water level. The ebb is stronger than the flood in the surface layer, the reverse is true at the bottom. This indicates that there is a tendency for the surface layer to move seawards, and for replacement by saline water flowing in along the bottom. In the western part of the Sound an admixture of bottom and surface water can be seen. Less than 1/15 of the volume of water flowing in through the wide eastern pass comes in via the East River in the west.

Water temperature. In the eastern part of the Sound, water temperatures may drop to 3° C in winter to rise to 19° C in summer, whereas in the western part of the Sound the winter minimum will be about 0° C and the summer maximum as much as 23° C. In the estuaries and closely inshore the annual range can be even greater.

Salinity. The salinity of Long Island Sound is noticeably lower than that of the open Atlantic Ocean, ranging from 23 to 31‰. The drainage basin is roughly 11 times the area of the Sound itself and the annual volume of fresh-water drainage averages 35% of the total volume of the Sound. Some 75% of the river water enters, however, in the more open eastern part of the Sound and is flushed out rather rapidly. Thus the salinity rarely drops under the 23% level in offshore sites.

Chemical composition. Analysis of the Long Island Sound water has shown an N : P ratio of 8 : 1, about half that to be expected in ocean water. The phosphate-P figures fluctuate from 0.2 μg at/l in summer to 2.3 μg at/l in winter, nitrate-N figures from practically zero in summer to 18 μg at/l in winter. Chlorophyll showed most of the time a value around 5 μg/l, but occasional peaks rose as high as 30 μg/l, with usually 8×10^6 cells per l, and 30×10^6/l during the chlorophyll peak.

Long Island Sound, with its mean depth of 20 m, appears to have a larger standing crop of phytoplankton and a greater basic productivity than a station in 70 m of water in the English Channel off Plymouth. The Sound is a kind of trap for plankton and nutrients coming in from the ocean in which filter feeders such as oysters play an important role.

The water is rather turbid in Long Island Sound, a Secchi disc disappearing from view at a depth of about 2 m.

Sea bed conditions. The sea bed of the oyster grounds consists predominantly of a rather hard sand—gravel mixture. When severe storms strike from certain angles, however, oysters may become buried in shifting bottom deposits.

Pollution. Since the coast of the State of Connecticut is rather densely populated and has urban agglomerations such as Stamford, Norwalk, Bridgeport, Stratford and New Haven, it is not surprising that pollution by domestic sewage is a serious problem for the oyster industry. A red line is drawn on the map to indicate the quality of the oyster grounds on the basis of bacteriological surveys. Inside this red line, seed oysters may be produced but such oysters must be transferred to grounds with cleaner water for further growth and fattening. No shellfish may be marketed from grounds situated inshore of the red line. There are a transitional group of leases which are closed for marketing during periods of heavy downpours of rain, but which can be reopened once the situation ameliorates.

A.5. Legal aspects

The Bloom Brothers Oyster Company is a private enterprise. The company is owner of most of the grounds on which it operates. This means that it has a perpetual franchise, for the grounds can be held indefinitely by the company, provided it pays the tax on them. The grounds fall within the jurisdiction of the town and the town charges a tax of US $2.00 per acre per year. The tax is reduced to $0.60 per acre per year (2% of its appraised value: US $30.00) if a formerly valuable ground is given up, returned to the State and then re-leased to another company if there is no competitive bidding. When a company gives up a piece of ground other companies may apply for it by sealed bid. The company that offers to pay the highest annual tax per acre is given rights to the ground. Thus annual taxes may occasionally run as high as US $15.00 per acre.

The Bloom Company owns most of its grounds in the Norwalk Westport area, but in addition to the grounds it owns, a few are leased. The company has its settling grounds at Southport, Bridgeport, Fairfield, Milford and New Haven, but uses only a small proportion of any of these. The Bloom Brothers have 4 788 acres of ground held under perpetual franchise under the jurisdiction of the Shellfish Commission of the State of Connecticut, and in addition 357 acres under lease, partly from the town and partly from the State. The total acreage of the company is spread over 94 plots of which only a small number are greater than 100 acres. The general information bulletin, issued by the Shellfish Commission gives a complete index of the grounds with owners, lessees and acreages. It also indicates the steps to be taken to become a lessee.

The plots are marked by wooden stakes. It is the duty of the company to purchase such sea marks and to place them correctly. The stakes are pushed into holes pumped in the bottom; sometimes they are held in place by a chain fastened to a large cement stone.

Surveillance is carried out by the marine police attached to each town along the coast of Connecticut and by special shellfish wardens hired by most coastal towns to guard against poaching on public grounds. They also guard private grounds. Naturally, company staff also keep an eye on what is going on on the company's grounds.

B. SEQUENCE OF OPERATIONS

B.1. Procuring oyster seed from public beds

Off Bridgeport and in the mouth of the Housatonic River are public seed oyster beds. The seed oysters are harvested here by individuals termed "natural growthers". They operate usually from skiffs powered by outboard motors, and use 1-bushel capacity dredges to collect the seed oysters (Fig. 15). Such a skiff with two men on board can harvest about 40 bushels of seed oysters per day. This seed is 1 or 2 years old. The "natural growthers" sell their catch of seed oysters to oyster farmers, who use them to stock their beds. The company pays US \$3.00 per bushel, but 10% of that sum is claimed by the State as tax. This money is used for planting shells as collectors on the natural beds under the supervision of the State. This source of seed oysters is quite important for the Bloom Brothers Oyster Company: in recent years they have bought some 30 000 bushels of seed.

B.2. Procuring oyster seed on private beds

The company uses some of its settling grounds to produce seed oysters by scattering oyster shells as collectors. At its dock there is a huge pile of shells, partly derived from the shucking procedure and partly composed of dead shells collected when fishing for marketable oysters. Tens of thousands of bushels of shells are available on the premises of the company (Fig. 16). Dur-

Fig. 14. "Natural growthers" tying bushel bags of oysters by the side of the Housatonic River. (Photo C.L. MacKenzie.)

Fig. 15. The equipment of the "natural growthers".

ing storage ashore the epibiontic organisms, which had settled on them in the Sound, will die and disappear, so that the shells are essentially clean when spread.

As the larvae of the American Atlantic oyster require clean cultch as a substratum, it is essential to time the shell planting operations carefully. Water temperatures this far north are not conducive every year to the larval development of this essentially subtropical species. Therefore, the Bloom Company decides not to plant any shells unless spatfall prospects are reasonably good.

Fig. 16. The company's shell pile.

B.3. Spatfall forecasts

For many years the Milford Laboratory of the U.S. Bureau of Commercial Fisheries issued settling forecasts based on the analysis of daily samples of plankton. When a great number of young oyster larvae makes its appearance in the water of the Sound it is not yet possible to be sure that this indicates good settling prospects, for several factors may interfere with larval development. Water temperatures of 20° C and lower protract larval life to such an extent that survival until settling will be poor under these conditions. It is assumed that apart from water temperature as such, a factor like cloud cover, possibly affecting the development of suitable food organisms for the larvae, may have an influence on larval development and presumably also sudden increases in the number of organisms predating on oyster larvae. Practical experience has shown that one should wait for the appearance of a fair number of umbo-larvae before issuing favourable settling forecasts. This means that settling will reach a peak some 4 days later, but since the Bloom Company has the equipment to spread the shells in a short space of time, they are in a position to base their policy for spat collecting operations mainly on the plankton reports.

The Milford Laboratory ceased to be a special shellfish laboratory a few years ago, its programme being shifted to environmental problems. Since 1970 spatfall prediction has been taken over by Long Island Oyster Farms, the largest company in the area.

Usually the best time for settling is the second half of July, but occasionally a set of commercial importance may come as late as September. This, for instance, was the case in 1971.

B.4. Sailing out the shells

A pay-loader with a capacity of about 10 bushels removes shells from the pile and empties them into a hopper. This feeds onto a conveyor belt that carries the shells to the boat[1]. The two company boats can hold about 2 000 bushels of shells each, and it takes one man, operating the pay-loader, 40 min to load a boat. A bushel contains some 500 oyster shells. The time required to run the boat to the settling ground differs: about 1 h for the Southport grounds, 4 h for the run from Norwalk to the New Haven beds. In addition to the captain, there are three men on the ship to wash the shells overboard with a hose and water pump. The Bloom Oyster Company spreads 1 500—2 000 bushels of shells per acre of settling ground. The grounds lie under 8—25 feet of water. When settling prospects are really good, the company will spread its whole shell pile, i.e. 30 000—60 000 bushels of shells. On an average the company produces some 5 000 bushels of seed per year from its own settling beds.

B.5. Dredging old shells out of the bottom deposits

Occasionally open dredges are towed over the oyster grounds carrying old shells. This is primarily to remove silt deposits, but also to dig out and turn over the old shells in order to offer the larvae their clean underside. This procedure may lead to some success, but as drills and starfish are not controlled this way, the spat which does settle will usually suffer heavy losses here. It is therefore doubtful whether such operations can be considered as remunerative.

B.6. Purchase of seed produced in a pond

To supplement the quantities of seed oysters from the public beds and from the company's own settling beds oysters are sometimes purchased from other sources. One of these, is a rather deep 23-acre brackishwater pond on Fisher's Island (N.Y.) situated in the easternmost part of Long Island Sound. This pond is closed off from the sea in the early summer to accelerate the rise in water temperature and to prevent oyster larvae, produced there by a mother stock, from escaping to the sea. Strings of scallop shells (74 shells with 2-inch plastic tube spacers strung on 8-foot sections of 14 gauge galvanized wire) are hung from rafts and usually manage to collect a good crop of seed. In the years 1965—1971 the company purchased 1 000—2 000 bushels of 10-month-old oysters per year at a price of US $10.00—12.00 per bushel. These were spread on the Company's grounds during May. Since the seed from the natural beds is much cheaper and usually readily available, the company does not plan to continue to purchase from this source.

B.7. Hatchery seed

There are now several hatcheries in the area, among which is one at Stratford, on the Housatonic River, operated by the Bloom Company itself. The latter hatchery produces 200—2 000 bushels of oyster seed per year. The company occasionally purchases hatchery stock; for example in 1967 2 000 bushels of spat were purchased from the Vanderborgh-Radel Hatchery in Oyster Bay, N.Y., at a cost of US $10.00 per bushel. This spat was spread on the beds during September, when it was only 6 weeks old. In 1969—1970 the company purchased 7×10^6 seed oysters as singles from the Budge Oyster Hatchery, Pigeon Point, California, at a cost of 3 per US $0.01. These oysters, however, measured only about 5 mm in diameter and had to be grown for 6 weeks on screen-bottom trays supported by rafts moored above the beds. When planted they measured 0.75—1 inch in diameter, but the trays fouled so rapidly that labour costs for thinning the oysters and cleaning the screens became prohibitive. It is, therefore, not planned to purchase such single spat again.

Fig. 17. Two pioneers in rearing shellfish larvae admire a batch of cultchless seed in the hatchery: left, the scientist, Dr V.L. Loosanoff; right, the director of Pacific Mariculture Inc. at Pigeon Point, Pescadero, California, Mr W.W. Budge. (Photo P. Korringa.)

B.8. Inspection of the spat on the settling grounds

Some 6 to 8 weeks after the settling season, a regular system of inspection is begun, with inspections of the spat which has settled on the planted shells spaced at intervals of a few weeks. This not only allows for timely action to be taken if predators make their appearance, but is also to see whether spat is being shifted by storms, and therefore requires transplantation to a safer ground in October.

B.9. Transplanting the seed

The rate of growth of American Atlantic oysters living along the coast of Connecticut is about 1 inch per year and as marketable oysters have a shell length of from 3 to 6 inches, they will be from 3 to 6 years old when sold. Most of the oysters are sold as 4 year olds with a shell length of about 4 inches and amount to 200—300 per bushel.

The Bloom company transplants its seed oysters from the settling grounds to the growing grounds, which are characterized by fast water currents, rich in food. The oysters are planted in water which is 5—18 feet deep and shel-

Fig. 18. Typical Long Island Sound oyster boat.

tered by the Norwalk Islands. Transplantation begins in September and October of the year for those shells which should be moved because they run the risk of being washed away by storms from unprotected shoal grounds. For those shells where this is not the case, transplantation is carried out the following spring, but preferably before about April 10th. This is because oysters which become covered by silt or sand during the course of the winter would smother to death if they were not dredged up before the water temperature rises above about 7°C.

A boat [1] (Fig. 18) can transplant some 1 500 bushels of seed oysters per day when the run is between Norwalk and New Haven (4 h) but two to three trips can be made when the distance to be covered is small (Norwalk—Southport). This procedure consists solely of transplanting oysters, without cleaning or grading. Again a jet of water is used to spread the seed oyster onto the new beds. The seed is spread at various rates depending on the count per bushel. When the count is as low as 500 to 800 seed oysters per bushel, they are spread at a rate of 800 bushels per acre, but when the count is as high as 10 000 to 14 000 per bushel they are spread at a rate of only about 300 bushels of material per acre, taking care to spread the oysters as evenly as possible. The company does not like to have more than about 1 500 bushels of seed oysters on an acre after growth ceases in the early winter. Handling leads to the breaking off of seed oysters from the collector shells and also to the breaking up of clusters, so that nearly all the oysters are singles on their final ground before marketing. The seed oysters are left on the new ground for 1 and sometimes 2 years. The activities of starfish and drills have to be checked during this period whenever necessary.

B.10. Transfer to fattening grounds

The Bloom Company transfers its oysters to special grounds for fattening during their final year before marketing. To acquire a good market value the oysters should be planted on the best fattening grounds, such as the company's plots 79 and 92. These are shoal grounds and well-protected from storms. The oysters are spread here at a rate of 500 bushels per acre in the spring of their final year as their fattening would be jeopardized if they were spread at a higher rate.

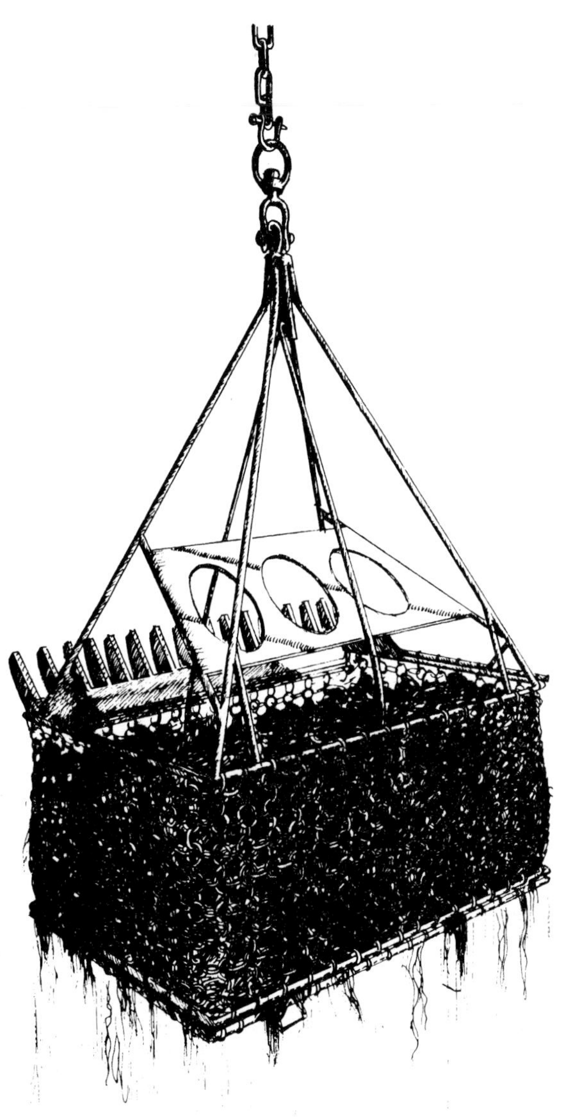

Fig. 19. Type of oyster dredge used by the Bloom Company.

B.11. Fishing and culling marketable oysters

There is no close season in the Long Island Sound oyster district, but invariably most of the oysters are sold in the winter months when their quality is at its best. One of the company boats is fully engaged in harvesting marketable oysters. When it is not too cold, the oysters are culled and graded on an 8 × 8 foot table, placed on the deck of the dredge boat, but in the colder months this is done in the shop ashore (Fig. 20). In this latter case the catch is just piled on deck, and when the boat arrives at the dock it is moored just below the bin which is in the loft of the shop. The oysters are shoveled into 5-bushel tubs and power hoisted into the loft where they are dumped into the bin. From here they are allowed to fall onto the culling and shucking benches.

Any clusters of oysters which remain are broken apart by culling irons and any oysters which are too small for the market are separated, to be re-spread on a clean bed and harvested during the following marketing season. Empty shells are removed to the shell pile.

Fig. 20. Headquarters of the Bloom Brothers Oyster Company with railway (left) and bin (right) above the shop. (Photo C.L. MacKenzie.)

B.12. Grading and shipping marketable oysters

The oysters are hand-graded by size for market. A bushel of oysters weighs 70—75 pounds. The so-called "medium" oysters run to 200 per bushel and the "half-shells" to 300 per bushel. Some of the larger oysters are shucked by hand, after which the meats are freed of any adhering shell particles in a "blower" (a large stainless steel tub containing fresh water through which air is blown; see Fig. 22). They are next put into 1-gallon cans, quickly refrigerated and then shipped to the market.

The Bloom Company shucks only about 10% of its oysters, the remaining 90% being shipped in the shell. These are predominantly of the "medium" category with some 20% "half-shells". After being washed by dipping them into a tub of fresh water, these oysters are packed in either wooden baskets or 1-bushel burlap bags. The company ships its packed oysters by truck within 12 h of packing. There are no storage basins ashore but, when packed, shelled oysters can be temporarily stored at 2—5°C in a cold room before travelling.

After arrival in the restaurants, most of the "mediums" will be shucked on the spot to be fried or to undergo further culinary preparation in the kitchen. The smaller "half-shells" are predominantly eaten in the raw state on the half shell.

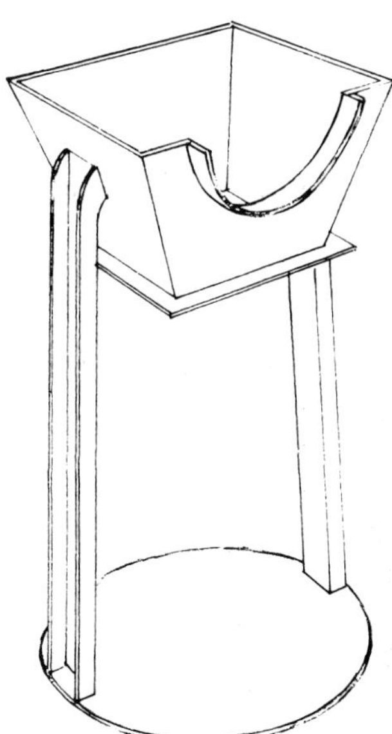

Fig. 21. Utensil used for filling bags with 1 bushel of marketable oysters each.

Fig. 22. The blower in which shucked oyster meats are washed. (Photo C.L. MacKenzie.)

B.13. Fishing and transplanting hard-shelled clams

As quite a large percentage of the gross income of the Bloom Brothers Oyster Company is as a result of the sale of the hard-shelled clam, *Mercenaria mercenaria*, and a good proportion of the sailing time of the company's boats has to be earmarked for fishing for clams, some remarks on this aspect of the company's operations are felt to be in order.

Hard-shelled clams, or quahogs, occur in great numbers on natural beds in several sections of Long Island Sound. They live at the bottom of the sea, but not on the surface of the bottom as do oysters; they live in the sediment and only their siphons protrude. Thus clams cannot be harvested using a normal oyster dredge. To fish clams, a special hydraulic clam dredge is used. This has a narrow blade, 6-inch teeth and operates using jets of water to

Fig. 23. One-gallon cans of shucked oysters ready for sealing and storage in a refrigerator. (Photo C.L. MacKenzie.)

soften the bottom in front of the teeth. The bag of the clam dredge can hold from 10 to 15 bushels of material. The "Cultivator", one of the company's boats, has a clam dredge installed on its port side, with a large pump fitted between the cabin and the stern, under the engine housing.

The peak season for fishing and shipping clams is during the months of June, July and August, which is exactly the opposite to that for oysters. Therefore, clam fishing and oyster farming go well together. The demand for clams is very great, especially those in the "little-neck" category, the main product of the company, and the somewhat larger "cherry-stones". The value per bushel of the larger clams, known as "mediums" and "chowders", is less. As the clams live in the bottom deposits and usually occur in lower densities than oysters, they are somewhat harder to harvest. The Bloom Company boat can, nevertheless, bag 25—35 bushels of clams per h. In summer, the clam beds are worked on during the early morning, to land and sell about 75 bushels of little-neck per day. As the "Cultivator" has an oyster dredge on her starboard side a load of oysters can always be collected if there is an order. During the 3 months mentioned, over 90% of the sailing time of the company's boats is spent fishing for clams, whereas during the remainder of the year more than 90% of the time is spent on oysters.

The clams, emptied from the dredge onto the deck, are picked out, tossed into 1-bushel baskets and later emptied into burlap bags. Picking clams requires considerably less time than sorting out oysters on the deck of a ship.

Although most of the clam industry could be described as solely harvesting from natural beds, there is a small-scale operation which can be described as partial clam farming. The Bloom Company found beds of little-necks on the public grounds in Norwalk harbour, but as the area concerned is within the red line, these clams cannot be marketed directly. Thus, after going through a legal battle to obtain permission, the company proceeded to fish these clams for transportation to the company's Darien beds nearby. Up to 700 bushels of material, containing clams of all ages, can be transferred in a 6-h trip of the company's boat. After living about 1 month in clean water, the clams can be taken up for marketing. Cleansing is the main purpose of the operation, not growth or fattening.

Some efforts have been made to farm clams based on hatchery stock. The very small clams produced by the hatcheries are, however, extremely vulnerable to the attacks of a variety of predators, and the survival rate is very low indeed. Rational exploitation and proper protection of the natural clam beds appear, for the time being, to be the more promising procedure.

C. FARMING RISKS

The planting of shells at the right time of the year to offer settling larvae a good substratum is an operation of major importance in oyster farming in Long Island Sound. However, even when spatfall is prolific, one cannot necessarily be assured of a good harvest of seed oysters, for enemies and adverse weather conditions may lead to very high mortality rates. Predator control is therefore a "must" in a modern oyster farm. The scientists and technicians of the Milford Laboratory have now obtained, not only a good insight into the causes of mortality in the different life phases of the oysters in Long Island Sound, but they have also developed, first in the laboratory and later in the field, adequate methods of control.

C.1. Hydrographic conditions

On some poorly sheltered grounds spatfall is often good, but since the shells carrying the spat are susceptible to being washed away by storms, they have to be transplanted at an early stage (September/October of the year of settling) to grounds which offer better protection. When spatfall is really good on such grounds, it naturally pays to use it well and to go to the trouble of transplanting the young spat.

On many beds it is quite common for the heavy shells carrying the small spat to become buried in sand and silt during the course of the cold winter months. It is a normal feature everywhere for oysters to disappear from sight during the colder months and return to the surface of the sea bed once the water temperature rises sufficiently. The specific gravity of a living oyster is lower than that of the bottom deposits. An oyster making active shell movements will, therefore, make its own way to the top of the sediment in spring, after having been in a dormant stage during the winter. Under fully natural conditions, spat will settle by preference on the clean new shoots of living oysters, so they have no trouble in coming to the surface in spring. Spat which has settled on the quite large and heavy shells of dead oysters, however, are not in such a favourable position, as the specific weight of the collector and spat combined is higher than that of the sediment. In winter, the spat is semi-dormant and survives even when buried somewhat by sand and silt, but if the oyster farmer does not come to its rescue in early spring (before about April 10th) the losses suffered may be extremely heavy. Dredging up shells with spat on in the early spring greatly reduces their mortality from smothering.

C.2. Predators

By far the most dangerous of the Long Island Sound oyster predators, is the starfish *Asterias forbesi.* Detailed studies of its feeding rate reveal that this is low in the winter, very high at the onset of summer and declines noticeably during its spawning season to rise again later in the year. The intensity of its settling in Long Island Sound has also been studied. Spawning begins in the middle of June, when the water temperature surpasses the 15°C level, and intensive settling may be expected from late June until the end of July, sometimes later still, the intensity of settling varying greatly from year to year.

Small starfish kill the spat; larger ones, oysters of greater dimensions. As the oyster beds are liable to become invaded by starfish in the course of the summer season, the boats of the Bloom Company check all their beds for starfish about once a week. During years when starfish are found to be numerous, this may even be twice a week. This checking does not take much time. About five short tows with a so-called ‘starfish mop’, taking a total of about 10 min, often done while the boat is travelling to an oyster or clam ground for harvesting, suffices. The starfish get entangled in the strings of waste cotton attached to the iron frame of the mop as it is dragged over the surface of the bottom. If the number of starfish detected on the beds happens to be low, they are removed by means of the cotton starfish mops and

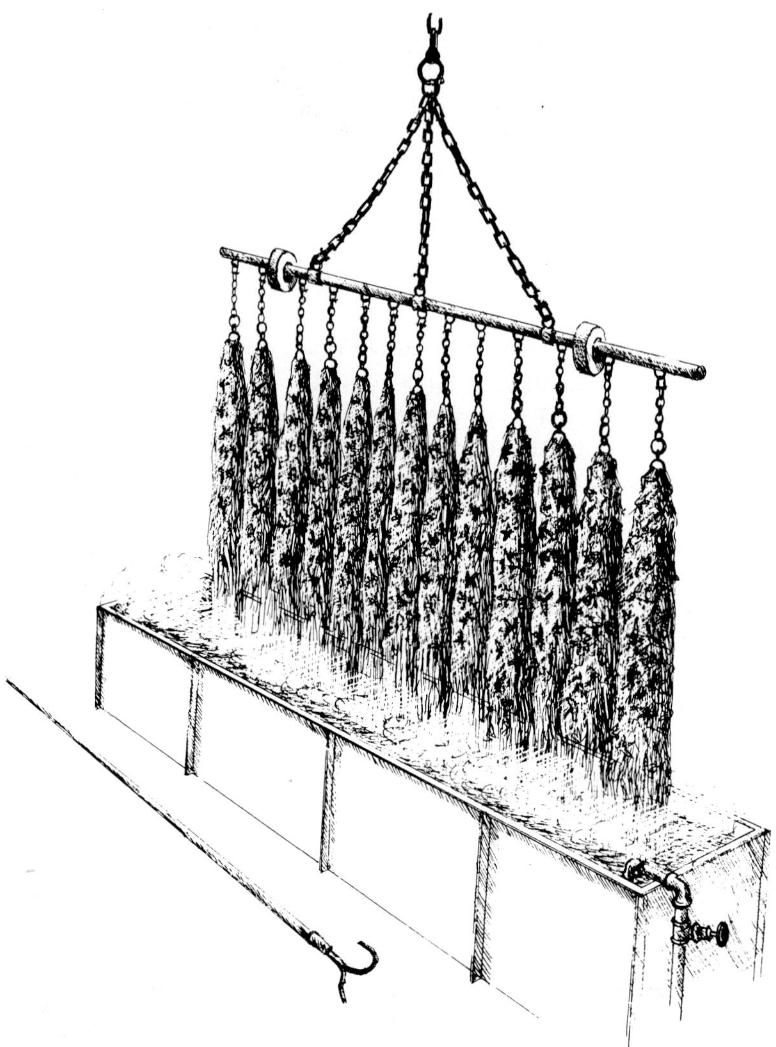

Fig. 24. The starfish mop is dipped into a tank of boiling water to kill the entangled starfish.

dipped in a tank of boiling water placed on the deck of the ship (Fig. 24). Sometimes starfish invade the grounds in such numbers that other methods of control have to be used. Occasionally starfish may be found to have encroached up to 100 feet into a plot before they are detected to be feeding on the seed oysters. Up to 50% of the seed oysters there may be killed in this way, whereas mortality from this cause may be less than 5% in the main part of the beds. Such a difference is logical, for starfish on feeding migration will linger longer where they find plenty of food.

An efficient method of starfish control, developed by the Milford Laboratory, is by the spreading of finely granulated quicklime, some 2 000 pounds per acre. During the period 1966—1967 the company under consideration efficiently controlled the starfish on its beds by means of quicklime, spreading each ground holding oysters on an average 1.5 times per year. During 1970—1971 there were far fewer starfish and the rate of treatment was thus much less.

Other predators causing substantial losses among the oysters grown in Long Island Sound are the Atlantic drill, the gastropod *Urosalpinx cinerea*, and the thick-lipped drill, *Eupleura caudata*. Oysters of all sizes may be attacked by drills but as the latter have no pelagic larvae the grounds are not invaded overnight, so to speak. When the ravages by drills are of a serious nature it is advisable to use chemical control. The Millford Laboratory scientists have experimented in drill control with carbamates and a product more widely used in the field known as "Polystream", a trade name of the Hooker Chemical Corporation for a mixture of polychlorinated benzenes. It is spread on the grounds as a granular product and kills a high percentage of the Atlantic drills and thick-lipped drills without noticeably affecting the oysters or clams. Immediately after the treatment, a slight residue may be found in the latter's tissues, but this disappears within 1 week. The treatment is only efficient on those grounds where the current velocities are rather low (0.9—2.7 km per h). Once they have been killed in an area, it takes the drills some years to invade it again. The costs for drill control using Polystream (US $200 per acre for one treatment) should therefore be spread over about 5 years. The increase in the yield of seed oysters was found to be remarkable after the drills had been adequately destroyed.

Other predators such as the mud crab, *Neopanope texana*, and the rock crab, *Cancer irroratus*, are of minor importance in Long Island Sound. Mud crabs may kill small spat which has settled on shells of up to 10 mm diameter and can overpower much larger oysters when they are not protected by a collector. Rock crabs can locally destroy some 10% of the oyster spat. The Bloom Company, however, does not attempt to control the mortality of oysters due to predation by crabs.

C.3. Competitors

Various benthic organisms may settle on the oysters or on the spat collectors and interfere with their feeding activities. Sometimes the young oysters are killed by smothering. Slipper shells, *Crepidula fornicata* and *Crepidula plana*, the jingle shell, *Anomia simplex*, and also the calcareous bryozoan, *Schizoporella unicornis*, are rightly considered as oyster pests by the Long Island Sound farmers, but their influence on the survival of seed oysters is undoubtedly of far less importance than that of drills and starfish.

Polydora, which causes unsightly mud-blisters in the shells of oysters in the regions further south is not a serious headache in Long Island Sound. Rarely can it be said that the market quality of Long Island Sound oysters has been reduced by *Polydora's* mud-blisters. The boring sponge, *Clione*, is also only occasionally found to honeycomb the shells of old oysters in this area.

C.4. Parasites and diseases

Although sometimes mortality among the recently settled spat is observed without it being possible to identify the cause, the oyster biologists working in the Long Island Sound region are convinced that parasites and diseases should be considered as a factor of far less importance in oyster survival than predators such as starfish and drills. Indeed, it was the control of these latter pests together with some other farming improvements, which led to the spectacular revival of the Long Island Sound oyster industry.

D. ECONOMIC ASPECTS

D.1. Rents

The Bloom Brothers Oyster Company has a considerable area of oyster grounds at its disposal: 4 788 acres under direct ownership, plus 357 acres of rented grounds. The company pays a total of about US $3 000 per year in taxes on its grounds.

D.2. Inventory items

The Bloom Brothers Oyster Company operates with two dredge boats. Both are flat-decked wooden boats powered by diesel engines. All the boats used in the area are rather old. They do about 10 knots and have a capacity of 1 000—1 500 bushels. The boats are equipped with oyster dredges of the standard cage type, which are lifted with booms. The engines have a useful life of about 15 years. A new engine, installed, costs about US $15 000. The dredges which cost US $150.00 each last about 15 years, but the dredge blade that holds the teeth has to be replaced two or three times a year. The chain bag on a dredge is replaced three times a year. The 150-foot tow chains, made of hard cam alloy, 1/2—7/16 inch in diameter, cost US $2.00 per foot and last about 2 years.

A new oyster boat, fully equipped, would now cost US $150 000—200 000, but a second-hand boat can be purchased for US $15 000—30 000.

Maintenance of a boat costs about US $5 000 per year and the ice sheeting has to be changed every 1—4 years depending on the amount of ice encountered. Torn sheeting can be patched. At its headquarters, the company at present operates out of one shop, measuring 80 × 200 feet. Recently the company purchased from the Radel Oyster Company, an adjoining oyster property that has a larger but older building, dock and yard. This building will be used for storing and repairing the equipment, the dock will be used for the boat, and the yard for storing a large pile of shells.

At its headquarters the company has four conveyor belts, each 30 feet long, for loading shells. These cost US $1 500 each and last about 15 years. A railway system and a car for carrying the shells from the ship and delivering them to the pile is located on the street side of the shop.

The company has further, a pick-up truck, costing US $2 500, with a useful life of about 5 years, and a pay-loader, costing US $8 000 which has an assumed life span of 10 years.

D.3. *Expendable items*

The huge quantity of shells planted each year as collectors does not figure on the budget of the company, since they are a waste product of the enterprise. Nevertheless, they represent a certain value as contractors sometimes buy them for various purposes. The company could not, however, sell its surplus shells in recent years, mainly because the plan for the State of Connecticut to spread shells on its public grounds did not materialize. Fuel is an ever recurring item. An oyster boat uses 20 gallons of fuel per day, costing US $0.20 per gallon, plus 0.5 gallon of lubricating oil per day, costing US $0.20 per gallon. The expenses for fuel for running the company's oyster and clam boats and for heating their shop on the dock amount to some US $300—400 per month. The great area of oyster ground necessitates the annual purchase of a fair number of sea marks. The company buys for this purpose an average of 1 000 stakes per year costing about US $1.75 each. The stakes last, at the most, 1 year.

D.4. *Purchase of seed oysters*

Every year the Bloom Company buys an appreciable quantity of seed oysters fished from the public beds by the "natural growthers". In recent years, the annual purchase of seed amounted to 30 000 bushels at US $3.00 per bushel. The more expensive seed from the pond on Fisher's Island and from the hatcheries has not been purchased in recent years, as there has been ample seed available from the public beds and from the seed beds where the company planted its own shells.

D.5. *Predator control*

For starfish control, for each acre 2 000 pounds of quicklime per application are required, costing, spreading included, US $25.00 per acre. On average, lime has to be spread 1.5 times per year. In the period 1966—1969 this led to an expense of US $37.50 per acre per year. In the period 1970—1971, with its lower starfish population, the cost for quicklime-spreading will have been some US $12.50 per acre per year.

A Polystream treatment given in 1966—1967 cost US $200.00 per acre, but as its effect lasts at least 5 years this expense can be calculated at US $40.00 per acre per year.

D.6. Personnel and wages

The company operates with ten full-time male workers, of which seven work on the boats and three in the shop, plus three part-time shuckers hired for a short season. There is also a part-time female bookkeeper. The full-time workers earn US $10 000—15 000 per year. Some work as many as 70 h per week. Oyster shuckers earn US $1.50 per gallon of oyster meat.

D.7. Running costs of a boat

It costs about US $100.00 per day to operate a boat, including the salaries of the captain and the deck-hands. If a boat transplants 3 000 bushels of seed oysters per day, this operation costs some US $0.033 per bushel. If a boat fishes 25—35 bushels of clams per hour, this work costs less than US $0.50 per bushel.

D.8. Farming costs

For predator control, US $37.50 per acre is necessary for quicklime and US $40.00 per acre for Polystream. If $2.00 for tax are added to this, the total expenses are approximately $80.00 per acre. As there are usually 1 200—1 500 bushels of oyster seed per acre these costs amount to US $0.05 per bushel per year. In reality these costs are lower, for during the final year before marketing there is virtually no control of starfish or drills to be paid for, since, by then, the oysters, are so much larger. All items include producing the seed, transplanting it twice, predator control, and taxes. Mr Clyde L. MacKenzie, biologist of the Milford Fishery Laboratory, estimates the costs of raising a bushel of oysters to market size to be US $1.25.

D.9. Cost of culling and packing oysters

Culling, grading and packing oysters, and getting rid of the empty shells is quite an expensive business, ranging from US $1.25 to US $3.50 per bushel, with an average of US $2.25 according to Mr MacKenzie. Evidently it costs more to prepare oysters in the shop for the market than it does to raise them on the grounds to a marketable size over a period of 4 years!

D.10. Sales

The Bloom Brothers Oyster Company sells its oysters to several places in the northeast of the United States, especially in the States of Pennsylvania, Rhode Island, Connecticut, Massachusetts, New York, and also to eastern Canada. The total sales amounted in recent years to some 25 000 bushels of oysters per season. As a bushel of oysters contains 200 to 250 specimens, the annual production amounts to $5 \times 10^6 - 6 \times 10^6$ oysters. Since up to ten men are involved in farming work, the number of oysters produced per employee amounts to roughly half a million, substantially more than is achieved in farming flat oysters in Europe.

The company received US \$13.00—16.00 per bushel for shelled oysters (90% of their production, predominantly in the "medium" category) and US \$14.00 per gallon for shucked oysters, with 9 pounds of oyster meat per gallon. They receive the latter price for the remaining 10% of their oysters.

It has been previously stated that some 66% of the company's income should be ascribed to the sale of hard-shelled clams. The price for clams has risen considerably during the past 10 years or so. Fishermen received US \$19.00 per bushel of little-necks some 10 years ago, whereas now they are payed US \$30.00 per bushel. "Cherry-stones" were sold for US \$22.00 per bushel in 1972. The value of the larger "mediums" and "chowders" was less. The Bloom Company predominantly sells little-necks. The Bloom Company, both in 1970 and 1971, sold some 20 000 bushels of clams which, expressed in weight, is about 800 tons.

E. GOVERNMENTAL ASSISTANCE

The Government assists the oyster industry in Long Island Sound in various ways. First of all it should be mentioned that the taxes paid for oyster grounds here are very low indeed, especially in comparison with the rents paid in European oyster districts. It can hardly be felt to be a burden on the budget of the farmers and gives them the opportunity of having more ground than they actually need.

Then there are the scientists and technicians of the government laboratory at Milford who carry out investigations on the various phases of the oyster's life, starting with its larval development, under both natural and laboratory conditions. The settling forecasts from the laboratory, based on frequent larval surveys, have been a great help in deciding if and when to plant shells. The investigations on oyster predation have also been of great practical importance. The scientists not only discovered the causes of the oyster losses suffered over the years of farming, but also developed practical methods for their control. One of the difficulties encountered in chemical control is the precautions required when a chemical product is used on organisms finally destined for human consumption. Therefore all the possible side effects of chemical control had to be studied before it could be used. Not only biological but also technical advice has been given by the Milford staff, for instance, on the construction of the dredge and on the efficient spreading of quicklime to control starfish. It should also not be forgotten that during the years that Dr V.L. Loosanoff was its director, the Milford Laboratory was the cradle for oyster hatchery techniques in the United States. After careful experimentation there, it was discovered how to control gonad maturation, spawning, and larval development so that it is now possible to produce clam and oyster spat in a hatchery on a large scale at almost any time of the year. The stage between settling and the oysters being large enough to be able to withstand the attacks of various predators is still the main bottleneck after actual hatchery operations. The heavy losses suffered during this phase or, alternatively, the high costs for labour and material if it is preferred to grow the juvenile shellfish on trays, still prevents large-scale application of hatchery techniques in areas such as Long Island Sound, where spatfall under fully natural conditions leads to reasonably good results in the average year. Though hatchery operations give the opportunity for genetic control and thus of developing strains of oysters and clams displaying desirable features, including fast growth and resistance to certain diseases, in the long run it is always the economic aspect of seed oyster production which makes oyster farmers decide which system they will use.

Another important aspect of government assistance to the oyster industry in Long Island Sound is in bacteriological control and the enforcement of the red-line system. For this, the Federal Food and Drug Administration and the State Public Health Laboratory, in Hartford, Connecticut, carry out the relevant programmes free of charge. The water on the oyster grounds is required to have a coliform count of less than 70 per 100 ml and the oyster meat to have a fecal coliform count of less than 230 per 100 g. For this purpose Federal Inspectors check both the oysters on the grounds and the water twice a year, while State Inspectors check the oysters in the shops at least once a week. Each bushel of shelled oysters and each gallon can of shucked oyster meat is shipped with a tag listing: the name of the company, the license number, the ground number and the date of harvesting. This means that it is always possible to trace the origin of the oysters. Occasionally, the market grounds of the company are temporarily closed because of pollution after heavy rains.

F. GENERAL IMPRESSION

Oyster farming in Long Island Sound is a typical example of a semi-culture based on rich natural resources. During the early part of this century, the production of marketable oysters reached a very high peak here, although farming operations were virtually limited to shell planting and transplantation of seed. The huge stock of mother oysters ensured a good spatfall all over the area in most years.

Gradually, however, the situation deteriorated. This was due to the encroachment of serious predators such as starfish and drills, poor maintenance of the beds, and irregular spatfall; the latter was partly due to a lower stock of mother oysters. These factors finally led to a partial collapse of the industry. Only a few companies, supported by the supplementary income obtained from clam fishing, battled their way through. These companies were assisted by the scientists and technicians of the Milford Laboratory who gave them the tools for predator control, issued spatfall forecasts, and who advised on technical improvement in farming techniques. Now oyster farming is again profitable in this area.

An archaic aspect of the oyster industry in Long Island Sound is that the best settling grounds are still the public beds, which cannot be rented and exploited by oyster farmers. The oyster farmers are, therefore, largely dependent on seed oysters bought from individuals fishing the natural beds (the so-called "natural growthers" who do nothing other than this), and on shell-planting operations carried out by the State and financed by the taxes levied on seed oyster sales. There is every reason to assume that a modern oyster farmer would keep the natural beds in better condition by spending more effort and money on predator control and cleansing procedures, and would thereby produce greater quantities of seed oysters per acre. That another category of people, other than the farmers, has the exclusive right to exploit the best settling grounds does not seem to be a very modern approach to efficient oyster farming.

The future of the Long Island Sound oyster industry is in several ways uncertain. It is certainly not a lack of oyster ground which presents a bottleneck to the possible expansion of the Bloom Brothers Oyster Company, for this company at present uses only 10% of its growing grounds and an even smaller percentage of its settling grounds. The very low tax for the grounds makes it possible to retain a huge acreage for possible future use. The company hesitates, however, to make an effort to drastically increase its production. At present the Bloom brothers can supervise every operation of oyster culture personally, and also do their marketing by telephone. The company makes a good profit as it is, whereas expansion would involve the delegation of authority to others, and perhaps, to a lesser degree of efficiency. They feel that before expanding they would want to be certain of the answers to two problems: pollution, and the market. The possibility of pollution always threatens the market grounds. Already, the company's market grounds have had to be closed from time to time because of pollution after heavy rain. The company is afraid to expand its seed stock, for the oysters would be unsaleable if pollution increased so much that the market grounds had to be closed permanently; it would mean that all the money invested would be lost. The market, used for many years to a small production of Long Island Sound oysters, absorbs the increasing quantities with some hesitation. That both the demand and the price have risen in the years 1972 and 1973 is, however, reassuring. It would probably not be easy to sell much more than the present 200 000 bushels produced in the area without an adequate campaign of product development. Some companies have already introduced a more attractive cardboard package for small consignments of oysters. There is a greater demand for shucked oysters than for oysters with shells, but shuckers are hard to find nowadays. It is not lack of capital which dissuades the company from expanding, but lack of skilled labour, the pollution threat, and limited market demand.

G. TECHNICAL DETAILS

G.1. The two dredge boats

The two company dredge boats, the "Cultivator" and the "Eban A. Thatcher", are built of wood. They are both 60 feet in length, 18—20 feet wide and draw 5—6 feet of water. They are flat-decked boats, with the wheel house located aft. They are equipped with G.M. diesel engines of 180 and 225 h.p., respectively.

For fishing oysters rigid dredges of the standard cage type, which have a door at the bottom for dumping, are used. The dredges of the Bloom Company have short bags. Observations by divers led to the improvement of the dredges, reducing the breakage of young oysters and ensuring that a higher percentage of oysters is gathered by the dredge. A characteristic feature of the modern dredge is that its teeth point forward at an angle of 15° in relation to the bottom.

The dredges are towed on a chain which has a length about three times that of the depth of the water, and are lifted by means of booms. The Bloom Company uses chains 150 feet long. The metal used for making the chain is 1/2—7/16 inch in diameter. The winches used for hoisting are especially made for oyster boats. They are worm-driven and have two drums. They work on power taken from the main engine. Both winches and engines are located below the deck.

H. BIBLIOGRAPHY

Crosby Longwell, A. and Stiles, S.S., 1970. The genetic systems and breeding potential of the commercial American oyster. Endeavour 29, (107): 94—99.

Davis, H., 1969. Design and development of an environmental control system for culturing oyster larvae. Proc. Conf. Artificial Propagation of Commercially Valuable Shellfish. — Oysters Coll. Mar. Stud. Univ. Delaware, Newark, Del., pp. 135—149.

Galtsoff, P.S., 1964. The American oyster, *Crassostrea virginica* Gmelin. U.S. Fish Wildl. Serv., Fish. Bull., 64: 1—480.

Galtsoff, P.S. and Loosanoff, V.L., 1939. Natural history and method of controlling the starfish (*Asterias forbesi*, Desor). Bull. U.S. Bur. Fish., 49: 75—132.

Loosanoff, V.L., 1961a. Recent advances in the control of shellfish predators and competitors. Gulf Caribb. Fish. Inst. Univ. Miami, Proc. 13th Annu. sess., November 1960, pp. 113—127.

Loosanoff, V.L., 1961b. Biology and Methods of Controlling the Starfish, *Asterias forbesi* (Desor). U.S. Fish Wildl. Serv., Fish Leaflet 520, 11 pp.

Loosanoff, V.L., 1964. Variations in time and intensity of settling of the starfish, *Asterias forbesi,* in Long Island Sound during a twenty-five-year period. Biol. Bull., 126 (3): 423—439.

Loosanoff, V.L., 1965. The American or Eastern Oyster. Bur. Commer. Fish., Fish Wildl. Serv., Circular 205, 36 pp.

Loosanoff, V.L., 1966. Time and intensity of settling of the oyster, *Crassostrea virginica,* in Long Island Sound. Biol. Bull., 130 (2): 211—227.

Loosanoff, V.L., 1969a. Maturation of gonads of oysters, *Crassostrea virginica*, of different geographical areas subjected to relatively low temperatures. Veliger, 11 (3): 153—163.

Loosanoff, V.L., 1969b. Development of shellfish culture techniques. Proc. Conf. Artificial Propagation of Commercially Valuable Shellfish — Oysters. Coll. Mar. Stud. Univ. Delaware, Newark, Del., pp. 9—40.

Loosanoff, V.L. and Davis, H.C., 1963a. Rearing of bivalve Mollusks, In: F.S. Russell (Editor), Advances in Marine Biology, Vol. I. Academic Press, New York, N.Y., London, pp. 1—136.

Loosanoff, V.L. and Davis, H.C., 1963b. Shellfish hatcheries and their future. Commer. Fish. Rev., 25 (1): 1—11.

Loosanoff, V.L. and Engle, J.B., 1941. Little known enemies of young oysters. Science, 93: 328.

Loosanoff, V.L. and Nomejko, C.A., 1951. Existence of physiologically-different races of oysters, *Crassostrea virginica.* Biol. Bull., 101: 151—156.

Loosanoff, V.L., Engle, J.B. and Nomejko, C.A., 1955. Differences in intensity of setting of oysters and starfish. Biol. Bull., 109 (1): 75—81.

Loosanoff, V.L., MacKenzie, C.L. and Shearer, L.W., 1960. Use of chemicals to control shellfish predators. Science, 131 (3412): 1522—1523.

McDermott, J.J., 1960. The predation of oysters and barnacles by crabs of the family Xanthidae. Proc. Penn. Acad. Sci., 34: 199—211.

MacKenzie, C.L., 1969. Feeding rates of starfish, *Asterias forbesi* (Desor), at controlled water temperatures and during different seasons of the year. U.S. Fish Wildl. Serv., Fish. Bull., 68 (1): 67—72.

MacKenzie, C.L., 1970a. Causes of oyster spat mortality, conditions of oyster settling beds, and recommendations for oyster bed management. Proc. Natl. Shellfish. Assoc., 60: 59—67.

MacKenzie, C.L., 1970b. Control of oyster drills, *Eupleura caudata* and *Urosalpinx cinerea,* with the chemical Polystream. U.S. Fish Wildl. Serv., Fish. Bull., 68 (2): 285—297.

MacKenzie, C.L., 1970c. Oyster culture modernization in Long Island Sound. Am. Fish Farm. Mag., May 1970, 4 pp.

MacKenzie, C.L., 1970d. Oyster culture in Long Island Sound 1966—1969. Commer. Fish. Rev., 32(1): 27—40.

Matthiessen, G.C., 1971. A Review of Oyster Culture and the Oyster Industry in North America. Contrib. no. 2528 Woods Hole Oceanogr. Inst., Woods Hole, Mass., 52 pp.

Riley, G.A., 1955. Review of the Oceanography of Long Island Sound. Pap. Mar. Biol. Oceanogr., Deep Sea Res. Suppl., 3: 224—238.

Chapter 3

FARMING THE AMERICAN ATLANTIC OYSTER (*CRASSOSTREA VIRGINICA*) IN LOUISIANA, U.S.A.

Example
Pausina Oyster Corporation.
Proprietor: Captain Baldo V. Pausina, 1361 Moss Street, New Orleans, Louisiana.
Period of observation: 1960—1972.

A. BACKGROUND

A.1. General principles

The natural beds of the American Atlantic oyster, *Crassostrea virginica* (Gmelin), originally fringed the Atlantic coast of North America from the Gulf of St Lawrence southward and round into the Gulf of Mexico. In many places they had already been exploited since prehistoric times. In due course European settlers discovered this rich source of food, and in the middle of the eighteenth century it had already been found necessary to impose restrictions on dredging in some places. Statistics show that in 1890 the United States produced the impressive total of over 180×10^6 pounds of oyster meat. Since then production has declined, mainly due to over-exploitation and erosion, the latter being associated with deforestation.

By 1940, the annual total yield had been halved to only 90×10^6 pounds of oyster meat. It was especially Chesapeake Bay, once the big producer, which lost much of its former glory. Many oyster areas experienced large fluctuations in the production of oyster meat, but remarkably enough, the State of Louisiana showed only minor fluctuations in the annual yield. Both in the period 1941—1959 and 1960—1965 Louisiana, with its 600 000 acres of oyster beds, produced on an average 9×10^6—10×10^6 pounds of meat. The Louisiana oysters grow in the bays of the marshy belt where the fresh water of the Mississippi, Atchafalaya, Sabine and Pearl Rivers mixes with the saline water of the Gulf of Mexico.

During the 1840's and 1850's immigrants from Dalmatia, then under foreign rule, settled in fairly large numbers in the Mississippi River Delta and it was these settlers, in whose home country oysters had been farmed since Roman days using the hanging form of culture, who realized that high quality oysters could be produced by transferring seed which settled on the natural reefs to beds where growth and fattening was much better, and experimented accordingly. In due course the settlers built camps on the site, one-roomed structures on piles at the four corners, raised about 10 feet above the ground for protection against the high tides and hurricanes, and watched over the oysters they had planted there (Fig. 25). This was the beginning of oyster farming in Louisiana and, even today, most of the oyster farmers in the delta are of Dalmation extraction, but they no longer live in camps on the spot.

Oyster farming in Louisiana is a semi-culture. Larval development is fully left to nature — the settling larvae are offered a suitable substratum by planting shells in the appropriate places. This operation, although partly carried out by the oyster farmers themselves, is largely, however, done by state agencies. The half-grown oysters are then, in due course, transferred to submerged parks where growth and fattening, because of the natural food supply, are most favourable. The production of seed oysters is mainly concentrated in the bays east of the Mississippi River, whereas most of the marketable oysters are grown on the oystermen's beds west of the river.

The farther south in the geographical range of the American Atlantic oyster, the more vigorous are the attacks of predators, parasites and diseases on the planted oysters. The most productive seed beds are those bathed in water of reduced salinity, where they are out of reach of the most notorious oyster enemies, but as the fastest growth, the firmest meats, the best flavour and the deepest shells are produced on beds near the Gulf shore, it is here that one finds the beds for producing marketable oysters, avoiding as far as possible the perilous warmer part of the year.

Fig. 25. Artist's view of Louisiana oyster camp some 20 years ago. (After an aquarelle by E.M. Schiwetz.)

Most of the oysters produced are marketed in Louisiana itself; the largest are sold to shucking houses, the medium sizes as counter oysters for raw consumption, the smaller oysters to canneries. Sometimes it is economically viable to ship certain categories of oysters to sea food dealers as far away as Maryland and Virginia.

A.2. Biology of the species

The American Atlantic oyster, *Crassostrea virginica*, is like all the *Crassostrea* oysters, adapted to subtropical conditions and requires quite high water temperatures (over 20° C) for spawning and larval development. Once planktonic, the larvae are not easily killed by fluctuations in water temperature, but at temperatures as low as 20° C their development is extremely slow, so that few, if any, will survive to settle. The larvae of this oyster can thrive in water with quite a wide range of salinities, but the rule that settling and survival are usually best in water of reduced salinity should not be explained in terms of the oyster's preference for water of lower salinity, but rather of the better survival in places where the most destructive enemies cannot reach them. The same holds good for the observation that most spat is usually found in the intertidal zone. Oysters settling somewhat deeper too easily fall victim to boring sponges, starfish and many other enemies which cannot live intertidally. In the southern part of this oyster's range these factors affecting survival are responsible for their pattern of distribution: in inshore water, preferably of somewhat reduced salinity, and often intertidally. An advantage of the southern region is that there is no interruption of growth in the winter.

In many respects, the biology of the American Atlantic oyster closely resembles that of other *Crassostrea* species such as the Portuguese oyster, the Pacific oyster and the Australian oyster, dealt with respectively in the chapters on oyster farming in France, in the State of Washington and in Japan, and in Australia. As a wealth of biological information on the American Atlantic oyster has been collected in the excellent treatise written by Dr P.S. Galtsoff: "The American oyster, *Crassostrea virginica* Gmelin" (Fishery Bulletin of the U.S. Fish and Wildlife Service, Vol. 64, 1964, 480 pp.) there is no need to discuss this topic further here.

A.3. Geographical situation

The headquarters of the company under consideration are located at the residence of Captain Baldo Pausina in the city of New Orleans, Louisiana, 30° 00′ N and 90° 03′ W. The company's ships have their home port at Lafitte, some 30 km further south, and the company's parks are scattered over a wide area, both in and around Barataria Bay, roughly 70 km south of New Orleans, west of the Mississippi River, and in the area of Boudreau Bay and Indian Mound Bay, roughly 70 km east of New Orleans, east of the Mississippi River.

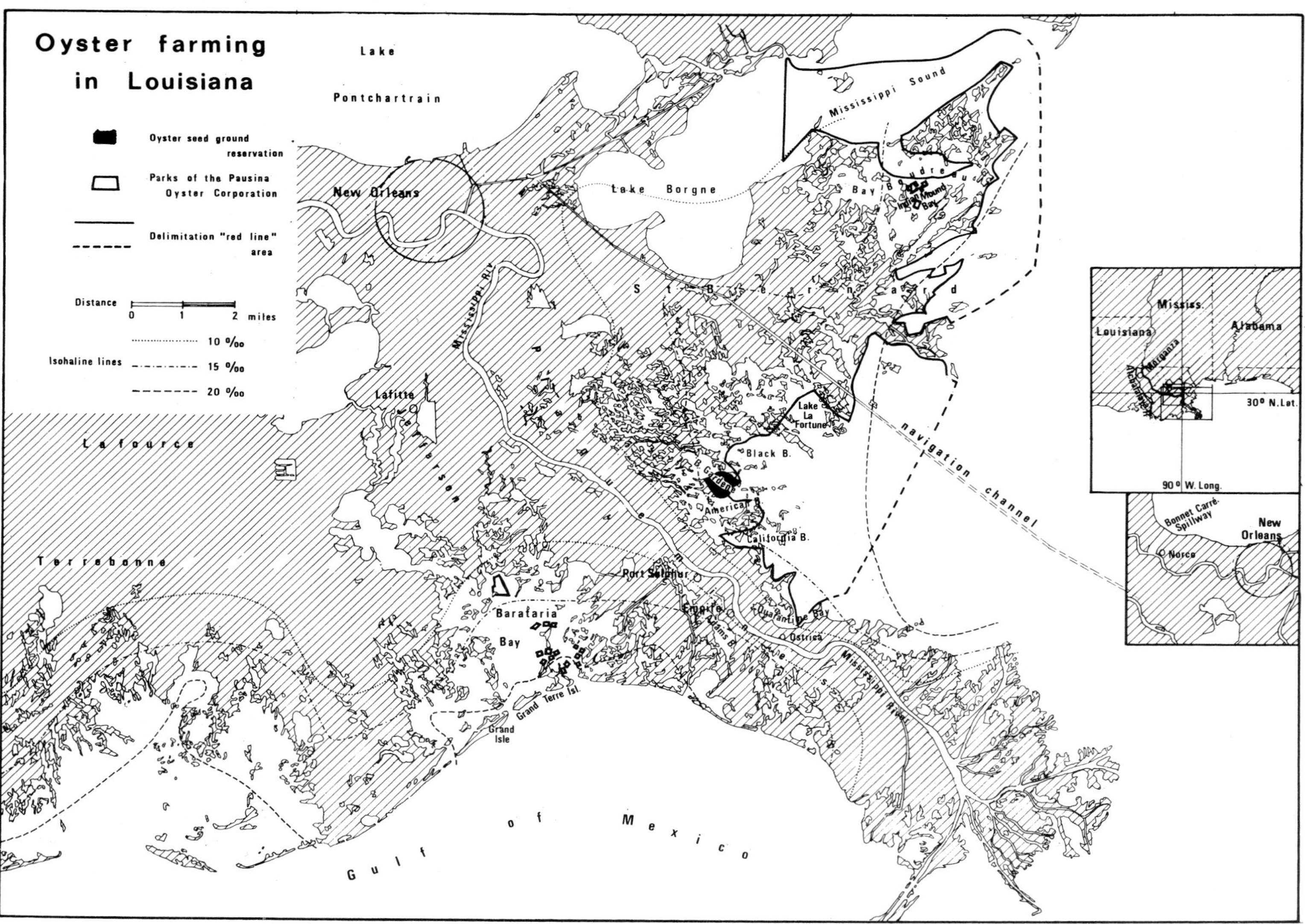

Oyster farming in Louisiana
Oyster seed ground reservation
Parks of the Pausina Oyster Corporation
Delimitation "red line" area
Distance
0 1 2 miles
Isohaline lines
10 ‰
15 ‰
20 ‰
Lake Pontchartrain
New Orleans
Lake Borgne
Mississippi Sound
Bay Boudreau
Indian Mound Bay
St Bernard
Mississippi Riv
Plaquemines
Jefferson
Lafitte
Lafource
Terrebonne
Lake La Fortune
Black B.
B. Garden
American
California B.
Port Sulphur
Empire
Adams B.
Quarantine Bay
Ostrica
Mississippi River
Barataria Bay
Grand Terre Isl.
Grand Isle
Gulf of Mexico
navigation channel
Louisiana
Mississ.
Alabama
Morganza
Atchafalaya R.
30° N. Lat.
90° W. Long.
Bonnet Carré Spillway
Norco
New Orleans

A.4. Hydrographic pattern

Maps of the coastal area of Louisiana show some 240 km^2 of marshes, predominantly located in the Mississippi River Delta, and its diversion, the Atchafalaya River. It is a complicated pattern of rather shallow bays of various dimensions, with bayous intersecting the area in a capricious way, and of marshland bearing a more or less dense vegetation, differing in character according to the salinity of the water. Only few roads penetrate deep into the marshland, large areas can only be reached by waterways. The upriver sections of the marshes are fresh. Near to the sea the water has a fairly high salinity, and in between the waters are brackish. The sea invades through many passes when hurricanes hit the coast, penetrating far inland. The rivers bring down an impressive volume of fresh water (on an average 650 000 $feet^3$ per sec) but occasionally the river floods, sometimes with disastrous results. The 1927 floods, during which as much as 3×10^6 $feet^3$ of water came down per sec, caused so much damage that extensive engineering works were undertaken to prevent such disasters occurring in the future. There are now two spillways for diverting the water in case the Mississippi River floods: the Bonnet Carré spillway at Norco, due west of New Orleans, which can divert 250 000 $feet^3$ per sec, and further north, in Pointe Coupée parish, the Marganza spillway which can divert 150 000 $feet^3$ per sec to the Atchafalaya river system. This latter river normally takes care of some 100 000 $feet^3$ per sec of Mississippi water.

Bays which have a salinity ranging from 15 to 20‰ are the most suitable for oyster farming. The most important grounds for the production of seed oysters are east of the Mississippi River. Most of the leased grounds for producing marketable oysters, on the other hand, are west of the river. Water salinity does not only show seasonal fluctuations and occasional deviations under the influence of hurricanes and floods; there is also a substantial general trend towards higher salinities in the entire delta. In the upriver section more and more dams have been constructed for flood control and power production, whereas, in the downriver section, the levees are in a continuous process of upgrading. Such works reduce the risk of floods but bring an ever-increasing percentage of river water straight down to the very mouth of the river, where it is discharged into the Gulf of Mexico, 140 km southeast of New Orleans, leaving an ever smaller percentage for mixing with the sea water in the bays and bayous. Another factor leading to the incursion of water of high salinity is the deep navigation channel which has been dredged from the southeast to the heart of New Orleans. In the last two decades changes in the salinity pattern have been particularly noticeable, many of the seed oyster grounds becoming gradually invaded by water of so high a salinity that several oyster predators and parasites soon infiltrated to such a degree, that the productivity of the reefs dropped alarmingly. Seed oyster production had to be shifted to grounds further away from the sea, where formerly no oysters occurred. On the other hand, typical denizens of brackish water, such as the clam *Rangia cuneata* (Gray), had to leave the areas of increased salinity. It disappeared completely, for instance, from Lake Borgne.

The oyster industry, faced with the changing salinity pattern, had to shift its activities away from the more seaward beds to grounds further from the Gulf, because formerly productive beds had lost their quality due to the invasion of predators and parasites adapted to the higher salinities. This led to a rather instable pattern, forcing the oystermen to apply for new grounds further from the sea, both for the production of seed oysters and for fattening marketable oysters, once the more seaward beds could no longer be used on a remunerative basis. It also forced the oystermen to rent more ground than they actually needed. The Louisiana Wildlife and Fisheries Commission, on the other hand, does all it can to monitor the hydrographic situation, by sampling the water frequently on a great number of stations, in order to follow the shifting pattern and whenever possible, to forecast what will happen next. Until 1973, the Lake Bonnet Carré spillway had previously last been used in 1947, and the Mississippi spillway, so far, not at all. It was, therefore, wondered whether the costly water regulating schemes were not based too much on the fear that the 1927 disaster might occur again as, up until this time, they had resulted only in detrimental effects on the oyster industry and many other fishing activities, as more and more of the fertile river water was poured directly into the Gulf, instead of increasing the productivity of the bays and bayous. At the beginning of 1973, however, the river flooded again, the water rising 9 feet within 1 hour. Both spillways did their work and huge volumes of fertile fresh water spread over the delta, reducing the salinity over a large area. Several oyster pests, not able to withstand such low salinities, were killed wholesale. Therefore, a series of good years are expected for the oyster industry, with reduced losses and water richer in phytoplankton which has developed on the nutrients brought down by the river and on the nutrients set free by biodegradation of all the organisms killed by the low salinity.

Depth. The waters where the oyster grounds are located are not very deep: up to 4 and 5 m in the seed production area east of the river, somewhat less deep on the beds where the marketable oysters are grown. Barataria Bay, is for instance, over most of its acreage only 2—3 m deep. The bottom consists of alluvial material and is predominantly muddy or clayish, except where stronger currents prevail, where it is more sandy.

Tides. The tides have a modest range in this region, usually from 30 cm at neap tide to 60 cm at spring tide. The current velocities are therefore quite low here and the wind may exert a greater influence on the actual height of the water level.

Water temperature. The greatest range of water temperatures occurs in the shallower parts of the marshes. Extreme values ranging from 0°C to 36°C have been recorded there. During an average year, the water temperature in

Barataria Bay, an important area for the production of marketable oysters, has a minimum of 13° C in March and a maximum of 29.5° C in August. This is characteristic of such subtropical areas. In the seed oyster area east of the river a winter low of 9.5° C and a summer high of 30° C can be expected. Water temperatures above 20° C will occur from April to November over the entire delta.

Salinity. The precipitation here amounts to some 150 cm per year, but it is the Mississippi and Atchafalaya Rivers, which drain slightly more than 1.3×10^6 miles^2 of land, which have the greatest effect on the salinity pattern. The saline belt of the marshes varies from 2 to 20 km in width. The vegetation of the higher grounds is characterized by a dense growth of *Spartina alterniflora* and *Juncus roemerianus*, and locally *Avicennia nitida* brushwood. On higher ridges there are live oaks profusely hung with garlands of Spanish moss.

The salinity in Barataria Bay ranged from 15 to 29‰ in the period 1967—1969 with peaks in winter and from 12 to 20‰ in the stations along the southeastern sector of the Mississippi River; slightly lower salinity was found at several stations sampled due east of the river.

Offshore a salinity range of 15—35‰ is found, mainly influenced by the quantity of water discharged from the Mississippi River.

Chemical composition. The nitrite, nitrate, inorganic phosphate and total phosphorus content are measured at a great number of stations in the scope of the monitoring programme of the Louisiana Wildlife and Fisheries Commission. In Barataria Bay, particularly important for the production of marketable oysters, up to 3 μg at/l of nitrite, with peaks in winter, up to 26 μg at/l of nitrate showing noteworthy peaks, up to 1.0 μg at/l of inorganic phosphate and from 1 to 5 μg at/l of total phosphorus have been recorded. In the same period (1967—1969) the seed oyster area east of the river showed somewhat lower nitrite and nitrate values and slightly higher figures for phosphorus compounds.

The turbidity varied from 0.30 to 1.00 m in both areas. Quantitative data on phytoplankton or chlorophyll content are not collected in the scope of the monitoring programme. The meat content of the oysters indicates that feeding conditions must be better, on average, in the areas west of the Mississippi River than in the "red-line" district east of the river, but from site to site widely differing patterns may be found.

Pollution. The oysters are grown far away from sewage outfalls, human population in the delta itself being very scarce. Although there is an oil industry of considerable importance both in the Delta itself and offshore, it is rare for the oysters to be affected by it. There have been occasions, however, when oysters have become tainted locally by clandestine dumping of drilling-mud containing lubricating diesel oil.

A.5. Legal aspects

The Pausina Oyster Corporation is registered as a small business corporation. Since the owner, Captain Baldo V. Pausina, who was born in Prpang in Dalmatia but has lived in the United States since 1908, formally retired as president in 1969, the board has consisted of his son Ralph (president), Captain Baldo V. Pausina (vice-president), his wife Katherina Pausina (secretary) and his daughter Dominica Pausina (treasurer).

The State of Louisiana distinguishes four categories of oyster ground: private and public oyster leases, oyster seed ground reservations, and "red-line" areas. The private leases in the hands of the oystermen, amount to some 130 000 acres, predominantly in the parishes of St Bernard, Plaquemines and Terrebonne. In the extreme west of the State are the 1 200 acres of public oyster grounds which are opened on a seasonal basis for tonging. Oyster seed ground reservations, totalling 16 453 acres and set up by Acts of Legislation in the late 1930's and early 1940's, are located in the parishes of Plaquemines, St Bernard, Jefferson, Lafourche and Terrebonne. Here the State plants shells as cultch and all the oysters produced on these grounds are for the use and benefit of the oyster industry. There are restrictions on the time, the quantity and the methods of taking such oysters to ensure proper maintenance and preservation of the area as a perpetual source of seed supply for the oyster industry. Harvesting is allowed only on alternate years to ensure a prolonged period of growing in low salinity waters. The old "red-line" areas in Plaquemines and St Bernard parish encompass 450 000 acres. These areas are set aside by the State and no new private leases are permitted within their boundaries. Here are some live natural reefs where the production of seed oysters can be improved by planting cultch material. Whenever the State authorities decide to do so, such areas are open for fishing on alternate years, whereas the remainder of the "red-line" reefs are open every year. The recent saltwater intrusion has reduced the effectiveness of this area by some 60—65% . For fishing on the oyster seed ground reservations and on the natural reefs during the periods the season is open, a licence is required: either a dredging licence (US $50), necessary whenever a boat operates a mechanical dredge in any public water, whether for seed oysters or marketable oysters and/or a tonnage licence. A dredging licence is not required for operating on private leases. A tonnage licence is required for the shipment or haulage of oysters of 3 inches in diameter and over, regardless of where the oysters come from. This licence involves a tax of US $0.50 per ton maximum loading capacity, but is rarely sold for quantities of less than 2 tons.

Oyster farmers can lease private oyster grounds on an annual basis for a 15-year period. For this, a completed application form has to be forwarded to the officer, in charge of oyster and sea beds in the area, at the New Orleans headquarters of the Wildlife and Fisheries Commission, indicating on a map which ground one would like to rent, and accompanied by a retaining fee. No grounds are allocated which are in the "red-line" area. The records are checked to see whether the ground under consideration is still available and whether or not oil or navigational interests should be given priority. If not, a surveying party will measure the ground on the spot, using surveyor's instruments and starting from triangulation marks. These marks are concrete pillars placed on higher ground, each bearing a brass plate with an inscription indicating its exact geographical position. The lessee has to pay, as a surveying fee, US $20 for 10 acres or less, US $30 for leases of 10—20 acres, and for any excess acreage US $0.50 per acre. He also has to place his own sea marks. These are 16—18 feet long and some 3 inches thick, made from either bamboo cane or pine saplings, or occasionally hardwood or willow. This accomplished, the plot is re-surveyed by state officials and the lessee receives his documents together with a "plat", a map showing the lease. He has to pay an annual rent of US $1.00 per acre. He can also "buy" grounds from other lessees. There are at present some 1 000 leases covering 130 000 acres, with 30 000 to 40 000 additional acres under application.

The Pausina Oyster Corporation has ten leases in Indian Mound Bay east of the Mississippi River, totalling 613 acres (plot 18422 with its 264 acres being the largest), and two leases in Boudreau Bay, totalling 11 acres. In Barataria Bay the Corporation has 23 leases totalling 699 acres. Only one of

Fig. 26. Oyster camp in Grand Bay, east of the Mississippi River, built adjacent to the mangrove vegetation, *Avicennia nitida*. (Photo P. Korringa, 1948.)

these plots (no. 18773, covering 430 acres) measures more than 35 acres. On lease 19731 is the old original oyster camp, formerly inhabited for purposes of surveillance, but since 1960 only used as a base for fishing trips.

There is no intensive police patrolling in this extensive area. Formerly many oystermen lived on their camps, armed with a rifle and a powerful searchlight, but although the camps are no longer used for this purpose, complaints of the theft of oysters are of rare occurrence.

B. SEQUENCE OF OPERATIONS

B.1. Fishing oyster seed on the state grounds

About 90% of the seed ground in the State of Louisiana is located east of the Mississippi River. Here are the large acreages of the so-called "red-line" areas, and also the "oyster seed ground reservation" of Bay Gardene (south of Black Bay). The Louisiana Wildlife and Fisheries Commission selects the appropriate sites for planting shells as cultch. Good grounds for planting shells are found in Black Bay, California Bay and Lake Fortune. As a rule the State uses the shells of the brackishwater clam *Rangia cuneata* as cultch. These are collected using a suction dredge in Lake Pontchartrain, where there are rich beds of these shells. The shells, brought to the selected site on a barge, are sprayed overboard using powerful water jets. About 30 yards^3 per acre are planted, and in total the state operations may cover each year up to three separate plantings of 0.5—1 miles^2 each. Shell planting is carried out in spring, as the spat settles in the month of May. Where shells have been planted, the beds are not opened before the September of the following year. The planting areas are clearly marked and posted.

Licenced oystermen may dredge up seed-covered shells from September 1st until the end of May. As they are informed where the shells have been planted under the auspices of the State, there is no need for a time-consuming search and they can start dredging straight away and, dumping the material on the deck, load their boats to maximum capacity.

Captain Pausina's two boats[1] have a capacity of 50 and 60 tons of material. It takes some 10 h to fill a boat with unsorted material, but as the season advances, it takes longer to fill a boat to capacity.

Usually Captain Pausina transfers most of the oysters fished on the grounds where the State planted shells to his leases in upper Barataria Bay; if the oysters are large enough, they are transferred directly to the fattening beds in lower Barataria Bay. For this, a ship has to cover a distance of about 100 miles. This takes about 8 h. From Quarantine Bay, a ship enters the Mississippi River through the locks at Ostrica. It next sails upstream to Empire, to pass through the locks there on the west side of the river to reach Adams Bay. From here, it finds its way through the bayous to the company leases.

B.2. Procuring seed oysters on private grounds

For the Pausina Oyster Corporation, the shells planted by the State in the bays east of the Mississippi River are only considered as a supplementary source of oyster seed, tapped when the production of seed oysters on the leases of the company falls short of expectations. For many successive years, the Pausina Corporation has operated on a large lease of excellent seed collecting ground (no. 18773) in upper Barataria Bay. This large bed is subdivided into sections, and shells are only planted on those sections from which the seed which settled in earlier years has been completely removed. *Rangia* shells, purchased from the suction dredgers of Lake Pontchartrain, are loaded on barges with a capacity of 700 yards^3. The Pausina Corporation usually buys three to four barge loads of shells each year for their spat collecting operations in Barataria Bay.

The shells have to be planted before May 15th as planktonic larva are at their peak values in May, and it takes a week to scatter the three or four barge loads over the appropriate sites. One barge load is scattered over some 10 acres of the lease.

To plant the shells the company uses powerful water jets produced by the pump installation on board (25 h.p. gasoline engine giving 30—40 pounds pressure, connected to a 2.5-inch hose with 1.5-inch nozzle); in addition, an extra high pressure pump (100 pounds pressure, 1-inch nozzle, gasoline engine 25—30 h.p.) is hired, which makes it possible to scatter a barge load of shells in 8—9 h. A tug later comes to collect the empty barge. *Rangia* shells, readily available in Louisiana, are popular collectors, as they produce single oysters. Occasionally oyster shells, a waste product from the culling procedure, are planted but the corporation does not buy any oyster shells from the huge piles found at the canneries. Oyster shells are more expensive than *Rangia* shells, as they are sold as the basic material for making chicken grit and for the construction of road beds. They are also too large, leading to clustering, and too heavy, leading to smothering in the sediment.

Late in the summer, the shells planted on the Barataria Bay lease are inspected. If an average of 250 to 300 small oysters on half a bushel of clam shells (somewhat less than one per shell) are counted, settling and survival are considered to be satisfactory.

B.3. Planting seed stock from state reserves

If spatfall falls short of expectations, the corporation supplements the stock with seed dredged from the state beds east of the Mississippi river. The impression is that spat which settled in Barataria Bay grows better than young oysters brought in from the state reserves. For planting the shells carrying young oysters use is again made of a powerful jet of water produced by

Fig. 27. Planting seed oysters with the shovel. (After an aquarelle by E.M. Schiwetz.)

the pump unit described previously. This is only taken on board when it is needed for this purpose. The material is simply washed overboard.

B.4. Growing marketable oysters

In brackish water the oysters are quite safe. In their first year growth is rather slow but as such notorious enemies as the drill, the drumfish and *Dermocystidium* stay away from low salinity areas, the young oysters can be kept there for a prolonged period. Mr Pausina does not start fishing the shells planted here before 3 years have elapsed.

The best oysters, nicely cupped and well filled with firm meat of perfect flavour, are, however, only produced on beds which are bathed by water of higher salinity. It is for this reason that the oysters grown in upper Barataria Bay are transferred to beds closer to the sea. For this purpose the Pausina Oyster Corporation uses its leases in lower Barataria Bay. Here, however, although growth is fast and fattening excellent, the risks are great, especially in the warmer season. The oysters are, therefore, preferably planted in September or October, for harvesting marketable oysters with a legal minimum size of 3 inches 4—5 months later.

Having been collected by dredging, either from privately owned ground or from the state reserves east of the river, the oysters are planted using a shovel, at a density of 300 barrels (= 900 bushels) per acre. When, several months later, the oysters are fished it will be seen that although the individual oysters are much larger, with a shell length of over 3 inches, the total tonnage has not increased. Many oysters fall victim to their enemies even in the colder season. If one barrel of marketable oysters is fished for every barrel planted, the farmer is more than satisfied. As a general rule, every 300 barrels planted yield some 250 barrels of marketable oysters.

Normally, Mr Pausina does not transplant all the oysters from his upper Barataria Bay bed when they are about 3 years old. Some stay there for 1 year longer and are then either transferred to the lower Barataria Bay fattening beds, or marketed directly as 4-year-old oysters.

B.5. Fishing marketable oysters

When the oysters are dredged from the fattening beds, each dredge load is dumped onto a sorting table to be culled immediately. Marketable oysters are put in metal baskets (43 cm high, 43 cm diameter at the top) for transfer into sacks holding some 85 pounds of oysters. All the oysters from the same beds are kept together, the sacks being piled up methodically. About 100

Fig. 28. View on deck of Bertoul Cherami's oyster lugger, showing dredge, stand, winch, chains, shovel and extreme right — the roller over which the dredge is hauled in. (Photo P. Korringa, 1948.)

sacks of oysters can be fished and culled per day by a three-man crew. Shells and small oysters are dumped on the deck to be replanted on the leases in upper Barataria Bay. Replanting on the beds in lower Barataria Bay would lead to serious losses in the following summer months.

B.6. Fishing for marketable oysters on the natural reefs

When the private beds become depleted of marketable oysters and if time allows, oysters are fished from the natural reefs east of the Mississippi River, in, for instance, Lake Borgne or American Bay. The grounds are prospected by 'sounding' them, i.e. probing the bottom with a pole while standing on the forward deck. If the impression is obtained that a productive reef has been found, the dredge is lowered to see whether fishing will be remunerative there. Again, the culling table is used to sort out the large 3-year-old marketable oysters, for packing in sacks, whereas smaller, 2-year-old oysters are dumped on deck either to be sold to the canners as steam oysters or for planting on one of the low salinity leases of the company. It should be remembered, however, that a much smaller quantity of marketable oysters will be produced from the natural reefs than from the private beds. On the latter 100 sacks of oysters can be harvested per day, fishing with a crew of three men, whereas from the state beds and from the natural reefs inside the "red-line" area a daily harvest of 50 sacks of marketable oysters is considered an excellent result.

B.7. Delivering marketable oysters

Early in the season, during the month of September, is the time to make the best catches on the public grounds. The yield declines as the season advances, especially on the public beds where many boats participate in oyster fishing. The Pausina Oyster Corporation, working with two boats, expects an average of two loads per boat a week, though harvests are greater during the month of September.

Usually the oysters fished in lower Barataria Bay are brought to Port Sulphur where the wholesaler awaits the boat at the appointed hour. Port Sulphur can be reached by road from New Orleans. The Pausina Corporation uses a conveyor belt with a 5 h.p. engine to transfer the sacks containing the oysters from the boat to the buyer's truck. It is the buyer who decides whether the oysters should be sold as counter oysters for raw consumption or as shucking oysters to be shucked, chilled and packed in tins. Excellent flavour is important for counter oysters, which should not be too large, whereas good meat quality and fair size are important for shucking oysters.

When the oysters are not of prime quality, either because they are too small, of irregular size or somewhat clustered, but with a good meat content, they find their way to the "steamers". This means that they are taken to a cannery at Harvey Canal, in the vicinity of New Orleans, a trip of some 5 h by boat. Again, the buyer should be previously informed of the time of arrival of the oysters. Sometimes oysters are taken to a landing stage at Lake Borgne. When a farmer has planted a smaller category of oysters on a given section of his lease, he knows beforehand that such oysters will find their way to the canneries. As a rule, quite a high percentage (75—80% of all the oysters produced in Louisiana) find their way to the steamers, among which are most of the 2-year-old oysters fished on the natural reefs.

It occasionally happens that the New Orleans wholesalers refuse to accept consignments of oysters in which there are too many under 3 inches in shell length or when they are too badly clustered. If, in such cases, the meat quality is nevertheless good, a trailer is hired to transport the oysters to the seafood dealers in Virginia and Maryland. There the oysters are shucked and sold raw, packed in gallons and pints and kept under refrigeration. This happens particularly in the spring, when the first quality stock becomes depleted. Again, oysters are only shipped to the canneries when the buyer has ordered them.

C. FARMING RISKS

In a subtropical region, such as the coast of Louisiana, spatfall may be profuse because it is favoured by high water temperatures, but for the same reason, the attacks of oyster enemies of various description will be more vigorous than at higher latitudes. The presence of productive natural reefs next to extensive dead reefs, indicates that ups and downs were a normal feature in this oyster area from time immemorial. Since the early days of oyster farming there, the Louisiana oystermen have experienced repeated reverses, which are apparently beyond their control and of which the causative agencies were poorly known. It is always difficult to find out what has happened under water, especially when practically invisible microscopic organisms play an active part in killing oysters, and so, like everywhere else in the world, the oystermen were inclined to blame industrial pollution for the serious losses their stocks suffered from time to time. In the light of the rapidly expanding oil industry in the Mississippi Delta, which started in the early 1930's, it seems only logical that many oyster farmers pointed an accusing finger at the oil industry when heavy mortality struck their oysters. Lawsuits began to pile up, the oystermen alleging that oil operations were damaging their business. There was, however, no scientific evidence to prove their case and the State of Louisiana's Conservation Department was at that time too poorly equipped, both with manpower and money to undertake large-scale research projects on the causes of oyster mortality in the Mississippi River Delta.

The oil companies against whom suits had been filed decided to organize research in this field. This ultimately led to what is known as Project 9 of the

Fig. 29. Field work during the Project 9 investigations of the Texas A & M Research Foundation. Culling and measuring oysters to be put out in trays in English Bay. (Photo P. Korringa, 28-6-1948.)

Texas A & M Research Foundation, directed by Dr S.H. Hopkins and guided in the field by Dr J.G. Mackin. A large number of scientists and technicians were engaged in these studies, the field headquarters being located on Grand Isle. The author of this book was, in fact, a consultant there for a short while in 1948. As the research was carried on for over 10 years (Projects 9 and 23) a wealth of information on the subject has been collected. Therefore, we are better informed on the risks in oyster farming in Louisiana than in most of the other oyster areas in the world.

C.1. Hydrographic conditions

It has already been explained in the section dealing with the hydrographic pattern of the Louisiana oyster district that sudden and long-term changes in salinity are of considerable influence on the total oyster industry. Oysters survive best in water of reduced salinity but attain their best quality in high salinity waters. In water of high salinity, mortality may strike so hard during the summer months, that it is strongly advisable to only keep the oysters there during the winter season, whereas the juvenile stock should be kept in relative safety further away from the open sea.

Fig. 30. The author acted for some time as a consultant in the early phase of the Project 9 investigations. Here, he is seen inspecting oysters attacked by *Polydora* in Bassa-Bassa Bay. (Photo S.H. Hopkins, 26-6-1948.)

The salinity shifts observed in recent decades forced the oystermen to apply for a greater number of leases than they really needed to grow their oysters. This was to enable them to experiment and to move their oysters to a safer place when increasing salinity threatened to inflict serious losses.

Apart from the salinity factor, mention should be made of the effect of hurricanes. For the Pausina Oyster Corporation, hurricane Camille (1969) led to such a serious deposition of sand on their leases east of the Mississippi River that these beds could not be used for oyster farming for several years in succession. By repeated dredging, followed by the planting of shells, it is hoped to be able to restore these beds in due course. Similar effects were suffered on some of their leases in Barataria Bay when hurricane Betsy struck in 1965.

C.2. Predators

A very serious predator is the black drum (*Pogonias cromis* (L.)) a fish reaching 4 feet in length, which destroys countless oysters, particularly in the warmer part of the year when it invades the coastal waters. The drum does not operate in water of a salinity lower than 25‰. Another notorious oyster predator, locally perhaps even worse than the drum, is the conch, also called the drill or Gulf oyster borer, a gastropod, *Thais haemastoma* (L.). Small specimens of the drill make neat holes straight through the oyster's shell to consume the meat, so that their evil deeds can easily be traced, but larger specimens overpower the oysters with a toxic material produced by the hypobranchial gland, which paralyses the oyster. One drill can kill and devour about 30 oysters per year and they occur locally by the tens of thousands. The drill cannot survive in low salinity water (under 15‰), which makes the upriver beds quite safe for the oyster. Many beds bathed in high salinity water had to be abandoned for oyster farming because of drill attacks. When a flood, such as that of January—February 1973, forces the drills away from such beds, it is hoped that they can be used again for years afterwards, as this drill has no pelagic larvae so that it takes years to repopulate the lost ground.

Other predators, amongst which is the stone crab, *Menippe mercenaria*, appear to be of minor influence as oyster enemies.

C.3. Parasites and diseases

A few of the larger parasites, for example the trematode *Bucephalus haimeanus*, have been encountered in the oysters of Louisiana, but their activities could not be associated with the large-scale oyster mortalities repeatedly observed. Very little was known about the microscopic enemies of oysters when Project 9 of Texas A & M started. The sporozoan *Nematopsis ostrearum* was often found in great numbers in the tissues of Louisiana oysters. It exchanges its host with that of the little mud crab, *Panopęus herbstii*, but experimental investigations demonstrated that it cannot be blamed for killing oysters.

The discovery of the parasitic fungus *Dermocystidium marinum* (Mackin, Owen and Collier) was the most important result of the efforts made by the research team in Louisiana. It was clearly demonstrated that this parasite could be held responsible for devastating losses among the oysters. It appears that *Dermocystidium* does not thrive in low salinity waters, hence the relative safety of upriver oyster beds, that it particularly attacks oysters from their second summer onwards, and shows hardly any activity at water temperatures of 18°C and lower. This knowledge has made it possible to avoid heavy losses among farmed oysters by selecting places and seasons where oysters will not be attacked by this devastating parasite.

C.4. Competitors

Several organisms, though not intending to kill oysters, may inadvertently interfere with their well-being. One such is the mudworm *Polydora websteri*, which often makes its burrows in oysters' shells. This may lead to unsightly mud-blisters in the shell margin, sometimes even real honeycombing, rendering the shell brittle and the oyster exhausted from having to secrete new shell material to keep pace with the boring activities of *Polydora*. Thus, this polychaete worm is certainly an oyster enemy, though not responsible for the heavy losses which sometimes occur. The same can be said of the boring sponge, *Clione*, which in Louisiana is not so wide-spread as elsewhere in American oyster districts. *Martesia*, a boring clam, is of limited importance as an oyster enemy.

C.5. Pollution

The evidence produced by the intensive multidisciplinary research carried out by the team of scientists under the guidance of Dr S.H. Hopkins, revealed that the increased activities of the oil industry could not be blamed for the ups and downs in the oyster industry. Neither did it lead to deterioration in the other fisheries or to a decline in the general productivity of the delta district. The very fact that the Louisiana estuary represents one of the few places where marine fauna and oil have co-existed, though significant quantities of oil have occasionally been lost, and where the renewable resource productivity remains high, makes this area most interesting for detailed investigations on oil pollution. The general conclusion, drawn from the available evidence by Mr L.S. St.Amant of the Louisiana Department of Wild Life and Fisheries, that the marine ecosystem must be extremely resilient or well-buffered in order to continue operating so well, must be accepted. The large-scale oyster mortalities in Louisiana did not bear any relation to pollution with oil or bleed-water, but local tainting of oysters has been observed to render marketing impossible. In such cases one could usually trace the phenomenon to clandestine dumping of drilling mud lubricated with diesel oil.

D. ECONOMIC ASPECTS

D.1. Rents

The Pausina Oyster Company has over 1 300 acres of oyster ground on lease, more than they actually use for oyster farming, but this allows for a dynamic policy when the salinity pattern changes. For this acreage, the corporation has to pay a rent of US $1 730 per year. For newly acquired ground, annual surveying costs have to be paid in addition. A rent of US $15 per month has to be paid for the shoreline section at Lafitte where the ships have their headquarters and landing stage.

D.2. Inventory items

The company fleet consists of two dredge boats, the "Indiana" built in 1945 and the "Captain Baldo" built in 1964. The "Indiana", measuring 65 feet and equipped with a 135 h.p. diesel engine cost, when built, US $16 980 for the ship and US $7 200 for the engine. Today one would have to pay US $1 000 per foot for a boat equipped as an oyster dredger, and US $17 800 for a comparable engine. The "Captain Baldo" measures 50 feet and is equipped with a 165 h.p. diesel engine. In 1964 it cost US $72 000 and the engine, US $12 000. Several years after its construction the cabin was remodelled at a cost of US $10 000. Both ships should have a long useful life if properly maintained, but although the "Indiana" still has the engine with which it was originally installed, it is safe to expect the engine to last 10 years. Maintenance means a new coating of submarine paint four times a year, an absolute necessity in this area with heavy fouling. This costs US $1 000 per treatment, including the paint. The upper structure is painted once a year by the boat crew. The total costs for painting, repairing and ship-yard work amounted, in the year 1972, to US $7 281. The engine requires overhauling every 5 years, at a cost of about US $2 000. Each ship is equipped with two dredges, with a life span of about 1 year, and costing US $180 each. The steel chains for operating the dredge have a life span of 2 years. These are 75 feet long and cost US $150 each (US $0.70 per pound).

Compared with the fleet, the other inventory items are of only minor importance. The Corporation has two cars predominantly used for business, a necessity as the headquarters are now in the city of New Orleans and no longer at the camp in Barataria Bay.

Additional inventory items are the 25 h.p. high pressure pumps on the ships and the conveyor belt ashore equipped with a 5 h.p. engine for unloading the ships.

D.3. Expendable items

Every year the company buys three to four barge loads of *Rangia* shells to be used as collectors. One barge load costs US $1 800, delivered on the planting spot. Every year some 600 poles, costing US $0.50 each are bought for use as sea marks. The boat engines consume 8 gallons of diesel oil per h, amounting to some US $5 000 per year for both ships combined. In addition, the two company cars consume an appreciable volume of gasoline per year, amounting to US $1 500. In 1972 US $756 and 472 for repair and insurance of the cars were paid, respectively. The hire of high pressure pumps for planting shells costs US $50 per week. Sacks for packing oysters cost US $0.40 each and the company produces 30 000 sacks of oysters per year; however, the sacks can be used more than once. Sacks for transporting oysters out of the State are used once only.

Miscellaneous expenses, including the renewal of equipment such as shovels and baskets are estimated at some US $1 000 per year.

D.4. *Personnel and wages*

The company operates with a staff of six, of which four are permanently employed. Administration is carried out by the directors of the corporation. The wages for workers in the field amount to US $400—500 per month, social security payments included. For compensation insurance the employer also has to pay US $750 per man per year. The food provided free of charge for the crew whilst on board, amounts to US $5 500 for both ships combined.

D.5. *Sales*

The company produces some 30 000 sacks of oysters per year, predominantly from the leases. Only 2 000 to 3 000 sacks are produced from the wild reefs east of the Mississippi River. Oysters of high quality, either for use as counter oysters or for shucking and packing in gallon tins in ice, are sold at US $5 per sack, holding some 250 oysters or 85 pounds of oysters in the shell. When the oysters are used for canning ("steaming") they are sold at $0.20 for 4 2/3 ounces of oyster meat. The exact amount of money received is computed by the capping machine, which automatically counts the number of cans filled with meat from a given consignment of oysters. A good meat content means a fair price for a sack of oysters. For the oysters which are not accepted by the local canneries, and which are therefore transported to the sea-food dealers in either Virginia or Maryland, the buyer has to estimate US $1.25 per sack transportation costs, some 400 sacks being loaded in one trailer. The price obtained for these oysters fluctuates between US $4 and 4.50 per sack. It may be advantageous to produce oysters on purpose for this special market, for they require considerably less manual labour for culling on board ship. In the light of rising labour costs it may, therefore, be more profitable in future to produce this type of oyster for US $4 per sack than high quality oysters for US $5 per sack.

E. GOVERNMENTAL ASSISTANCE

As has been stated in the section dealing with hydrographic conditions, the Louisiana Wildlife and Fisheries Commission carries out an elaborate monitoring programme in order to follow the shifting hydrographic pattern. A large number of samples is taken and analysed at regular intervals. A special field station operating from Grand Terre has been established for this purpose. The data obtained are not only of interest to the oyster industry but also for those concerned with various other aspects of fishery and wildlife.

In addition, the New Orleans headquarters officials carry out various investigations of a biological and technical nature on behalf of the oyster industry. The planting of shells as cultch on the public beds east of the Mississippi River is a continuous operation, paid for and directed by the State of Louisiana.

The rent and surveying costs for the leases are low and put hardly any strain on the oyster farmers' budget. The State Board of Health carries out the sanitary control, free of charge. If any oyster beds are found to be contaminated by either domestic or industrial sewage, they are closed. The Pausina Oyster Corporation operates in bacteriologically impeccable areas.

F. GENERAL IMPRESSION

Louisiana is certainly one of the most productive oyster regions in the world and the most important in the United States. The system of oyster farming practised here is rather simple, requiring only a limited amount of manual labour. The basis of the high productivity achieved is a huge area of sheltered, shallow, oyster ground, the bottom of which consists of a mixture of clay, sand and shell debris, washed by water of reduced salinity, rich in nutrients and phytoplankton. It is the delta character of the area which provides its rich source of oyster food.

That the system of farming can be rather simple is due to the availability of *Rangia* shells as collectors. *Rangia* shells are of precisely the right dimensions for use as cultch. Larger shells, such as oyster shells, lead to clustering and thus inferior quality oysters. They are also rather heavy when they become oyster-plus-collector, which makes it more difficult for the oyster to maintain its position on top of the rather soft sediment. Collectors of a smaller size than *Rangia* shells are less suitable, as the settling larvae show a marked preference for objects with a surface area greater than 6 cm^2. As the average number of young oysters found on *Rangia* shells is between one and two, no time-consuming declustering procedure is necessary.

The oysters grow fast in the southern area. At the end of the year in which they first settled as tiny spat, they may have reached a shell length of 2 inches and 1 000 oysters would then fill one and a half sacks. At the end of their second year the shell length of planted oysters is about 3 inches and 1 000 oysters will then fill three sacks.

Serious problems in the Louisiana oyster industry are the shifting salinity pattern and the presence of several dangerous oyster enemies such as the drum, the drill, and the parasitic fungus *Dermocystidium marinum*. The shifting salinity pattern forces the oystermen to continually experiment with new leases depending upon the rise and fall in salinity. This means that they need more ground than they actually plant with oysters. Good foresight is a prerequisite for a highly dynamic planting policy. It is feared that the continuing engineering works, which will lead more and more Mississippi water straight into the Gulf of Mexico, will eventually result in reduced oyster productivity in the delta area.

Scientifically based information is of paramount importance to the Louisiana oyster industry. As such, the monitoring service of the Louisiana Wildlife and Fisheries Department should be mentioned, which gives the oyster farmers a good insight into the shifting hydrographic pattern, and also, the biological studies which led to a better understanding of the causes of devastating mortalities and thus to farming methods which avoid such risks. At the time the scientists of the Texas A & M Research Foundation started their studies, the attitude of the oyster farmers, hoping for compensation from the oil industry on the basis of their lawsuits, was rather hostile, but now they have realized that the insight gained can be used profitably to reduce the losses among planted oysters.

As the oyster farmers no longer live in their camps in the marshes, which were almost completely cut off from civilization, there is now a more frequent exchange of information with the authorities of the Louisiana Wildlife and Fisheries Department, much to the benefit of the entire oyster industry.

It is interesting to note that the Louisiana oyster industry is, for the greater part, in the hands of farmers and wholesalers of Dalmation descent, whereas most of the other oystermen are "cajuns" of French-Canadian extraction.

The price of marketable oysters here is much lower than that of oysters of the same type marketed in the northeastern part of the United States. The quality of the Louisiana oyster is of the same standard as that of the oysters grown further north, but a disadvantage is that the highest quality are only available for about 3 months of the year, from late winter to early spring. Other factors affecting the price are the under-developed marketing system which is related to the subtropical climate, the limited demand for raw oysters and the scarcity of good shuckers.

G. TECHNICAL DETAILS

G.1. Dredge boats

(1) The "Indiana", dating from 1945, measures 65 feet in length with a maximum breadth of 17 feet and a draught of 4.5 feet. The hull is made of the rot and insect-resistant wood of the swamp cypress *Taxodium distichum*, 2.25 inches thick. The superstructure is made of pinewood. It is a typical Louisiana oyster lugger, with a spacious flat deck (9.5 m long) in front of the wheel house and cabin, surmounted by a sun awning. The engine is a 135 h.p. "Atlas" diesel. There is an auxiliary engine for generating electricity. The

Fig. 31. The "Captain Baldo" on the wharf at Lafitte. Part of the planking partition on the port side has been taken away. Note shape of sun awning, cut out for operations with the hydraulic winch. (Photo P. Korringa.)

Fig. 32. Hydraulic winch and auxiliary steering wheel on the fore-deck of the "Captain Baldo". (Photo P. Korringa.)

Fig. 33. The dredges used on the "Captain Baldo" have hard metal caps on their teeth to avoid undue wear. This dredge is displayed on the culling table. (Photo P. Korringa.)

boat is equipped with two dredges, both 6 feet wide. The steel-framed dredges carry 22 teeth in front and are each equipped with a "shoe" to facilitate the passage of the dredge over the rollers mounted on the sides of the ship. The dredge bag is of iron rings on the lower side and of nylon netting on the top. The bag can be opened with a handle for dumping the oysters on deck. The dredges are hauled by power taken from the ship's engine by a 75 feet long, 7/16 gauge, 3 B steel chain wound on a drum standing in the middle of the deck. At this spot there is also an extra wheel for steering the boat during dredging operations. The sides of the fore-deck can be built up by means of planks, thus increasing its loading capacity. The boat can carry 800 sacks of oysters.

(2) The other dredge boat, which is of more recent construction (1964), is the "Captain Baldo", measuring 50 feet in length with a maximum breadth of 19 feet and drawing 35 feet. This boat is also built of 2.25-inch swamp cypress wood and the deck and superstructure of pinewood. It resembles the "Indiana" in several respects but has a greater carrying capacity: 1 000 sacks of oysters containing about 85 pounds of oyster each. Apart from the spacious front deck where oysters can be stored up to the wheel house, there is a 70 cm wide storage space on both sides of the wheel house, cabin and galley.

Here too, the sides can be built up using 135 cm wide planks. The main difference in appearance is due to the cut-out sun awning (Fig. 31). This is necessary, for this lugger hauls its dredges with a hydraulic winch and booms (Fig. 32), not over a roller at the side of the ship. The ship's engine is a 165 h.p. GM 761 diesel. On the forward deck are the winch for operating the dredges and the extra wheel for steering the ship during dredging operations. Additional equipment which should be mentioned are a radio-telephone and an echo-sounder, and, for the comfort of the crew, a refrigerator and a television set. There are two bunks in the cabin and two in the wheel house. The 20 teeth of the dredge, each 15 cm long and 16 mm thick at its upper end, have welded-on pieces of a specially hardened metal, 2.5 mm thick on the front side of their tips which prolong their useful life (Fig. 33). The results of dredging are dumped on culling tables placed at both sides of the deck. These tables measure 160 × 100 cm by 85 cm high and are made of multiplex wood covered with aluminium.

H. BIBLIOGRAPHY

Anonymous, 1956. Scientists stalk oyster killers. The Humble Way, published by Humble Oil and Refining Co., Houston, Texas, 12 (2): 11.

Anonymous, 1956. Oysters and oil. The Humble Way, published by Humble Oil and Refining Co., Houston, Texas, 12 (3): 11.

Barret, B.B., 1971. Phase II, Hydrology, and Phase III, Sedimentology. In: Cooperative Gulf of Mexico Estuarine Inventory and Study, Louisiana. La. Wildl. Fish. Comm., New Orleans, 191 pp.

Galtsoff, P.S., 1964. The American Oyster, *Crassostrea virginica* Gmelin. Fish. Bull. Fish Wildl. Serv., Vol. 64, 480 pp.

Galtsoff, P.S., Smith, R.O. and Koehring, V., 1935. Effects of crude oil pollution on oysters in Louisiana waters. Bull. 18 U.S. Bur. Fish., 48: 143—210.

Gunter, G., 1949. A Summary of Production Statistics and Facts Related to Development of the Oyster Industry of Louisiana, with a Brief Comparison with other Gulf States. Publ. No. 2, Texas A & M Res. Found., 28 pp.

Hopkins, S.H., 1954. The American species of Trematode confused with *Bucephalus (Bucephalopsis) haimeanus.* Parasitology, 44: 353—370.

Hopkins, S.H., 1956. Notes on boring sponges in the Gulf Coast estuaries and their relation to salinity. Bull. Mar. Sci. Gulf Caribb., 6 (1): 44—58.

Hopkins, S.H., 1956. Crabs as predator of oysters in Louisiana. Proc. Natl. Shellfish Assoc., 46: 177—184.

Hopkins, S.H., 1956. Our present knowledge of the oyster parasite "Bucephalus". Proc. Natl Shellfish Assoc., 47: 58—61.

Hopkins, S.H., Mackin, J.G. and Menzel, R.W., 1953. The annual cycle of reproduction, growth and fattening in Louisiana oysters. Conv. Pap. Natl Shellfish Assoc., 1953, pp. 39—50.

Mackin, J.G., 1961. Oyster diseases caused by *Dermocystidium marinum* and other microorganisms in Louisiana. Publ. Inst. Mar. Sci., 7: 132—229.

Mackin, J.G. and Hopkins, S.H., 1961. Studies on oyster mortality in relation to natural environments and the oil fields in Louisiana. Publ. Inst. Mar. Sci., 7: 1—131.

Mackin, J.G. and Sparks, A.K., 1961. A study of the effect on oysters of crude oil loss from a wild well. Publ. Inst. Mar. Sci., 7: 230—261.

Matthiessen, G.C., 1971. A Review of Oyster Culture and the Oyster Industry in North America. Contrib. No. 2528 Woods Hole Oceanogr. Inst., 52 pp.

MacGraw, K.A. and Gunter, G., 1972. Observations on killing of the Virginia oyster by the Gulf oyster borer, *Thais haemastoma*, with evidence for a paralytic secretion. Proc. Natl. Shellfish Assoc., 62: 95—97.

Perret, W.S., 1971. Phase IV, Biology. In: Cooperative Gulf of Mexico Estuarine Inventory and Study, Louisiana. La. Wildl. Fish. Comm., New Orleans, La., pp. 33—175.

Perret, W.S., Barrett, B.B., Latapie, W.R., Pollard, J.F., Mock, W.R., Adkins, G.B., Gaidry, W.J. and White, C.J., 1971. Phase I, Area description. In: Cooperative Gulf of Mexico Estuarine Inventory and Study, Louisiana. La. Wildl. Fish. Comm., New Orleans, La., pp. 5—27.

Prytherch, H.F., 1940. The life cycle and morphology of *Nematopsis ostrearum*, sp. nov., a gregarine parasite of the mud crab and oyster. J. Morphol., 66 (1): 39—65.

St. Amant, L.S., 1970. Biological effects of petroleum exploration and production in coastal Louisiana. Santa Barbara Oil Symp., Univ. Calif. Publ. Mar. Sci., pp. 335—354.

St. Amant, L.S., 1973. Some considerations of the chronic effect of petroleum in the marine environment. Unpublished, 13 pp.

Sprague, V., 1971. Diseases of oysters. Annu. Rev. Microbiol., 25: 211—230.

Chapter 4

FARMING THE PORTUGUESE OYSTER (*CRASSOSTREA ANGULATA*) IN THE MARENNES-OLERON REGION, CHARENTE MARITIME, FRANCE

Example
Monsieur Gilles Georgeon, oyster farmer at Mornac-sur-Seudre, Charente Maritime.
Period of observation: 1969—1971.

A. BACKGROUND

A.1. General principles

The term "marennes" has an almost magic sound in the oyster world. It indicates to the epicurist, the highest peak in quality and flavour, above all when the gills of the oysters display the green hue ascribed to the pigment called "marennine". Although natural beds of the flat oyster (*Ostrea edulis*) were once prolific in the Charente Maritime, this area has for centuries, above all, been renowned as a fattening district. Oyster farming is usually considered as the application of techniques for collecting spat using artificial collectors, which started in France in the time of Coste, in the middle of the nineteenth century. However, it is quite correct to state, that oyster farming in France dates back much further, when it is recalled that special ponds were in use for fattening oysters taken from natural beds, long before that era. When the local natural beds of flat oysters became depleted, fair-sized oysters were introduced from other areas, both in France and abroad, for a rather short stay in the fattening ponds, known as "claires". These claires, which once served as salines for the production of sea salt, can be counted here by the tens of thousands. They are especially numerous along both banks of the River Seudre, where they cover a length of some 16 km, in a band from 500 to 1 500 m broad. Also north of the town of Marennes, and on the east coast of the Isle of Oléron between St Trojan and Boyardville there are many thousands of claires. The total area of claires in the Charente Maritime is estimated at some 1 300 ha. The original use of claires for making salt was dropped only gradually. Up to 1939, salt was still produced in various ponds on the Isle of Oléron. For a long period both flat oysters (*Ostrea edulis*) and Portuguese oysters (*Crassostrea angulata*) were fattened in the claires. The former were invariably purchased from the Morbihan, the latter more often introduced directly from natural beds in Portugal. When natural beds of this latter species came into being in the

Gironde Estuary, these became an important source of oysters for stocking the claires. Nowadays flat oysters are hardly used at all in the claires, the whole industry having switched over to the cheaper *Crassostrea* oyster. Production of marketable flat oysters in the whole Charente Maritime district now fluctuates between 5 and 10 tons per year.

In addition to the claires there are about 20 000 small oyster parks covering a total area of 2 300 ha, laid out on the extensive intertidal flats between the Ile d'Oléron and the mainland. The intertidal grounds belong to the State, but the claires are invariably private property.

Though many oysters are introduced for fattening from other districts, a serious effort is made to procure spat in the area itself, utilizing a variety of collectors. The spat procured here belongs exclusively to the species *Crassostrea angulata*. Oyster farming in the Charente Maritime is a semi-culture, larval development and the provision of food for oysters of all ages being fully left to nature. There is a clear-cut differentiation between the following phases: procuring the spat ("captage"), growing oysters to a fair size ("élevage"), and fattening ("affinage"), after which the oysters are harvested, graded, stored and shipped.

The company under consideration participates in all three phases, but concentrates on fattening, to which end they use both intertidal parks and claires. The company works practically exclusively with *Crassostrea* oysters and only on an experimental scale with a very small tonnage of flat oysters purchased in the Morbihan. There are thousands of oyster farmers and many hundreds of companies shipping marketable oysters in the area, but the company under consideration is probably the most important of all.

A.2. Biology of the species

The Portuguese oyster, *Crassostrea angulata* Lmk, differs in several respects from the European flat oyster, *Ostrea edulis* L. Its shell is elongated instead of round, and more deeply cupped, with a marked purple pigmentation of the muscle scar. An unmistakable difference is the presence of a promyal chamber, a slit which guides part of the water passed through the gills to the exhalent chamber on the right side of the body and is between the adducter muscle and the umbo. This promyal chamber facilitates the passage of water and keeps the exhalent chamber clean of invading sediments which makes it possible for such oysters to live in more turbid water and on softer ground than can flat oysters. Another noteworthy difference is that *Crassostrea* oysters are oviparous, expelling their eggs directly into the surrounding sea water, whereas *Ostrea* oysters are larviparous, i.e. they practise incubation, by keeping their larvae on their gills for some time before releasing them.

The Portuguese oyster not only thrives in rather turbid water and on rather soft ground, but can also endure a much wider range of salinities. Flat oysters suffer at salinities under 25‰, but Portuguese oysters can live, grow and fatten even when salinities are as low as 15‰, and can stand still lower salinities for a certain period, or intermittently as happens with the tides in many estuaries.

The Portuguese oyster and related species are, therefore, often found closer inshore and higher in the estuaries than are flat oysters. It has even been thought that Portuguese oysters will not thrive at all in high salinity water and that their larvae could only develop normally in sites having a certain admixture of fresh water from rivers or submarine wells. Spatfall is, however, often observed in places where the salinity is almost equal to that of the open ocean, and the assumption of Ranson that the larvae must have been transported there in pockets of brackish water seems to be unfounded. Moreover, not only have natural beds of this species been found in the Adriatic Sea, not far from Trieste, but also in the vicinity of the Balearic Islands where high salinities prevail. It is, therefore, more reasonable to conclude that the Portuguese oyster has a wider ecological range than the flat oyster, at least as far as salinity is concerned. In respect of other environmental factors the Portuguese oyster may, on the contrary, be more exacting than the flat oyster. For spawning, it requires higher water temperatures than *Ostrea edulis:* it does not spawn unless the water temperature has been 20° C or higher for several days, and its larvae will not develop and settle at temperatures below this level. Thus Portuguese oysters will always settle several weeks later than flat oysters in areas where both species occur together, which makes it possible to procure either one or the other on the collectors by correctly timing sailing out. The high temperature requirements make it clear why the settlement of Portuguese oyster spat is only rarely observed north of the Loire river, even when appreciable numbers have been relaid for growth and fattening. It is, on the other hand, a noteworthy fact that *Crassostrea angulata* can stand low water temperatures very well, better in fact, than the flat oyster. This is the more remarkable because this species is never faced with freezing weather in places where it occurs naturally. The author recalls an observation he made that Portuguese oysters had suffered badly from freezing weather high in the intertidal zone of the Bay of Arcachon after the severe winter of 1946—1947, not because their living tissues could not stand the low temperatures, but because freezing of the chalky deposits had led to the shell being burst!

It is, therefore, possible to re-lay Portuguese oysters at higher latitudes without running the risk of losing them in the winter. The risk has to be run, however, that they will develop an unpleasant oily flavour, from retaining their eggs and sperm, if the water temperature does not rise high enough in summer. It is, therefore, advisable to plant them rather high in the intertidal zone, so that they may be washed for some time in the comparatively warm water arising from the incoming tide passing over grounds warmed by the sun during spells of fine weather. The flavour of the Portuguese oyster, faintly reminiscent of cucumber, is unmistakably different from that of the flat oyster, even when the latter has been grown in the very same water.

The Portuguese oyster was originally only known on the west and south coasts of Portugal and Spain, a rather limited geographical range. As mentioned previously, it has in recent years also been found in appreciable numbers at two rather isolated places in the Mediterranean, some distance from the Atlantic Coast. A very remarkable feature is the close resemblance of the Portuguese oyster to the Japanese oyster, *Crassostrea gigas* Thunberg. On the basis of the features of the larval shell, it has even been surmised that they are one and the same species. However this may be, the hypothesis that it was originally brought to Portugal on the hulls of ships returning from Japan is not very plausible to anyone who has inspected hulls of ships for oysters, and who knows that the hulls of the ancient wooden sailing vessels had to be scraped clean several times during the long journey to and from the Orient. On continental sites in the Charente Maritime department fossil and subfossil oyster shells have been found, so closely resembling those of the Portuguese oyster that it seems more logical to assume that this species showed a wider range long before the dawn of history, but that in time, it disappeared from the French coastal area. Arcachon oyster farmers brought it in again from Portugal, after having depleted the beds of flat oysters in the estuaries of northern Spain. In the year 1868 the "Morlaisien", one of the ships transporting Portuguese oysters, had to seek shelter in the Gironde Estuary during a gale which lasted several days. When the oysters deteriorated they were thrown overboard, although not all of them were dead, and they have since found an almost ideal habitat there. Thus, profuse natural beds in due course came into being. From there the Portuguese oysters spread gradually further north, but have not proceeded to any extent beyond the Loire River, because of too low water temperatures there in the summer.

A.3. Geographical situation

The company under consideration has its parks on the intertidal flats east of the Isle of Oléron, both adjacent to the island and to the continental shoreline. The Isle of Oléron is on the French Atlantic coast, north of the Gironde Estuary, its axis is roughly southeast—northwest, from 45° 48′ N, 1° 08′ W to 46° 04′ N, 1° 24′ W. The company has its claires on two sites on the east coast of the Ile d'Oléron, due east and northeast of the town of Dolus, and also near to Mornac-sur-Seudre, in the upriver section of the Seudre Estuary, close to its headquarters at 45° 44′ 45″ N, 1° 02′ 40″ W, some 10 km north of the city of Royan.

A.4. Hydrographical pattern

Depths. The oyster farming area between the Ile d'Oléron and the continental coast largely consists of vast and broad intertidal flats, bisected by a

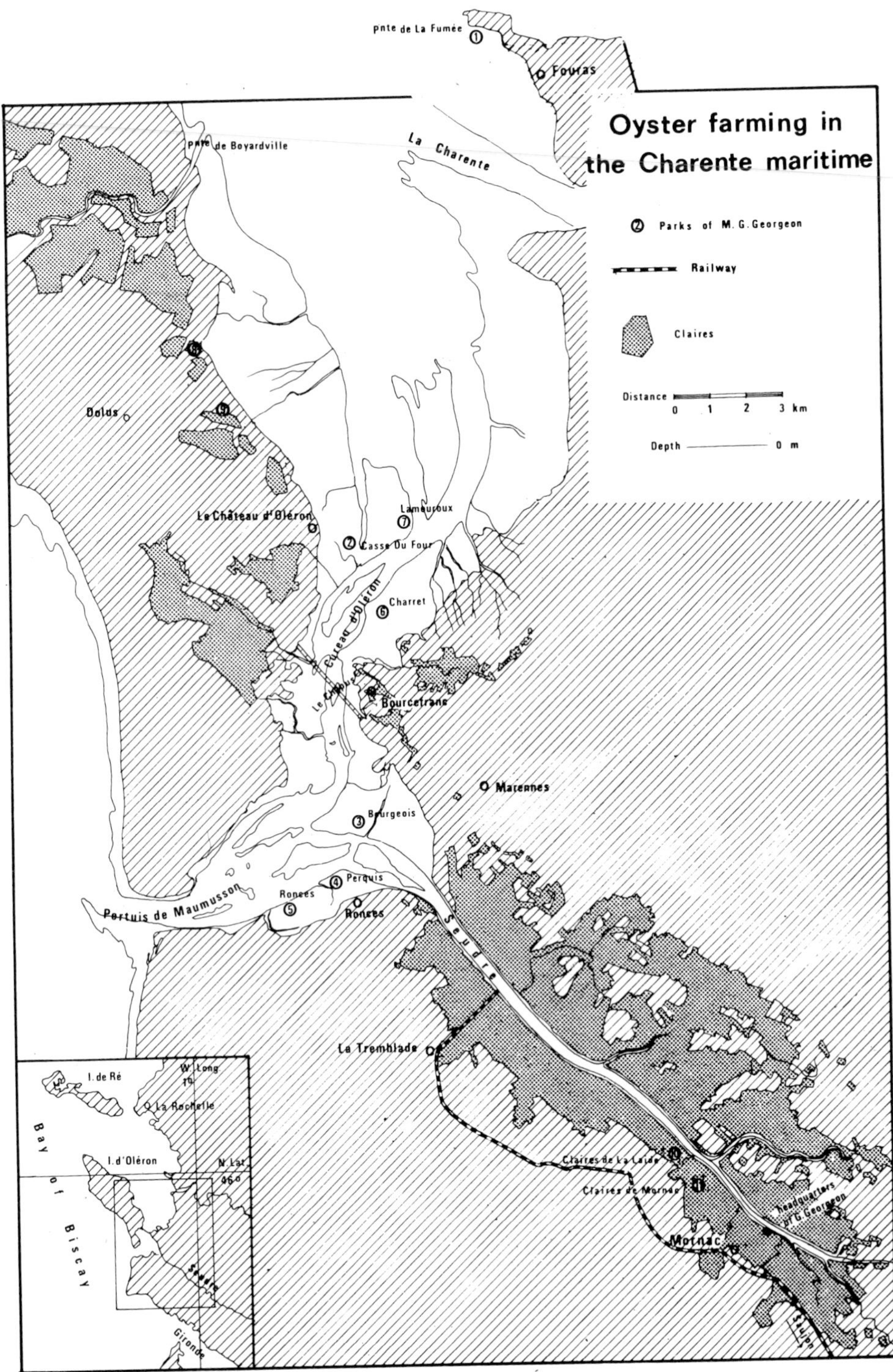

Oyster farming in the Charente maritime
Parks of M. G. Georgeon
Railway
Claires
Distance 0 1 2 3 km
Depth 0 m
pnte de La Fumée
Fouras
La Charente
pnte de Boyardville
Dolus
Le Château d'Oléron
Lameuroux
Casse Du Four
Charret
Coureau d'Oléron
Bourcefranc
Marennes
Bourgeois
Perquis
Ronces
Pertuis de Maumusson
Seudre
La Tremblade
Claires de La Laide
Claires de Mornac
Headquarters of G. Georgeon
Mornac
I. de Ré
La Rochelle
I. d'Oléron
Bay of Biscay
Gironde

channel called "Coureau d'Oléron" which, towards the south, is continuous with the Pertuis de Maumusson, the strait which separates the island from the mainland. Towards the northwest the area narrows gradually towards the Pertuis d'Antioche beyond Fort Boyard and the Ile d'Aix.

Tides. The tide comes in from the Pertuis d'Antioche in the northwest attaining a speed of up to 2 knots at spring tides. On the ebb tide, a fair amount of water regains the open Atlantic by way of the Pertuis de Maumusson, but the bulk finds its way back to the Pertuis d'Antioche. At La Tremblade, at the entrance to the Seudre Estuary, the tidal range is 4.00 m at spring tide, and only 1.80 m at neap tide.

Water temperature. In the open sea, water temperatures are about the same as those recorded for the Pertuis Breton, ranging from about 8°C in winter to 20°C in summer, but closer inshore, the differences can be greater in both directions. Especially in the upriver section of the Seudre River and high on the tidal flats, temperatures well above 20°C can be observed in midsummer.

Salinity. Though salinities are quite equable in the Pertuis d'Antioche, ranging from 33 to 35‰, precipitation can lead to rather low salinities in the inshore section, especially in the upriver section of the Seudre. Most of the time the rivers Seudre and Charente discharge modest volumes of fresh water, but during the rainy season the run-off can be much greater. The claires do not easily suffer from low salinities as they only take in water at high tide, and in the best claires the intake is limited to a few days around spring tide. The effect of high salinities may be more serious when, during a period of drought and strong evaporation, combined with a prolonged spell of low tides, the salinity in the claires increases to 40‰ and over. It has sometimes happened that oyster farmers have had to try to save their oysters in the claires by pumping in water from the Seudre River.

Plankton and turbidity. Little is known about the exact quantity and quality of the phytoplankton in the water bathing the oyster parks east of the Isle of Oléron. In the claires, in which the water is stagnant for prolonged periods, phytoplankton development may differ quite a lot from that in the open water. Depending upon the depth of the claires, on their bottom conditions, on the maintenance pattern, on the degree of flushing, and on the contribution of nutrients from the land, quite large individual fluctuations can be expected. The diatom *Navicula ostrearia*, in particular, gives reason for concern. When this diatom flourishes, the oysters attain the desired green hue associated with their delicate flavour. The ways of the diatom, however, are rather capricious and the factors affecting its bloom are still poorly known. Despite efforts to create good conditions, oyster farmers experience time and again that only some of their claires become green, often only 10%. It is said that a higher percentage developed this desired flora in former years and the decline is attributed to some form of pollution.

The open water is very turbid and, in fact, comparable with that of the

Pertuis Breton. The silt swirled up from the bottom deposits by the wind and tide causes this turbidity. Fortunately, Portuguese oysters can cope with such conditions and are able to collect edible matter from the sea water even when this is heavily loaded with silt. In the claires the conditions are quite different, as the water is stagnant for many days in succession, giving the silt an opportunity to settle. A disadvantage, however, is that this settling of silt brought in with the spring tide, leads to a gradual rise in the bottom of the claires, making it necessary to remove these deposits every few years if the claires are to be kept in good condition for oyster farming.

Sea bed conditions. The area is known for its muddy bottom into which the human foot can easily sink. Thus, on many parks special wooden footwear is used to enable workers to walk on them. Although the rivers Charente and Seudre both bring down some silt, the bulk has been discharged during the course of ages by the Gironde, and is perpetually being moved by tides and currents. Oysters and other filter feeders tend to consolidate finely dispersed silt particles, which leads to the silting up of places where they congregate in large numbers.

A.5. Legal aspects

The firm under consideration is a private enterprise of which Monsieur Gilles Georgeon is the proprietor.

The parks on the intertidal grounds belong to the State. M. Georgeon uses his parks (which are marked on the chart) as follows:

For catching spat:

(1) A 1.5-ha park south of the Pointe de la Fumée, due west of the town of Fouras off the northern bank of the Charente Estuary. The tidal coefficient here ranges from 75 to 80, which means that the park is only exposed around spring tide, for an average of some 13 days per month. (This park is number 1 on the chart.) M. Georgeon has to pay the standard rent of FFr 132 per ha prevailing in this area. This rent is expected to double in the near future, for not only is the government going to raise the standard rent per hectare, but in addition, the farmers will have to pay a special fee for product development ("taxe de publicité") based on the number of hectares actually in use.

For rearing oysters:

(2) Casse du Four, due east of Le Chateau off the Isle of Oléron. This park measures 2 ha and has a tidal coefficient of 100, which means that it can only be worked on foot at spring tides — a few days per month. This park is used for re-laying of 18-month oysters.

(3) A park of 0.45 ha on the Banc de Bourgeois, right in the Seudre Estuary. The tidal co-efficient is 80—90 which means exposure at spring tide only.

(4) A park of 0.09 ha with a tidal coefficient of 70 on the Banc de Perquis off the town of Ronce-les-Bains.

(5) A park of 0.25 ha with a tidal coefficient of 80 on the Banc de Ronce, due west of Ronce-les-Bains. This park is rented from a colleague.

(6) A park of 0.18 ha with a tidal coefficient of 90 on the Banc de Charret on the flats on the continental side, north of the town of Bource-franc.

(7) On the Banc Lamouroux situated between the channels leading to the Pertuis d'Antioche east-northeast of Le Chateau on the Isle of Oléron, three parks of 0.15 ha each, one with a tidal coefficient of 70, and two of 90.

For fattening oysters M. Georgeon can make use of several groups of claires. The claires do not belong to the State but are private property, belonging either to M. Georgeon himself or to someone from whom he rents them:

(8) Prise de Videau on the Isle of Oléron, northeast of the town of Dolus, 4 ha of privately owned claires. These claires were purchased about 8 years ago.

(9) Prise de Méré somewhat further south on the Isle of Oléron, 5 ha of claires rented for a fee of FFr 10 000 per year.

(10) Prise de la Laide, due north of the town of Mornac-sur-Seudre, on the left bank of the river. Here M. Georgeon owns 200 claires measuring 40 × 12 m each. The claires are of the "claires de sarretière" type, named after the halophyte locally known as sarre (= *Salicornia*). The claires are situated close to the river bank, have not been dug, but were constructed by raising a low bank around them. They take in water when the banks overflow and there is a tidal coefficient of 70.

(11) Claires de Mornac, known as "claires de marais", dug in the saltings somewhat higher up the river bank. They take in water through special inlets at a tidel coefficient of 60. M. Georgeon owns 150 of such claires at Mornac, each measuring 40 × 12 m.

In addition, M. Georgeon has at his headquarters a yard with 600 m^2 of sorting and packing sheds, a 400-m^2 storehouse for various materials, and almost 1 000 m^2 of concrete storage basins for oysters, with a pump equipped with an 8 h.p. electric motor, capable of pumping 200 m^3 of water per h to fill the basins when the tide does not come high enough.

Apart from the usual "gendarmes maritimes" there are no paid watchmen on the parks. There is no need for them, as there are always so many people working on their small parks at low tide that they would easily spot a trespasser. At low water spring tide up to 5 000 boats may be seen on the parks in this area. At neap tides there are fewer workers, but even then it would be difficult to steal oysters unobserved.

B. SEQUENCE OF OPERATIONS

B.1. Procuring the spat

a. Preparing the collectors. The main types of collector used in the area are shell strings, slabs of slate, and scrap iron. All these materials are placed on some kind of support to keep them off the muddy bottom. Most of the collectors are concentrated along the banks of the Seudre River and on the intertidal flats adjacent to the east coast of the Isle of Oléron. M. Georgeon uses shell strings, scrap iron, and also a new type of plastic collector. This is not to produce all the oysters he needs for his claires, but rather to avoid his staff being idle during the slack season. He even sells most of the spat collected, as he is short of good ground for rearing them.

Shell strings, known as "chapelets" are made up from the oyster shells produced by the company, using the waste material left over after cleaning and sorting. No shells are bought for this purpose. Female workers make a hole in the shells using a pointed hammer. A worker can perforate some 50 kg of shells per h (2.5 baskets containing 20 kg each). Galvanized iron wire, gauge 15 (1.5 mm diameter) is used to string the shells which are alternately placed convex and concave side upwards ("tête-bêche"). The wire is twisted at the extremities of the strings to keep the shells in place. The shell strings are 1.20 m in length. One basket of shells (20 kg) is sufficient to make seven strings, and an experienced worker can make 20 to 22 strings per h. The company makes some 5 000 strings each year, which are first temporarily piled in the yard.

These shell strings have to be supported by frames constructed of 18-mm diameter iron bars. These rectangular frames measure 300 × 80 cm, with one cross-bar in the middle to provide greater strength. The six slanting legs with horizontal "feet" are each 60 cm in length.

Collectors made from scrap iron consist either of round iron bars, having a diameter of 16—20 mm cut into 1.20-m lengths (weighing some 0.60 kg each) and placed on similar supporting frames, or of scrap iron of any kind (box-mattresses included) placed either on frames or on iron tripods. The iron tripods are constructed of bars 60 cm long and 18 mm in diameter, again curved horizontally at their lower extremities to prevent them sinking in the mud. Such tripods are spaced at intervals of 60 cm.

Plastic collectors consist of four plastic tubes each 1.5 cm in diameter and 1.20 m long, kept together with three plastic cross-pieces so that the interspaces are about 12 cm. The plastic tubes are finely grooved along their lengths and need no lime coating to serve as collectors. They are placed in groups of ten (40 tubes) on the same types of iron frames as the shell strings and the scrap iron, and are attached to the frames with iron wire.

b. Sailing out the collectors. The best time for sailing out the collectors

Fig. 34. M. Georgeon holding up a "chapelet", a shell string locally used for collecting oyster spat. (Photo P. Korringa.)

depends on water temperature and on the appearance and development of the oyster larvae. The "Institut Scientifique et Technique des Pêches Maritimes" keeps the oyster farmers informed on settling prospects. Usually sailing does not start before the month of July, but should be completed before August 15th. Collectors, of all the types described, are loaded on the two "chalands" belonging to the company. These chalands are of the usual flat-decked type, 10 m long, 3 m broad, made of pinewood and each equipped with a 18 h.p. Evinrude outboard motor. These engines are only used on the spat-collecting site. For the 35-km voyage to the spat-collecting park at

Pointe de la Fumée, the chalands are towed by the company motor boat [1]. It takes about ten trips to take out all the material — first the frames and the sea marks for marking the area, later the shell strings and the other collectors. Each trip out takes about 3 h, followed by about 2 h of work on the site, and finally a return voyage, with the tide, again of 3 h.

c. Maintenance and thinning out of the collectors. Each month M. Georgeon visits his spat collectors at Pointe de la Fumée at spring tide, going by car to the town of Fouras and taking along his rubber waders. The shell strings require little maintenance, but the iron bars, the scrap iron, and the plastic collectors eventually require thinning out. In April or May of the following year, the iron bars, now covered with spat, are attached to the frames with galvanized iron wire at intervals of about 20 cm, to give the oysters sufficient space to grow. The scrap iron, piled up on frames and tripods, 40—50 cm deep, needs spreading out over a greater number of supports after spatfall has taken place, but often mussel seed settles so profusely on it that the oysters get little chance to develop. For this reason M. Georgeon has not obtained satisfactory results using scrap iron over the past 4 years. Plastic collectors may also suffer from the heavy settlement of mussel seed. When they carry a sufficient number of oysters, they are attached to the frames with galvanized wire in a single layer. This operation is carried out in April or May. When the spat on the plastic collectors and on the iron bars has not been ousted by mussels and has been thinned out properly, oysters with a weight of 25 kg per 1 000 at 18 months, and 50 kg per 1 000 when they are 30 months old can be expected. Such oysters are easily taken off and may be sold, though up to 50 tons per year are used for further growth on M. Georgeon's own parks in the Casse du Four.

Shell strings carrying oyster spat, ranging from 2 to 30 per shell, are not left on the frames for further growth. In March or April they are taken away. The iron frames being left on the site, unless they require a thorough cleaning due to being covered with mussels. If M. Georgeon intends to plant the shells with spat on a park, for which he chooses the park on the Banc de Ronce, he cuts the iron wires on board the ship, and scatters the shells on arrival at the park. However, as he is short of good grounds for rearing spat, he usually sells the strings covered with spat either to other oyster farmers in the region, or to those working in the Etang de Thau (on the Mediterranean coast of France) or in Brittany. In 1970, strings were all sold to Brittany for a price of FFr 3.00 each. When the strings are destined for sale the iron wire, of course, is not cut.

B.2. Rearing the spat collected with shell strings

The shells carrying spat are preferably planted on a park with a tidal coefficient of 60—70. There, the young oysters can be expected to develop thick, strong shells, whereas the shells would be thin and brittle if the spat were planted on deeper ground. The shells carrying spat are planted quite densely, almost touching each other. To prevent them being washed away by the current, the park is fenced in, for which end M. Georgeon uses iron wire netting, with 3.5-cm hexagonal meshes, supported by iron pickets. This wire has to be renewed every year. It is advisable to provide shelter, using rows of stones or sticks, on the more exposed sites in the park. To avoid the shells with spat being washed into heaps, the parks are subdivided into compartments with low fences of plastic-covered wire netting. It is still advisable to inspect the parks containing young oysters rather frequently.

The young oysters are left on the park for a year. They are harvested in the spring or, if growth has been fast, in the autumn of the year they were planted. They are then brought to the headquarters where they are separated with a heavy knife. As some oysters are damaged by this procedure, it is advisable to place them for some days on a tray in a basin. These oysters now weigh between 10 and 30 kg per 1 000 and can be used for the next step, "demi-élevage". They are usually re-laid on the park in the Casse-du-Four. M. Georgeon purchases such oysters when his own production is insufficient. The smaller category, weighing 10—20 kg per 1 000 cost FFr 1.20—1.50 per kg, the regulars, weighing 25—35 kg per 1 000, FFr 2.00—3.00 per kg. As the latter category can reach marketable size the same year, a higher price has to be paid for them than for those which have to be reared 1 year longer.

B.3. Growing oysters for re-laying ("demi-élevage")

To stock his parks on the Banc de Perquis, the Banc de Charret, and the Banc de Bourgeois, M. Georgeon buys a considerable tonnage of 3-year-old oysters every year. About 30 tons of oysters of French origin, weighing some 30 kg per 1 000, are purchased partly from other farmers in the Marennes—Oléron district and partly from oystermen exploiting the natural beds in the Gironde Estuary. In addition, from 30—50 tons of oysters, weighing 30—40 kg per 1 000, are imported from the Sado Estuary in Portugal and from the Spanish estuaries in Andalusia. M. Georgeon prefers to buy oysters for relaying in the heavier weight categories; the official limit of 40 kg per 1 000 for imported oysters cannot always be observed very precisely. The larger oysters are used for stocking the claires, but the bulk of the oysters, which are purchased in March, April or May, are destined for the parks on the intertidal flats (Fig. 35), including all the stock imported from Portugal and Spain. The oysters are planted quite densely: 1 ton per acre, which corresponds to 10 kg per m^2, exactly the same figure as that for mussel farming on parks in The Netherlands. These parks are fenced in with iron wire netting having 3.5-cm hexagonal meshes and supported by iron pickets, 50 cm long, placed at 1-m intervals. A 6—7 m long sea mark is placed every 10 m.

Fig. 35. Oyster parks laid out on the intertidal flats of the Isle of Oléron seen from the bridge at low tide. (Photo P. Korringa.)

These fences are made to prevent the oysters being washed away from the park, not as a defence measure against crabs, which would not be able to destroy oysters of the size planted here. Fishes such as the "tère" (the sting ray *Trygon pastinaca*) can, however, be destructive here. Therefore, a mass of willow twigs are placed on the parks, which make it impossible for the rays to "land".

Every spring tide a crew of six workers visits the oysters on these parks, making use of the boat and always taking a small rowing boat along with them. There is a lot of work to do: spreading oysters which have been thrown into heaps by waves and currents, picking out starfish, placing willow twigs for defence against the rays, and in cases where sand or silt threatens to smother the oysters, harrowing the entire plot. For this latter purpose M. Georgeon uses a special harrow [2] which is drawn along with the aid of a 3 h.p. petrol engine over the whole breadth of the park. A similar harrow can be operated with a hand winch. In this area harrows are never dragged behind a boat.

Fig. 36. Densely planted Portuguese oysters grow well on one of the parks at la Tour du Phare, east of the Isle of Oléron. (Photo P. Korringa.)

B.4. Harvesting oysters from the parks

In principle, oysters scattered on the parks in the spring are harvested in the autumn of the same year. They then weigh 50—60 kg per 1 000. Harvesting is carried out manually, the workers using special forks with nine, slightly curved 33-cm long prongs and a 20-kg basked ("manne") (Fig. 37). When the water goes out far enough, one worker can collect 50 baskets of oysters per tide. The oysters are transported on board the two company chalands to the headquarters at Mornac-sur-Seudre, towed behind a motor boat. On arrival, the oysters are graded by four to five female workers, who clean off the spat and any other organisms which may have settled on the shells, and eliminate the empty shells. When the oysters are fairly clean, a worker can grade 60 baskets of oysters (a little over 1 ton) per day, but when the oysters carry appreciable numbers of spat on their shells, as is often the case with oysters of French origin, only 30 baskets per worker per day can be handled. This work is carried out from September to the middle of November. The clean oysters are then brought to the claires for further fattening.

Fig. 37. Harvesting oysters with fork and basket on a park near the Isle of Oléron. The numerous twigs planted on the parks serve to keep down fish predation. (Photo P. Korringa.)

B.5. Growing marketable oysters on trays

A variant of oyster farming, cultivation on trays, is also practiced by M. Georgeon. For this, he uses his parks on the Banc Lamouroux, a 2-h sail from the headquarters, where each year he places some 1 000 frames of the same type of construction as those used for supporting the collectors. On these frames he places the trays complete with oysters, although not earlier

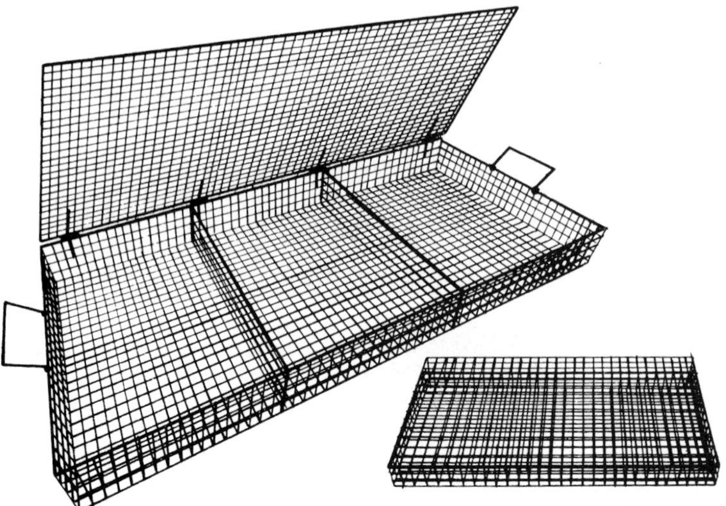

Fig. 38. Trays used for growing oysters on the Banc Lamouroux.

then June the 15th. This is in order to try to avoid the settlement of mussel seed. He uses three types of tray: (a) the traditional wooden tray with wire netting (this will be replaced by plastic netting when worn out); (b) trays made entirely of 2.5-cm square mesh wire netting, measuring 1.50 × 0.60 × 0.12 m and subdivided into three compartments (Fig. 38), the trays being closed with a lid of the same material; (c) smaller, all-plastic trays subdivided into two compartments and measuring 1.00 × 0.50 m. One tray is placed upside-down as a lid on each tray (a) carrying oysters. The oysters are put in the trays one layer thick, which means 22—23 kg of oysters weighing some 40 kg per 1 000 for the larger trays. Each spring tide, four or five workers, often accompanied by M. Georgeon himself, go to the trays to maintain them, which includes hand-picking out starfish. Harvesting begins during the month of September, trays and frames being taken along on the chalands, towed by the motor boat. M. Georgeon has a special clientele throughout the season for the bigger oysters thus produced.

B.6. Fattening ponds or "claires"

The claires, the fattening ponds with a clay bottom, are generally 40 m long and 12 m broad, but the local topographical situation may sometimes lead to divergent sizes. They require laborious maintenance. Before they can receive a new lot of oysters after a season, their clay bottom has to be exposed to the air for about 2 successive months. This operation, "grâlage", is usually carried out in the spring. For this the claire is drained at a low spring tide, after which the inlets and overflows are carefully closed. The clay soil has to

Fig. 39. Typical scene at Chaillevette with claires, sheds and boats of oystermen; the Seudre River can be seen in the background. (Photo P. Korringa.)

desiccate until it shows cracks. It is not precisely known why desiccation is a prerequisite, but it can be assumed that a variety of organisms which live in the submersed clay soil die and that both microbiological and chemical processes lead to a turn-over such that the nutrients trapped in the soil again become available to the phytoplankton. The next step is called "douage" and gives the floor of the claires the desired shape, slightly convex. With a wooden shovel, a "pelle à douer" [3], a thin layer of silt is dug away from the edge of the claires over a breadth of 1 m, and smeared over the inside of the embankment (Fig. 41). This can only be done when the clay is sufficiently stiff, and a wooden tool is more practical for doing this than an iron one. The convex floor shape is required, as the shallow gulley thus created, the "doue", collects most of the sediment which settles in the claire when it is filled; at the same time it facilitates the drainage of the claire when the time comes to harvest the oysters. Finally, the floor of the whole claire is carefully levelled using a "rouable", a type of scraper consisting of a wooden blade, measuring 59 × 10 cm, attached perpendicularly to a 2.5-m long wooden shaft. All this takes one man about 1.5 days per claire, included cutting the vegetation on the banks of the claires. Special attention is paid to the overflow ("derase") which feeds the claire from the channel when the sluice gate

Fig. 40. Claires for fattening oysters on the Isle of Oléron. (Photo A.C. Drinkwaard.)

is opened at the seaward end. To drain a claire, the "chantier", the claire bank, has to be cut using a narrow steel spade called "une ferré"[4]. Nowadays, however, many claires are provided with a deeply laid drainage pipe to let the water out.

When the claire is ready the sea water is let in; first a thin layer, for absorption by the dry bottom, with more following later. A cream-coloured film, called "humeur", develops on the bottom of the claire. Thus this operation is called "mettre en humeur".

In spite of the annual maintenance, or "douage" a claire may gradually silt up. Once in 10—20 years, it is necessary to dig away a thicker layer of clay and for this an iron spade, known as "pelle à piquer" [5], is used. A path of boards is made in the claire so that a wheelbarrow can be used to collect the material which has been dug out. It is very heavy work and even a strong man will not be able to cover more than 30 m^2 per day, including the removal of the clay.

The ideal level for a claire is such that the overflow comes into effect at a tidal coefficient of 70—80, which means that new sea water flows in only occasionally, during a few days at spring tide. A higher coefficient brings the danger of too high salinities during periods of drought, and low spring tides.

Fig. 41. "Douage" — digging away a thin layer of silt from the edge of the claire and smearing it on the inside of the embankment. (Photo P. Korringa.)

Once a claire has been filled with water it is necessary to wait until the next spring tide before proceeding to plant the oysters. Only a few oysters are planted per claire if the high quality oysters called "spéciales de claires" are required. These must stay in the claires during the whole summer season. M. Georgeon estimates that 3 to 4 oysters per m^2 is the maximum that can be planted and also that only the best oysters should be selected for this purpose. Some of the claires can be reached by van, but in other cases it is necessary to transport the oysters to the site in a small boat called a "plate" [6] (Fig. 42). This can carry a load of 600 kg of oysters and three men. When empty this lightweight boat can be carried over the banks ("chantiers"). A special shovel, or "pelle à éparer" [8], is used, to spread the oysters evenly over the claires. As stated above, the hope is that there will be a lush development of the diatom *Navicula ostrearia*, which gives the oysters the desired green hue and excellent flavour, but often the farmer is disappointed. For no obvious reason many claires fail to go green. Of the claires used by M. Georgeon, those on the Isle of Oléron show a better "verdissement" than those near Mornac-sur-Seudre, possibly because in the case of the latter the water is often of somewhat lower salinity. The green colour may appear within a few

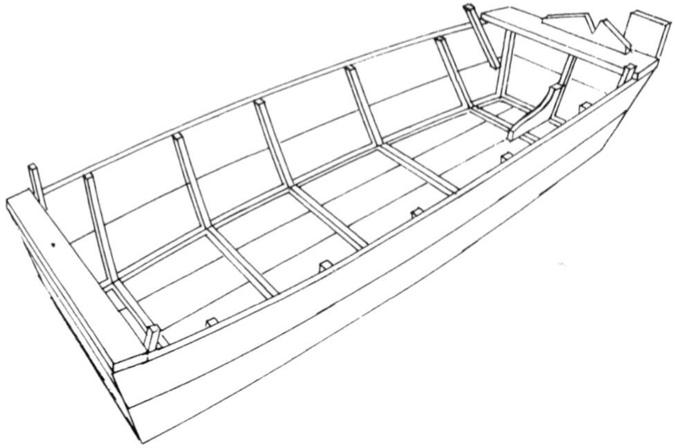

Fig. 42. Very lightweight boat used in the claires.

weeks, but if it has not appeared by September, it will not develop at all that year.

During the summer season the oysters grow and fatten on the muddy bot-

Fig. 43. Typical low-tide scenery on the Isle of Oléron with claires, sheds of the oystermen and oysters in baskets on a landing stage. (Photo A.C. Drinkwaard.)

tom of the claire. Each spring tide brings in some new water loaded with silt, nutrients and plankton, making the water slightly turbid. Within a few days this sediment has settled, so that the water becomes clear again.

When the oysters have acquired the desired quality, whether they are green or not, they are harvested from the claire. This is usually carried out during the month of September. Immediately afterwards, oysters collected from the parks are brought to the same claire and planted, but much more densely, 600 kg per claire, thus six or seven times as many as were planted in June. The quantities planted, about 75 kg per claire for producing "spéciales de claires" and about 600 kg per claire for oysters planted in September, are related to the claire as a whole. The "doue" is always kept free and sometimes the oysters are planted over only half the surface of the claire, but then, of course, at a greater density per square metre. The oysters planted in September will not grow appreciably while in the claires, but their shells will become harder and stronger, and they may, moreover, fatten a little. Also the somewhat lower salinity may lead to inflation of the soft tissues, which makes the oysters look plumper. With luck, they may even have a slight greenish tinge. The oysters thus produced and harvested later in the year, are known as "fines de claires".

Fig. 44. Artist's view of harvesting oysters from a claire; a "commode" is being used to transport baskets of oysters.

B.7. Harvesting oysters from the "claires"

There are different ways of taking the oysters from the claires. When the oysters have acquired the desired green hue an effort is made to give a second batch a chance. It is for this purpose that half of the claire is reserved at the beginning. Care is taken to disturb the bottom as little as possible during the harvesting of the first crop.

A practical way of harvesting oysters from a claire is by making use of long-shafted forks. The claire is carefully drained, leaving a layer of about 40 cm of water, after which two men proceed to harvest the oysters using the "fourche", the 23-cm broad fork with nine slightly curved prongs 33 cm long. The claire is entered at the short end, the first worker wading out in a straight line, about 2 m from the long bank on his left. He works with his fork from left to right, clearing a strip about 2 m wide, depositing the oysters in a single row some 3 m from the long bank. The second worker wades

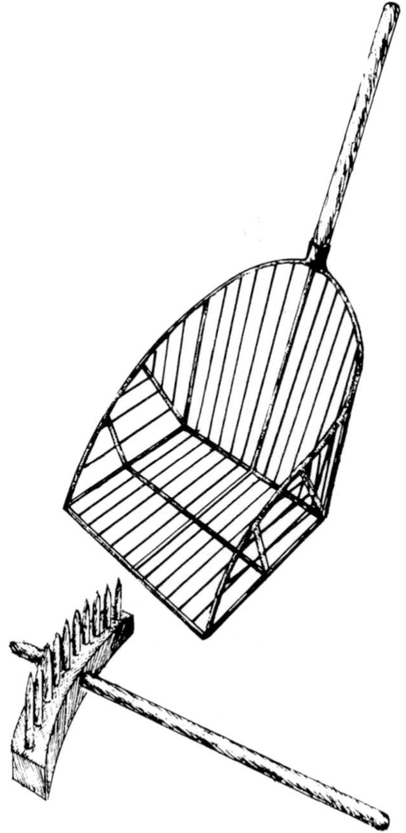

Fig. 45. The "truelle", a scoop into which the oysters are raked in a claire, and rake.

out about 4 m away from the left bank and works with his fork from right to left, depositing the oysters collected from his 2-m strip in the same row as the first worker. As the "doue", the shallow gully around the claire, is kept free of oysters, and if only half of the claire had been stocked with oysters the two men will accumulate all the oysters planted in one single row. A third man collects the oysters in baskets. The baskets are then put in the "commode" [7], a rectangular, 94 × 65 cm wooden box which sledges on the mud and is pushed by its vertical handles (Fig. 44). The oysters planted rather densely in September as the second crop, producing the "fines de claires", are always harvested in this way. Before transferring them to the headquarters, the baskets of oysters are thoroughly shaken under water to wash away most of the mud. A small "plate" boat is used for transporting the baskets of oysters harvested from the "claires de sarretière", whereas those from the "claires de marais", which are surrounded by a more substantial embankment, can be taken away by van.

Another way of harvesting oysters from the claires, usually practiced when the oysters to be harvested are so widely dispersed that only a few occur per square meter of bottom surface, involves complete drainage of the claires. For this, workers wade out into the claire with a short-shafted rake in one hand and a trellis scoop, a "truelle", in the other (Fig. 45). The oysters are raked into the scoop and deposited in baskets, placed either in the "commode" or on the "plate".

B.8. Washing, grading, and storing the marketable oysters

On arrival at the headquarters the oysters are put in the washing machine which carries them on a conveyor belt, under jets of water, to the machines which grade them according to weight (Fig. 46). M. Georgeon has two such machines installed, one into which a female worker is required to place the oysters one by one, the other equipped with an automatic distributor. It requires three workers to operate this production line, one of whom feeds the oysters into the washing machine and takes away the metal baskets filled with sorted oysters. This installation can handle up to 250 baskets containing 20 kg of oysters per day, i.e. 5 tons.

The graded oysters are stored in the large concrete storage basins in the company yard. They are not put on trays but spread out in a thin layer on the floor of the basin. Special care is required when green oysters are handled as they are apt to lose their precious green colour if repeatedly exposed to air.

B.9. Shipment of marketable oysters

The oysters are taken from the storage basins by fork and put in metal baskets. A fork-lift truck carries these baskets to the packing shed. After a

Fig. 46. Washing and grading machines installed at M. Georgeon's headquarters. The automatic grading machine (right) is equipped with an automatic distributor. (Photo P. Korringa.)

last washing, the oysters are carried on a conveyor belt high above the long packing table. An adjustable distributor ensures that oysters of a given weight category land gently on the assigned section of the packing table. Normally four female workers are kept busy packing the oysters in rectangular boxes made of thinly cut poplar-wood and covered with a plaited lid of the same material, fastened with staples. Since most of the oysters have to be shipped in small quantities of 50 or 100 oysters, packing is a time-consuming operation. M. Georgeon has already worked on an experimental scale with plastic containers for the shipment of oysters. To spread the labour over the peak season it would be useful if some kind of perforated baskets could be used for storing oysters awaiting shipment under water. In the height of the season, November and December, the company employs as many as 60 female workers for packing oysters. At this time of the year two men begin at 5 o'clock in the morning taking the oysters from the storage basin, the women coming in at 8 o'clock and working 9—10 h a day, after which some male workers clean up. Having been provided with an "étiquette sanitaire", the boxes are put in a cool storage room before they are transported by vans or trucks to the railway station, or are personally collected by buyers. The railway from La Tremblade is probably the only one in the world constructed especially for the transportation of oysters. Some oysters are carried by van to buyers in the neighbourhood.

C. FARMING RISKS

C.1. Hydrographic conditions

Occasionally gales may do some damage, but when the trays on the Banc Lamouroux are properly attached to their supports, catastrophic damage is a rare occurrence. Salinities may rise too high in the claires in periods of drought and low spring tides. This harms the oysters about once in 10 years. For farmers with a large number of claires in use, pumping in Seudre water to keep pace with evaporation is hardly feasible. It is always wise to keep quite a good layer of water in the claires, over 1 m deep, to reduce the effects of downpours of rain and evaporation. Occasionally intrusion of mud into the shell cavity of the oysters is observed, leading to nasty mud-filled blisters inside the shell, if the oysters survive. Sub-optimal conditions which prevent the oysters from coping with the intruding silt are to blame for this inconvenience. For instance, spells with extreme water temperatures, particularly where there is too dense a population of oysters on a park or in a claire.

C.2. Predators and competitors

Starfish may kill the oysters, but repeated inspection and hand-picking will avoid catastrophic losses. Starfish do not invade parks which are frequently exposed at low tide. They may, however, play havoc among the oysters in the trays if not eliminated in time. Shellfish-eating fishes, such as "tères" (*Trygon pastinaca*), "aigles" (*Myliobatis aquila*), and Sparid fishes such as the "dorade" (*Aurata aurata*) may destroy a lot of oysters but planting great numbers of twigs on the parks cuts down the losses appreciably. Birds such as the oyster-catcher (*Haematopus ostralegus*) are blamed for devouring oyster spat on high grounds.

Mussel seed may be a serious competitor, smothering the oysters, both on shell strings and other collectors, and in the trays. Repeated inspection and cleaning can keep pace with mussels in the trays, but not on the collectors.

C.3. Parasites and diseases

As everywhere in the world, the oyster farmers of the Charente Maritime fear most of all the mysterious diseases which threaten their oysters and which are so difficult to control. In recent years they have suffered serious losses from the so-called gill disease, which raged in the area in 1967 and 1968, and inflicted losses of up to 30 and 40%, but disappeared again in later years.

Even more serious was the outbreak of another disease, the cause of which was in all probability some kind of micro-organism, in the year 1970. M. Georgeon observed the first victims of this disease in his trays on the Banc Lamouroux in July 1970, but gradually it spread over the whole area, first attacking the bigger oysters only, but later all categories. In 1971 the situation was truly catastrophic, the losses rising to 100% on some parks.

Although intensive scientific research has been carried out to identify the causative micro-organism, there is little that can be done to control such diseases, even if the culprit is found. A fortunate coincidence was that spat of the Japanese oyster, *Crassostrea gigas*, which had been introduced on an experimental scale in the 1966—1967 season, was found to have excellent growth, largely surpassing that of the local oyster *Crassostrea angulata*, so that a consignment of 20 tons of spat was introduced in the 1968—1969 season. The Japanese oysters appeared to be invulnerable to the new disease. This offered a chance to take action. Experience gained on the Atlantic coast of Canada has shown that it takes a very long time before a resistant stock can take over after a microbial disease has hit hard. The scientists of the French Fisheries Institute advised the importation of a consignment of large Japanese oysters, which can be found in British Columbia, in an effort to collect spat from this resistant species. Despite the risk of introducing new pests or diseases, the introduction of these oysters was, under the circumstances, the best that could be done. Fortunately the Japanese and the Portuguese oysters resemble each other in so many respects that the environmental conditions in the Charente Maritime will certainly appeal to the Japanese oyster, and the oyster-eating public in France will no doubt accept this species on its table.

D. ECONOMIC ASPECTS

D.1. Rents

The fees paid to the State for renting parks in the intertidal zone are not high (FFr 132 per ha) and, as most of the parks in this area are quite small, this does not put too heavy a burden on the farmers' budget. However, they must reckon with the doubling of taxes in the years to come. Renting a claire is more expensive, as they are private property and much in demand. For the 5 ha of claires at Prise de Méré M. Georgeon has to pay a fee of FFr 10 000 per year.

D.2. Inventory items

The claires the company has as private property are of considerable importance. It should be taken into consideration that an appreciable capital has been laid out for the purchase of claires. The price for a 40 × 12 m claire fluctuates between FFr 800 and FFr 1 500, but prices as high as FFr 4 000 and FFr 5 000 have been paid for claires in perfect condition, i.e. those regularly acquiring the desired green diatom vegetation.

The headquarters' yard has some important buildings, such as the 600-m^2 sorting and packing shed, the 400-m^2 storage shed and the 1 000-m^2 storage basins equipped with a pump. The more important apparatus at the headquarters are the two automatic sorting machines manufactured by David Frères at Tonnay-Charente (Charente Maritime), costing FFr 14 000 each, (plus tax), the washing machine costing FFr 8 000, and the "SINEX" brand distributor costing FFr 9 000. The 10-m long wooden motor boat equipped with a 100-h.p. diesel engine is another inventory item, but as it is only used for transportation and not for dredging, its useful life should be quite long — at least 20 years. A similar lifetime is estimated for the engine. The two wooden chalands of 10 × 3 m are very sturdy and if regularly coated with submarine paint should have a life of 10 years at least, probably more. The two 18-h.p. outboard motors for the chalands will last 6—7 years. The rowing boats, and the small craft used in the claires, do not amount to much expense. The wooden bottom of the "plate" wears rapidly, due to the use of the shovel, and has to be renewed every 4 years. Of considerable importance, however, are inventory items such as the fork-lift truck costing FFr 25 000 with an estimated lifespan of 10 years, the 7-ton truck, the 2-ton truck, and the 800-kg carrying capacity van, all having estimated useful life of 6 years. These vehicles are not used for transporting packed marketable oysters over long distances, but are particularly for the transportation of oysters and material to and from the claires on the Isle of Oléron.

In addition, the company uses 100 iron frames for supporting collectors and 1 000 for supporting trays. These are made by the local blacksmith for FFr 35 each. Next there are several hundreds of iron tripods, also made by the local blacksmith and every year about 100 more are bought. These should last about 10 years. The company now has in use, on an experimental basis, 100 plastic collector units, which have already served for several years in succession.

The number of wooden trays in use in the field amounts to 2 500. The plastic netting having 16-mm square meshes which will be used in due course to replace the metal wire netting, costs FFr 120 per 50 running m. The company also has 800 all-iron trays and a small number of plastic trays, the latter on an experimental basis. No trays are used in the storage basins. The company has 800 to 900 metal baskets ("mannes") and every year buys some 100 new ones. The posts to support the fences around the parks last between 5 and 6 years.

D.3. Expendable items

Every year the company buys 6 000 m (300 kg) of iron wire for making shell strings, plus 20—25 tons of scrap iron for use as collectors. The iron wire netting for the fences around the parks must be renewed every year. In addition, about 60 oak sea marks of 6—7 m length are purchased annually. The boat requires 10 l of diesel oil per h sailing. Petrol is required for the outboard motors and the harrow, and electricity for the operating pumps, washing and sorting machines. The costs for sanitary control tickets are low, (FFr 0.13 each) but every package of oysters has to carry one.

Every year some 25 000 wooden boxes costing FFr 0.60—1.50 each, according to size are bought for packing the oysters. By far the most important item in the list of expendables is, of course, the purchase of oysters of various categories, among which are the 30 tons of Portuguese oysters for relaying, produced in France, costing FFr 4.30 per kg in the 30—40 kg per 1 000 weight categories, and 30—50 tons Portuguese oysters imported from Portugal and Spain, costing FFr 3.40 per kg for the 40 kg per 1 000 category. The company under consideration does not produce all the marketable oysters it ships on its own parks. To supplement the stock some 30 tons or more of unsorted marketable oysters are purchased from small farmers in the area. For these oysters a price of FFr 4.30 per kg for the 30—50 kg per 1 000 weight category is payed, but for heavier oysters, considerably less.

D.4. Personnel and wages

It follows from the description above that the company under consideration operates with quite a large staff. Seven men are engaged on a permanent basis, most of whom work in the field, plus seven female workers at the headquarters. Madame Georgeon, although not on the payroll, works very hard herself, both in making shell strings and sorting oysters, and in surveying the packing of the oysters. It is she who supervises the hiring of the many extra workers taken on during the winter season, all of whom are under 40 years of age, and she has a keen eye for working speed. The men in the period of observation earned FFr 36.00 per day, social taxes included, the women FFr 26.95.

D.5. Sales

On an average M. Georgeon's company ships 400 tons of marketable oysters per year, which indicates that his firm is the largest in the whole area. The prices are set every year by the local syndicate of oyster farmers, but in reality the oysters are sold at a discount of 5—10% of the official price. The categories of oysters sold are: "portugaises spéciales de claires", those which sojourned the whole summer in the claires and should have the green tinge; "portugaises fines de claires", those which sojourned several months in the claires, often from September onwards but which are rarely green; "portugaises fines parquées", those which come straight from the parks where they were grown in trays or on the ground and are never green. For the 1970—1971 season the official prices per 100 oysters packed in boxes were, expressed in FFr:

Weight per 1 000	Spéciales	Fines	Parquées
100	76.00	—	—
90	—	60.50	56.00
75	57.00	—	—
70	—	46.00	43.00
60	46.00	—	—
55	—	37.00	34.50
50	35.00	—	—
45	—	29.50	27.00
40	29.00	—	—
35	—	23.00	21.00

The larger oysters are sold throughout the year, the smaller ones more particularly during the height of the season in November and December.

E. GOVERNMENTAL ASSISTANCE

The Institut Scientifique et Technique des Pêches Maritimes has a small branch laboratory at La Tremblade. Here scientific investigations are carried out to advise the oyster industry, particularly as regards settling prospects, but also to some extent on predators, parasites and diseases. The same laboratory takes care of the control of salubrity. On the basis of the bacteriological analysis of their product, the oyster farmers obtain the certificate of cleanliness required for shipment of oysters. It is difficult to express in terms of cash the value of public confidence in the safety as regards salubrity of this delectable product.

F. GENERAL IMPRESSION

Oyster farming in the Charente Maritime is one of the most fascinating examples of farming the sea in the whole world. The quantities of oysters shipped from the Marennes—Oléron district are truly impressive: 20 000 tons per year, but the whole oyster trade amounts to a higher tonnage still: 25 000—30 000 tons, which is explained by the large-scale exchange of oysters between the various oyster farming centres.

Another impressive aspect is that the method of fattening oysters in claires, which can lead to the most exquisite flavour imaginable, is centuries old and was practised long before oyster farming on parks in private use and collecting spat on artificial collectors was initiated in the middle of the nineteenth century.

The very large number of oyster farmers (some 2 300) working here on very small plots indeed makes the system somewhat precarious. There are now 12 000 registered boats in the area, all small craft. Some may not be used any more for oyster fishing, but thousands of boats are seen to leave for the oyster beds each spring tide. The French system of "inscrits maritimes", described in the chapter dealing with oyster farming in Brittany (Chapter 3, Volume III), led to drastic splitting of the suitable ground here into units, each supporting one family, which are too small to withstand the various economic shocks which are unavoidable in such enterprises. The disastrous oyster mortality of 1971 will, no doubt, have put many farmers out of business here.

Too much work has to be done by hand and the possibilities for mechanization are very limited. Considering the number of oysters planted in a claire, nobody would undertake construction of such ponds nowadays. Fortunately, historic development in the area left posterity an enormous number of claires. It is a remarkable fact, giving a warning to others, that such a large enterprise as that of M. Georgeon buys most of the oysters it needs for growth and fattening from other farmers in France, and also from abroad. M. Georgeon does collect spat and subsequently grows the spat for 1 more year, not so much in order to produce the oysters he needs, but rather to keep his staff from being idle during the slack season. Exactly the same situation has arisen and is described in two other cases: oyster farming using shells as collectors in The Netherlands (Chapter 2, Volume III), and the huge mussel enterprise in the Ría de Arosa in Spain (Chapter 4, Volume I). Evidently it is more economic to buy the primary material from small farmers, who do not count their working hours or the working hours of the members of their families participating in the venture, than to produce it oneself with the aid of hired hands.

Another aspect worth noting is the large number of extra hands required during the peak of the season. In the light of the general tendency towards full-time employment this gives reason for concern.

A company such as that under consideration is economically strong enough to take action when an unforeseen oyster mortality strikes: it can import oysters from elsewhere, in this case including even Japanese stock. For many years the natural beds of Portuguese oysters in the Gironde Estuary yielded a rich supply of oysters for re-laying, but the productivity has declined due to overfishing, poaching and pollution. The Sado Estuary in Portugal appears still able to produce sufficient quantities of oysters for re-laying although there is also reason for concern there, as really rich years now only occur occasionally. The efforts being made to raise more oysters for export on appropriate sites on the Atlantic coast of Andalusia (Spain), especially in the vicinity of Cadiz, in which French oyster farmers play a leading part are interesting. Though a dearth of flat oysters led to a complete switch to *Crassostrea* oysters in the Marennes—Oléron area, and thus to the virtual disappearance of the famous true "marennes" grown in the claires, the results with Portuguese oysters, and later perhaps with their Japanese counterparts, are interesting enough to encourage continued oyster farming in the claires. The caprices of the diatom *Navicula ostrearia*, which shows lush vegetation in only 10—15% of the claires are, however, somewhat disturbing. Better knowledge of the factors affecting its development would be of great practical use. It is highly desirable that its ecology should be studied in greater detail, for a better insight into this subject might very well lead to better control of its growth.

G. TECHNICAL DETAILS

G.1. The motor boat

Both the hull and deck of the boat, which measures 10 m in length, 3.50 m at its greatest breadth and draws 1.20 m of water, are made of pine. The wheel-house is aft. The diesel engine is a 100 h.p. Boudoin DK4.

G.2. The mechanical harrow

The harrow the company uses has a hexagonal frame with short sides fore and aft of 45 cm. It has an overall length of 1.10 m, and a maximum breadth in the middle of 1.40 m. It has 30 teeth each 25 cm long. A 3-h.p. petrol engine, installed on a metal frame, is used to drag the harrow over the whole breadth of the parks with a returning mechanism on the other side. The fixed elements of the installation can be shifted systematically, so that a whole park can be harrowed.

A smaller type of harrow is available for operation with a hand winch.

G.3. "Pelle à douer"

This is a shovel with a wooden blade 30 cm long and 20 cm broad, tapering to 17 cm at its upper end. It is especially designed for chipping off a thin layer of clay from the bottom of a claire.

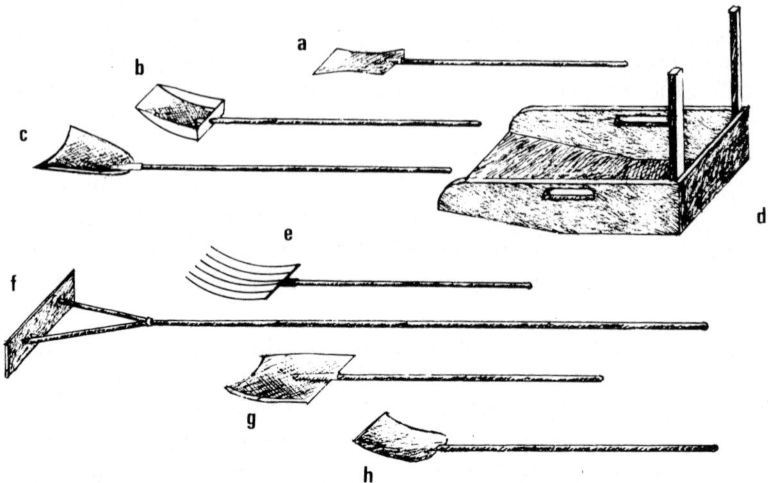

Fig. 47. Various utensils for use in the claires: (a) "la ferré", for digging in hard clay; (b) wooden bailer; (c) "pelle à douer", a wooden tool for chipping off thin layers of clay; (d) the "commode" for transporting baskets of oysters in a claire; (e) oyster fork with blunt teeth; (f) "rouable" wooden tool for levelling the bottom of the claire; (g) "pelle à éparer" for planting oysters in a claire; (h) "pelle à piquer" for digging in clay.

G.4. *"La ferré"*

This is a spade with a narrow steel blade 32 cm long and 13 cm broad at its extremity, 9 cm in the middle section and 11 cm where it is attached to a 1.50-m wooden shaft. This tool is used for cutting the banks and for digging in hard clay.

G.5. *"Pelle à piquer"*

This tool is a shovel with a slightly concave steel blade 27 cm long and 20 cm broad at its extremity. Its sides are rounded where it is attached to a 1.50 m wooden shaft. It is used for digging away thicker layers of clay from the bottom of a claire.

G.6. *The "plate"*

The "plate" is a light boat of simple construction made of deal. Almost rectangular in shape, it has a length of 6 m and a breadth of 2 m. It can accommodate three men and 600 kg of oysters.

G.7. *The "commode"*

This vehicle, used for carrying baskets of oysters over a muddy claire, is just a low wooden box 94 × 65 cm, sloping upwards at its front end. It has no side walls but two handles, placed vertically at the rear corners, to facilitate dragging the commode along the muddy bottom of a drained claire.

G.8. *"Pelle à éparer"*

This is a slightly concave shovel, with a steel blade measuring 32 × 27 cm, used for planting oysters.

H. BIBLIOGRAPHY

Bachrach, E., 1935. Le bleuissement des diatomées et le verdissement des huîtres. Rev. Trav. Off. Pêches Marit., 8: 112—113.

Baron, G., 1938. Etude du plancton dans le bassin de Marennes. Rev. Trav. Off. Pêches Marit., 11: 167—170.

Bierry, H. and Gouzon, B., 1939. Les Huîtres de Consommation. Biologie, Elevage et Production, Valeur Alimentaire, Salubrité. Baillière, Paris, 144 pp.

Borde, F. and Borde, J., 1938 *Ostrea edulis* et *Gryphaea angulata*, caractères communs et caractères différentiels. Rev. Trav. Off. Pêches. Marit., 11: 503—514.

Dantan, J.L., 1914. L'huître portugaise (*Gryphaea angulata* Lmk) tend-elle à se substituer à l'huître indigène (*Ostrea edulis* L.)? C.R. Acad. Sci., 158: 360—362.

Dubreuil, B., 1950. L'industrie Coquillière en France. Etude Administrative et économique. Imprimeries Réunies, Senlis, 148 pp.

Fraiches, F., 1865. Guide Pratique de l'Ostréiculture et Procédés d'Elevage et de Multiplication des Races Marines Comestibles. Librairie scientifique, industrielle et agricole, Eugène Lacroix, Paris, 176 pp.

Korringa, P., 1957. On the supposed compulsory relation between oviparous oysters and waters of reduced salinity. Année Biol., 33: 109—116.

Lafuste, J., Le Dantec, J., Marteil, L. and Trochon, P., 1957. La reproduction de l'huître portugaise (*G. angulata* Lmk) dans les centres de captage de la côte atlantique. Rev. Trav. Inst. Pêches Marit., 21: 401—414.

Lambert, L., 1932. L'acclimatation de la portugaise sur les côtes françaises. Rev. Trav. Off. Pêches Marit., 5: 343—365.

Lambert, L., 1938. Les gisements naturels d'huîtres indigènes (*Ostrea edulis*) et d'huîtres portugaises (*Gryphaea angulata*) sur les côtes françaises. Rev. Trav. Off. Pêches Marit., 11: 465—476.

Lambert, L., 1950. Les Coquillages Comestibles, Huîtres, Moules, Coquillages variés. "Que sais-je?" 416. Presses Universitaires de France, Paris, 127 pp.

Lambert, L., Faideau, F. and Bluteau, R., 1929. Ostréiculture et Mytiliculture sur le Littoral Centre-Ouest. Jean Foucher, La Rochelle, 78 pp.

Moreau, J., 1968. Lec facteurs de verdissement de l'huître en claires: le milieu hydrobiologique et benthique et ses variations. Rev. Trav. Inst. Pêches Marit., 32: 369—385.

Ranson, G., 1926. L'huître portugaise tend-elle à remplacer l'huître française? Notes Mém. Off. Pêches Marit., 47: 1—11.

Ranson, G., 1941. Les conditions de la distribution de *Gryphaea angulata* Lmk sur les côtes de l'Ile d'Oléron. Bull. Mus. Hist. Nat. Paris, 13: 179—186.

Ranson, G., 1943. La Vie des Huîtres. Histoires Naturelles I. Gallimard, Paris, 261 pp.

Ranson, G., 1948. Ecologie et répartition géographique des Ostréidés vivants. Rev. Sci. Paris, 86: 469—473.

Ranson, G., 1949. Quelques observations sur la biologie de *Gryphaea angulata* Lmk. Bull. Mus. Hist. Nat. Paris, 21: 574—579.

Renard, J., 1951. L'huître. Editions Compagnie Française du Papier Industrialisé, Imprimerie A. Davy, Paris, 103 pp.

Chapter 5

FARMING THE PORTUGUESE OYSTER (*CRASSOSTREA ANGULATA*) IN THE BAY OF ARCACHON, FRANCE

Example
Monsieur Edmond Daubric, oyster farmer and shipper at Gujan-Mestras, Gironde.
Period of observation: 1965—1970.

A. BACKGROUND

A.1. General principles

The Bay of Arcachon is virtually the birthplace of the French oyster industry. Although Coste's first large-scale experiments for producing oyster spat using artificial collectors may have taken place in the Bay of St. Brieuc, on the north coast of Brittany (1858), it was in Arcachon that models for the first parks were laid out and where lime-coated tile collectors first came into use on a practical scale. Since the year 1857 two species of oyster have been farmed in the Bassin d'Arcachon — the European flat oyster, *Ostrea edulis* L., and the Portuguese oyster, *Crassostrea angulata* Lmk. In principle, this is still the case but the stock of flat oysters is, for the time being, at a rather low ebb. In the Bassin d'Arcachon lime-coated ceramic tiles, piled up in wooden crates, are used exclusively as collectors. The farming operations are similar to those described for oyster farming in Brittany (Chapter 3, Volume III), but lack the refinements of the latter. After detachment, the spat is planted on parks in the intertidal zone, transferred in due course to other intertidal parks and then thinned out as the oysters grow. Virtually all the farming operations are carried out by hand.

The quantities of oysters thus produced are, however, insufficient. Therefore larger companies, such as the one under consideration, place supplementory collectors in the Gironde Estuary, and participate moreover in fishing on the natural beds in that area. Further, they buy Portuguese oysters for re-laying, both from the Marennes—Oléron area, and directly from the Sado Estuary in Portugal.

As in the Marennes—Oléron area, the oyster grounds are split up into a large number of small parks and most of the 1 800 oyster farmers produce only 25—75 tons of oysters each annually. Barely a dozen sell more than 100 tons of marketable oysters per year.

Oyster farming, Arcachon style, is classed as a semi-culture, as larval development and the provision of food for oysters of all ages is left fully to nature.

A.2. Biology of the species

As regards the biology of Portuguese oysters the reader should refer to the description of oyster farming in the Marennes—Oléron area (Chapter 4). A special variety of flat oyster, known as the "gravette", was formerly characteristic of this area, but has long ago disappeared.

A.3. Geographical situation

The Bay of Arcachon is located in the southwestern part of France, on the Atlantic coast, some 50 km west-southwest of the city of Bordeaux. It is triangular in shape and is open to the Atlantic Ocean at its southwestern corner. The sides of the triangle each measure about 18 km. At high tide the water covers some 15 000 ha, at low tide only about 5 000 ha. The west and southwest of the bay are bounded by a cordon of sand dunes, whereas to the east and northeast the bay is bounded by pliocene sands.

The southwestern tip of the basin, at Cap Ferret, is located at 44° 37′ N and 01° 12′ 30″ W, the northern tip, at Arès, at 44° 49′ N and 01° 09′ 10″ W, and the eastern tip, at Le Teich, at 44° 38′ 30″ N and 01° 03′ W. The headquarters of the company under consideration are to be found at Gujan-Mestras at 44° 38′ 30″ N and 01° 05′ 25″ W.

A.4. Hydrographic pattern

By far the larger part of the Bay of Arcachon is taken up by intertidal flats. Due north of the city of Arcachon, there is a circular-shaped island called "Ile aux Oiseaux", about 2 km in diameter. The gap which links the bay to the Atlantic Ocean is 2—3 km wide but strewn with sand bars, and therefore hazardous for navigation. Further inwards it splits up into two main channels which branch repeatedly towards the eastern part of the bay. It is the intertidal grounds, locally called "crassats", which are used for oyster farming.

Tides. The tidal range is quite great in the Bassin d'Arcachon, ranging from 3.90 m at spring tide to 2.00 m at neap tide, leading to tidal currents of up to 2 m per sec in the channels. At spring tides the water travels over a much greater distance than at neap tides, but in general it performs an oscillating pattern, with a limited degree of flushing by ocean water. Thus both temperatures and salinities show a gradient from southwest to northeast, and oyster larvae are retained in the basin for quite a long time.

Water temperature. As the Bassin d'Arcachon is on the whole very shallow, the temperature of the water is strongly affected by local weather conditions. Thus in winter the water in the bay is colder than that in the ocean, whereas in summer it is warmer. This tendency is more pronounced as one approaches the eastern shoreline. In mid-winter the average water temperature is about

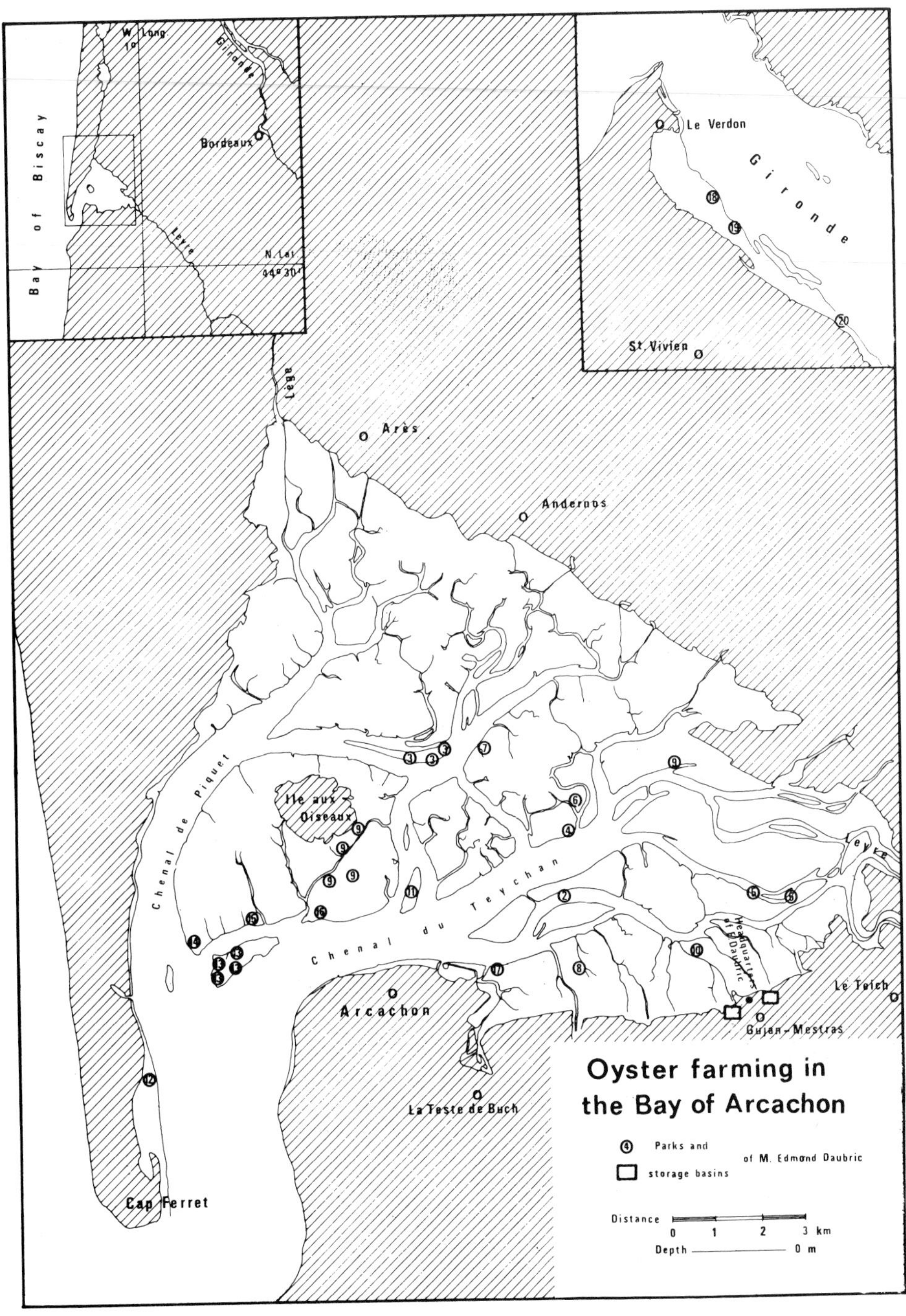

Bay of Biscay
W. Long. 1°
Gironde
Bordeaux
Leyre
N. Lat. 44°30'
Le Verdon
Gironde
St. Vivien
Leyre
Arès
Andernos
Chenal de Piquet
Ile aux Oiseaux
Chenal du Teychan
Headquarters of E. Daubric
Le Teich
Arcachon
Gujan-Mestras
La Teste de Buch
Cap Ferret
Oyster farming in the Bay of Arcachon
Parks and
storage basins
of M. Edmond Daubric
Distance
0 1 2 3 km
Depth 0 m

8°C in the bay, in severe winters lower still, whereas the winter average for the open ocean is about 12°C. In mid-summer, July and August, the water in the bay goes beyond the 22°C level for some time practically every year (excellent for Portuguese oyster larvae which do not grow at all at temperatures of 20°C and lower) compared with 20°C in the ocean. From May to November water temperatures are above 15°C, which favours the growth of oysters. The difference between air temperature and water temperature, which affects oysters in the intertidal zone, are greatest in February and very small in July.

Salinity. The salinity in the Bay of Arcachon is somewhat lower than that prevailing in the open ocean. It usually ranges from 30 to 33‰ at high water, but occasionally a serious drop, down to 20‰, sometimes even to a still lower figure, which may last for weeks in succession is observed. This is caused by the contribution of fresh water from the land, coming in via the River Leyre in the southeast, the River Lège in the north, both draining a vast area of the "Landes", and from a large number of streams which enter the bay along its eastern shore. In addition, phreatic water seeps into the bay more consistently. Local precipitation is normally more than 700 mm per year, occasionally over 1 000 mm per year. Heavy downpours of rain can be expected in the winter months, from November until February, and it is then that low salinities are observed. The limited degree of flushing of the water in the bay ensures a rather long duration of periods with low salinities.

Although the Portuguese oyster can stand low salinities much better than the flat oyster, a serious, and particularly a rapid drop in salinity may lead to heavy losses, especially when this happens during periods of reduced oyster vitality.

Plankton, turbidity and sea bed conditions. Le Dantec has studied the seasonal pattern of phytoplankton in the bay and demonstrated that net-plankton reveals a rich flora of diatoms throughout the year, be it that some species show their maximum in winter and spring and others in summer or autumn. He also measured the quantity of phytoplankton in Harvey units and his figures indicate that nanoplankton prevails during certain periods. Practical experience shows that the plankton is rich enough to support a huge population of oysters. Usually the water has a characteristic greenish hue, and unless gales swirl up the muddy bottom of the intertidal grounds, the water is remarkably clear. Most of the intertidal grounds have a bottom consisting of small-sized particles, ranging from clayish mud, via sandy mud to muddy sand, whereas in the channels sandy bottoms prevail, the more so as the open sea is approached. A thin film, very rich in microscopic life, is often observed on top of the mud flats. It is assumed by Le Dantec that primary production in the bay itself is of considerable importance as a source of food for the oysters, and that the slight but gradual contribution of fresh surface and phreatic water from the hinterland favours plankton development.

A.5. Legal aspects

The company under consideration is a long-established private enterprise, in which M. Daubric works together with his two sons, the wives of all three of them giving real support by actively participating in the work. In addition, a number of hired hands are employed. As is usual in France, the intertidal grounds belong to the State, represented by the "Domaine Public Maritime". The "Port Autonome de Bordeaux" is the agency which is responsible for leasing the parks to the oystermen. M. Daubric has the following parks in use, all indicated on the chart:

For spat collection ("captage"):

(1) A 0.20-ha park at Ilet de Branne.

(2) A 0.06-ha park at Arrouillats.

(3) Three concessions measuring 0.05, 0.10, and 0.15 ha, respectively, at Lahillon, for farming flat oysters.

(4) A 0.28-ha park at Bourrut.

(5) A 250-m strip, with a total surface area of 0.12 ha, along the channel at Carguefond.

For the further growth of oysters ("élevage"):

(6) Two parks together measuring 1 ha at Petché.

(7) A 0.40-ha park at Garrèche.

(8) A 1-ha park at Maouréou.

(9) Four parks, together measuring 1.5 ha in the Estay de Gahignon.

(10) A 0.30-ha park at Larros.

(11) A 0.25-ha park at Mapoutchet.

For fattening oysters ("affinage"):

(12) A 0.10-ha park at Cap Ferret.

(13) Four parks, together measuring 1 ha on the Grand Banc, destined for flat oysters.

(14) A 0.35-ha park at Le Courbey.

(15) A 0.25-ha park at La Réousse.

(16) Two parks, together measuring 0.55 ha at Pelourdey.

(17) A 0.42 ha park at Lucarnan, destined for flat oysters.

In addition, M. Daubric collects spat on shells, packed in bags, on three concessions with a total area of 1.30 ha on the left bank of the Gironde Estuary, namely:

(18) 0.30 ha at Cheyzin.

(19) 0.50 ha at Cabiraux and

(20) 0.50 ha at Charmailles, between 45° 28′ N, 01° 00′ W and 45° 25′ N, 0° 55′ W.

At the headquarters in Gujan-Mestras the company has two storage basins measuring 0.25 ha each, a 200-m^2 sorting and packing shed, plus a 0.05-ha yard. One of the basins can make use of a well producing salt water with a salinity of 22‰. This salt ground-water is used in periods of heavy downpour and reduced salinities, particularly for storing the more sensitive flat oysters. For this it is oxygenated by pumping it over cascades, the only remaining inconvenience being a slight iron deposit on the oyster shells.

The rent to be paid for the parks amounts to FFr 1.40 per are (1 are = 0.01 ha), which was raised to FFr 4.50 per are in 1974.

Official surveillance is, as is usual in France, carried out by the gendarmes maritimes, in charge of the whole coastline of the Gironde Département. In addition, eight to ten sworn-in volunteers keep an eye on what goes on in the oyster parks but, exactly as in the Marennes—Oléron district, theft is virtually impossible because of the great numbers of people working on the parks at low tide.

B. SEQUENCE OF OPERATIONS

Procuring the spat with tile collectors

B.1. Liming the tiles

The ceramic tiles used as collectors in the Bassin d'Arcachon are somewhat different from those used in Brittany and in The Netherlands. They are slightly curved and taper (see Fig. 50); they are 50—52 cm in length, 14 cm broad at one extremity and 18 cm at the other. Their height, thickness (2 cm) included, is 6—7 cm. Such tiles weigh 2.5 kg each when dry. The company in question buys its tiles from a factory in Gironde, west of La Réole, some 50 km southeast of the city of Bordeaux.

In order to prepare new tiles to serve as collectors, they have first to be thinly coated by bathing them in a mixture of lime and water. After thorough drying they get a second, but thicker coating by dipping them in a mixture of lime, sand and water. Tiles which have been used as collectors before are given the thicker coating without an undercoat.

The mixture for the second coating is prepared in the "douille", a trough made of 3-cm thick pinewood, measuring 105 × 105 cm at the top, 88 × 80 cm at the bottom, with a height of 85 cm. Slaked lime (100 kg) is poured into it (slaking having been performed earlier in a concrete pit) together with 45 kg of sea sand, and 70—80 l of sea water. A shovel or wooden stirrer is used to mix the material. One by one the tiles are taken up with a "crochet" (Fig. 48), an iron clasp with wooden handle, and dipped in the mixture. A group of two or three people work together, piling up the tiles in heaps of 50 to let them dry in the air. The quantity of mixture mentioned is sufficient for about 1 000 tiles. M. Daubric uses a somewhat thinner coating of lime than most of his colleagues in Arcachon, because once in every 4 or 5 years

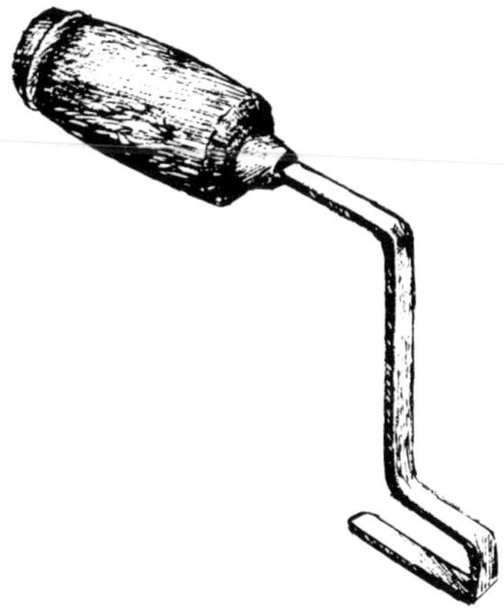

Fig. 48. The "crochet", the utensil for dipping tiles in the lime mixture.

freezing weather hits the area, and when the tiles carrying the spat are exposed at low tide, a thicker coating may be so much affected that it drops off after thawing, whereas a thinner coating stays on after a spell of frost.

B.2. Placing the crates called "ruches"

The oyster farmers of Arcachon place their tiles in a different way to those of Brittany. They use simple wooden open-work crates [1] known as "ruches", which are placed on the park for a few days, sometimes a fortnight, before the tiles are taken out by boat. The tarred crates, made of cheap scrap wood, purchased from the local sawmills, are constructed in such a way that they can be folded up, which makes it easy to transport them to the park on the deck of a "chaland", the flat rectangular lightweight wooden boat measuring 10 × 3 m, in use in all the French oyster districts. On arrival at the site, the "ruches" are placed on four round pinewood poles, driven into the sediment and sticking out some 40 cm, and then fastened to these poles through the bottom battens with iron nails.

B.3. Sailing out the tiles

In deciding the date for placing the tile collectors in the crates, the settling forecasts of the branch laboratory of the French Fisheries Institute at Arcachon are taken into account. According to the old-timers this will be "lorsque la vigne a fleuri" (when the vines are in flower). If one wishes to collect the spat of the flat oyster, *Ostrea edulis*, the tiles have to be taken out late in June or early in July, to a selected park in the western part of the basin. For M. Daubric, this means his park at Lahillon (3) not far from the Ile aux Oisseaux. Portuguese oysters, *Crassostrea angulata*, spawn later, at

Fig. 49. "Ruches" filled with limed tile collectors on the intertidal flats of Le Courbey in the Bay of Arcachon. (Photo P. Korringa.)

higher water temperatures. To catch Portuguese oyster spat, the tiles are not sailed out before the second half of July, sometimes even early in August, and preferably to a park selected in the southeastern part of the basin. For M. Daubric this means his parks at Ilet de Branne, Arrouillats, Bourrut and Carguefond (numbers 1, 2, 4 and 5, respectively, on the chart).

When the tiles are placed in the crates, the first layer is put lengthwise, and each of nine succeeding layers crosswise to the previous one; ten layers in all (Fig. 49). It takes about 100 tiles to fill the whole crate, the exact number depending on whether it is decided to put two or three rows next to each other in the layers placed lengthwise in the crates. Four poles, 140–170 cm in length are placed obliquely under the top batten of the long side of the crates as supports. If the crates, which have no lid, were left open on the upper side, the tiles would move and even break when waves hit them in stormy weather. To keep the tiles fixed in position, the oyster farmers place a thick layer of "brande" on top of them. "Brande" is the local name for *Erica scoparia*, a type of heather abounding in the pine forests of the region, which has both tough and flexible black branches. The "brande" is, in turn, secured by placing the "endorts" (six strips of wood) over it and putting one end under the top batten and nailing the other end into the batten at the opposite side of the crate. Thus nothing can happen during rough weather and, at the same time, the top layer of tiles is well protected against overheating by the sun.

B.4. Maintenance of the tiles in the "ruches"

Though gales can do no damage, the oyster farmer inspects his tiles regularly, especially when prolonged high water temperatures favour the settlement of ascidians, bryozoa, and sponges. If such fouling organisms threaten to become a nuisance to his young oysters on the tiles, the farmer opens all his crates and brushes his tiles thoroughly, one by one, a treatment the spat, well protected by its shell, can survive. As a rule brushing has to be done at least once during the course of the summer season, sometimes twice. M. Daubric usually mixes 3 kg of copper sulphate to every 100 kg of lime used for coating his tiles, and claims that this reduces fouling.

B.5. Procuring oyster spat with shell collectors and scrap iron

M. Daubric uses his three parks on the left bank of the Gironde Estuary to produce Portuguese oyster spat using both shells and scrap iron as collectors. The shells used, a by-product of his own plant, are put in bags of plastic netting having square 17-mm meshes, the "wire" having a diameter of 1.5 mm. The bags are long (90 cm) and cylindrical (17 cm diameter) and can contain some 8 kg of shells. These collectors are prepared at the headquarters; three men filling the bags with shells, and a female worker doing the basting. A group of four can fill 600 to 800 bags per working day. About 5 000 bags with shells are taken overland by truck to the Gironde Estuary, where M. Daubric has a flat decked boat, measuring 10 × 3 m equipped with a 16-h.p. "Couach" petrol engine, at his disposal. The bags have to be placed on a support, for which M. Daubric uses the very same type of iron frames as have been described for spat collecting in the Marennes—Oléron area. The bags are fastened to their supports with galvanized wire. About seven bags are attached to each metre of frame.

Scrap iron is used as a collector in the same way as has been described for M. Georgeon's enterprise (Charente Maritime), use being made of iron frames to support the 25 tons of iron purchased for collectors annually.

B.6. Detaching the spat from the tiles

The tiles are usually kept in the "ruches" on the parks until late in May or early June. Then both tiles and "ruches" are loaded on a chaland and taken to Gujan-Mestras. The young oysters are not detached individually, as in Brittany and The Netherlands, but the whole layer of lime is scraped off using a slightly concave iron blade, 5 cm broad and 7 cm long, attached to a

Fig. 50. An Arcachon oyster farmer inspecting his tiles in September. (Photo P. Korringa.)

wooden handle. For this, the tiles are placed, one by one, on a kind of table specially designed for the purpose, the "table de détroquage" [2], and both sides scraped from top to bottom (Fig. 52). Both spat and lime fall through the slit in the bottom of the table, and are either collected in baskets or just simply piled up on the deck of the chaland where these operations are carried out. Two workers can scrape about 1 000 tiles per working day. As it is not the custom in Arcachon to sell recently detached spat to other oyster farmers, there is no need to sort or to count it.

Fig. 51. Still life on the stern of an Arcachon oyster boat showing tiles garnished with young oysters ready to be detached, shovel, broom, "brande" and lunch basket. (Photo P. Korringa.)

B.7. Planting the spat on a park

All the scrapings from the tiles, a mixture of oyster spat and lime particles, including the debris of algae, barnacles, ascidians and other invertebrates, are, without sieving, sorting or washing, transferred to a fenced-in oyster park. They are scattered with a shovel directly from the chaland over one of M. Daubric's parks used for further growth. The fences for these are either of galvanized wire netting or plasticized metal netting, 30 cm high, with pickets 1 m apart. On top of each picket is nailed a horizontal board, 18 cm broad, well-tarred to make it smooth, and protruding above the water. This board serves to keep the crabs away. Further protection for the oyster parks in the Bay of Arcachon is provided by the "piniots" (Fig. 53), long hedges of densely placed branches to keep out marauding fishes such as "tères" (*Trygon pastinaca*), "aigles" (*Myliobatis aquila*) and "gueulles pavées" (*Pagrus pagrus*). M. Daubric prefers to use 4—5 m long branches of oak or false acacia (*Robinia*) for his piniots. He inserts, depending on their size, seven to ten branches per running metre, with the aid of a motor pump with a hose and iron pipe.

Fig. 52. Scraping oyster spat from the tile collectors on a "table de détroquage". Pieces of lime and spat are collected in the box placed under the table. (Photo P. Korringa.)

The number of young oysters planted on a park is not counted, but use is made of a rule of thumb; that the material scraped from about 10 000 tiles should be scattered over 0.25 ha of park, which means, on an average, some 2 000 young oysters of 10—20 mm diameter per m^2. M. Daubric selects one or two of his parks used for "élevage", for the further growth of his oysters, for planting the spat. Every spring tide the park with the young oysters is inspected on foot by a worker armed with a fork to destroy any crabs he finds.

B.8. Planting spat obtained with oyster shells

The bags with shells placed in the Gironde Estuary do not stay there for very long. During November they are picked up, together with the iron frames supporting them, loaded, first onto the boat, then onto the truck, and taken to the company headquarters at Gujan-Mestras. From there they are immediately taken to one of the parks in the bay which M. Daubric uses for spat collection, where they are again placed on iron frames. This is done because growth is better in the Bay of Arcachon, and surveillance

Fig. 53. A fence of "piniots" around an oyster park in the Bay of Arcachon serves to keep out marauding fish. (Photo P. Korringa.)

and maintenance give fewer problems when the oysters are near to the headquarters than in the more distant Gironde Estuary.

The following April, the bags are opened in order to scatter the shells with spat onto one of the parks earmarked for growing young oysters. Some of the shells are transferred to plastic bags having a rather flat shape and square 17-mm meshes, measuring 95 cm in length and 50 cm broad, and subdivided into three sections. These bags are again placed on the iron frames on one of the growing plots in the bay.

B.9. Transfer of "18 mois" oysters to other plots

When the young oysters produced on tiles have reached the age of "18 mois" (i.e. 18 months at the turn of the year), and which by then weigh 15—20 kg per 1 000, they are lifted with a fork at low tide. They are then taken to one of the "cabanes" (sorting sheds) at the headquarters, where, if two or more oysters have grown together, they are declustered. This is done with a special knife known as a "couteau à détroquer". Flat oysters are also separated from Portuguese oysters in those cases where both species have settled on the tiles. The Portuguese oysters are then divided into "large" and "small" categories. The oysters are next transferred to one of the parks used for further growth (élevage). This is also fenced in by 30-cm high wire netting and protected by piniots, but this time, the horizontal board on top of the fences to keep off marauding crabs is not required, as they cannot crack the shells of oysters this size.

The quantities of "18 mois" oysters planted are as follows: large Portuguese — 800 kg per are; small Portuguese — 500 kg per are; flat oysters — 500—600 kg per are.

The park containing the young oysters is inspected every spring tide, especially after a spell of bad weather when the oysters run the risk of being smothered in sand or silt. This is more likely to happen to Portuguese oysters than flat oysters, the latter appearing to have less difficulty in keeping themselves on top of the sediment. To rectify this, the farmer uses his harrow [3], which is moved systematically to and fro over the park with the aid of a 3 h.p. petrol engine, in the same way as has been described for the Marennes—Oléron area. A harrow with teeth 10 cm or 20 cm apart is used, depending on the quantities of oysters on the park.

The oysters which are obtained using shell collectors (the shells having been either planted directly onto a park or transferred to the flat bags placed on iron frames) having, at the age of "18 mois", reached a weight of 12—16 kg per 1 000, are also brought to the sorting sheds for declustering. They are then treated in the same way as the oysters obtained using tile collectors. If the oyster population on the "élevage" parks becomes too dense "dédoublage" is carried out. This means spreading the oysters over twice as large an area. As a rule, this is done only once in this phase of culture.

B.10. Fattening oysters ("affinage")

When the oysters have reached a weight of 30—40 kg per 1 000, which is usually 1 year after their planting as "18 mois", they are denominated "2 ans" (the oysters are 2.5 years old at the turn of the year), they are transferred to the parks, numbered 12 to 17 on the chart, in the southwestern section of the Bassin d'Arcachon. The intention is that they should become big and fat enough to be marketed at the end of the summer season of the same year. These fattening parks are surrounded with a low fence to prevent the oysters being washed away by waves and currents, and protected against fishes by piniots, in the same way as the others. About 800 kg of oysters are planted per are; somewhat less if the oysters are rather small.

At harvesting time, most of the oysters will weigh 55—60 kg per 1 000, but, when sorted, some 25—30% of so-called "boudeuses" will be found. These are oysters which did not grow very well, but may be plump enough to be eaten. Such oysters are normally sold for local consumption. However, this percentage should be kept in mind when referring to the economy of the enterprise.

Thinning out is not usual at this stage, but it is often necessary to use a harrow to keep the oysters on top of the sediment. This should, however, not be done shortly before the oysters are to be harvested.

The quantities of oysters grown in the ways described are far from sufficient for the tonnage of marketable oysters M. Daubric plans to produce. To reach his target he has each year to plant 400—450 tons of oysters on his fattening parks, of which only about 120 tons are produced using his own collectors. Therefore, he has to supplement his stocks, which he does in various phases of the operation:

Fig. 54. Harvesting oysters on a park in the Bay of Arcachon. The boxes into which the oysters are forked are picked up by boat as the tide comes in. (Photo P. Korringa.)

(a) By buying "18 mois" of 15—16 kg per 1 000, or oysters 1 year older, the so-called "2 ans" of 30—35 kg per 1 000, from farmers in the Charente Maritime.

(b) By buying Portuguese oysters fished from the natural beds in the Gironde Estuary.

(c) By himself participating in the fishing on the natural beds in the Gironde Estuary, which are opened for about 6 weeks per year. Dredging is then allowed with dredges measuring 80 cm in breadth. M. Daubric uses two such dredges, either equipped with a simple "knife" for use on a hard bottom, or with "teeth" for a softer bottom.

(d) By buying oysters of 35—40 kg per 1 000 for re-laying, directly from the Sado Estuary in Portugal. This latter is only done if the other three sources fail to produce the quantities required.

B.11. Harvesting of marketable oysters

The oysters stay on the fattening beds for a few months. For harvesting the oysters, the farmer, walking out onto the park at low tide, again uses the fork. The oysters are forked into iron baskets (cf Fig. 54) which are loaded, at the incoming tide, either onto the chaland or the motor boat, and transferred to the headquarters. Harvesting begins in September and continues for several months.

B.12. Cleaning, grading and storing the oysters

At the headquarters, the oysters are first thoroughly washed and then graded by weight using an automatic sorting machine of the type produced by the David brothers at Tonnay-Charente. The graded oysters are then transferred to the storage basin in which they are placed on 50 × 40 cm wooden trays, strung with galvanized wire netting. As the netting of the trays corrodes it is being replaced by plastic netting. By the end of the year M. Daubric normally hopes to have 140 tons of oysters stored in his basin.

B.13. Shipment of oysters

Most of the oysters are sold in small packages, usually chip boxes. It takes a considerable amount of work to pack the market oysters during the seasonal peak. To cut down on labour M. Daubric has purchased two special machines for fastening lids onto the chip boxes. One of these machines fastens packages of up to 10 kg in weight, using nylon cord; the other, used for the heavier packages, uses steel bands.

The company uses its own truck to ship oysters to customers, not only to those in the "Landes", "Pays Basque" and "Bordeaux" neighbourhoods, but also to buyers farther away, some as far as Paris. No extra charge is made for this delivery. A small percentage of M. Daubric's oysters travels by train.

Fig. 55. M. Daubric lifting a tray with oysters from his storage basin. Left, the old-timer M. André Mahéo. (Photo P. Korringa.)

C. FARMING RISKS

C.1. Hydrographic conditions

Although the Bassin d'Arcachon is, generally speaking, a well-sheltered oyster area, the oysters there are often affected by deviations from the normal climatic pattern. Since all the oysters are farmed on intertidal grounds, weather conditions affect them more readily here than in regions where oysters are grown sub-tidally.

The Arcachon oyster farmers have found that the flat oyster is, in many respects, more vulnerable than the Portuguese oyster. When winter strikes hard it is invariably the flat oysters which suffer most, and when the salinity drops to levels of 20‰ and lower it is again the flat oysters which suffer heavy losses, long before there is any trouble with the Portuguese oysters. As such conditions do occur every so often, the stock of flat oysters shows greater fluctuations over a period of years than that of the Portuguese oysters. This means that the economy of oyster farming in the Bay of Arcachon is primarily based on the production of large numbers of Portuguese oysters, and to a much lesser extent on a smaller production of the more expensive flat oysters.

The Portuguese oyster, in its turn, suffers more readily from being smothered by sediment when gales are raging, and if the oyster farmer does not come quickly enough to harrow them out, severe losses may ensue. The parks close to the entrance of the bay, where the older oysters are grown, suffer most from sand movements. If the oyster farmer comes rather late to the rescue he may find that so much sediment has penetrated between the oyster's valves that they cannot get rid of it. Such oysters may still survive but will suffer serious retardation in growth and have large unsightly mud-blisters in the shell.

C.2. Predators

Predatory fishes, of which sting rays ("tères", "aigles") are feared most of all, may devour large numbers of oysters. If no special measures were taken by the Arcachon oystermen heavy losses would be suffered year after year. Since the early phases of the oyster industry in the Bay of Arcachon, the oyster farmers there have protected their parks by planting "piniots", extensive branchwood hedges. This is a rather costly procedure, as the wood must be replaced from time to time, but the local oystermen can only then rest assured that they have not offered the fish free access to their parks.

Of the smaller sized predators, the drills (*Murex erinaceus*) can inflict the heaviest losses amongst the oysters. Here again, it is the flat oysters which suffer most. The same holds good for crabs (*Carcinides maenas*) which attack young specimens of the flat oyster more readily than they do small Portuguese oysters. Hermit crabs (*Eupagurus bernhardus*) are said to attack and devour oysters whose shells have been damaged during the declustering procedure. Starfishes cause hardly any damage on the intertidal parks.

C.3. Competitors

Among the invertebrates settling on and among the oysters in great numbers, competing for food and space, mussels (*Mytilus edulis*) and saddle oysters, locally known as "nacrées" (*Anomia ephippium*), annoy the oyster farmers most, as it takes a considerable amount of manual labour to eliminate these pests.

C.4. Diseases and parasites

Oyster farmers all over the world are far more afraid of the invisible enemies of the oyster than they are of predators which they can see with their own eyes, of which they can observe their ways, and against which they can take adequate measures for control. Microscopic parasites can suddenly and without warning wipe out whole populations of oysters, young and old, and even when a considerable amount of scientific research has been carried out, all that can be done, is to try to select and breed or introduce a resistant strain of oysters.

The oyster farmers of Arcachon have had much to endure from such microscopic pests in recent years. First of all, the juvenile flat oysters suffered heavy losses from an internal parasite, probably belonging to the genus *Dermocystidium*, identical, or at least similar, to that which attacks the flat oysters in Aber Wrach and Aber Benoit in the northwestern tip of Brittany. This led to a serious reduction in the quantity of flat oysters produced in the Bay of Arcachon. M. Daubric used to produce about 50 tons of flat oysters per year, but, despite all his efforts, he experienced a serious drop in production in the years following 1966, finally leading to the complete absence of flat oysters in his enterprise in 1970. Other oyster farmers experienced a similar disaster and it is questionable whether the flat oyster will ever appear again on a commercial scale in the Bay of Arcachon.

Unfortunately, the Portuguese oysters were not found to be invulnerable either. In the late nineteen-sixties a disease was noticed, which attacked the gills of Portuguese oysters, leading to the indentation of the gill edges, and in severe cases, even to the obliteration of whole gill blades. This disease made it, of course, increasingly difficult for the oyster to collect its food. In serious cases death struck on quite a large scale, especially on the oyster parks in the Charente Maritime. Just when it was thought that the danger was subsiding, a new attack was launched on the Portuguese oyster, but with different symptoms, and therefore presumably caused by another type of micro-organism. This began in the year 1970 and struck very hard in 1971, leading to oysters of all ages being almost completely wiped out on many parks, and putting hundreds of small oyster farmers into serious economic difficulties. The oyster farmers blamed industrial pollution of the water for this disaster, though they could not identify the source. It is clear, however, that such cannot be the cause, nor even an aggravating factor, for the Portuguese oyster is the only invertebrate which appears to suffer from this in the Bay of Arcachon, and many species of invertebrates thriving there are, without any doubt, less resistant to changes in the environment than the robust Portuguese oyster. The water in the bay has, moreover, its normal clean and green appearance. In addition, the disease made its first appearance on parks close to the entrance of the bay, far away from any source of pollution, and not only affected parks at Arcachon, but also Portuguese oysters grown in the Charente Maritime and in Brittany, in sites where pollution is out of the question. The authorities at the Institut Scientifique et Technique des Pêches Maritimes, aware of the serious consequences of the disease, and realizing that no effective method of control was possible, took the difficult but only feasible decision: to introduce, at the shortest possible notice, a large quantity of Pacific oysters, *Crassostrea gigas*.

Small scale introduction of this species in previous years had shown that it grows very well in the area, will be accepted by the oyster-eating public because of its striking resemblance to the Portuguese oyster, and is fully resistant to the disease. In the spring of 1971, large specimens of *Crassostrea gigas* were introduced by air from British Columbia to serve as mother oysters, both in the Charente Maritime and in the Bay of Arcachon, with the result that spat of this species settled on the collectors in appreciable numbers. In addition, fair quantities of spat produced in Japan were introduced by many oyster farmers in an effort to stock their parks with oysters resistant to the devastating disease.

It will be clear that the entire oyster industry in the Bay of Arcachon was seriously afflicted by these events, and this is the reason why the "period of observation" for the chapter dealing with oyster farming in Arcachon, closes with the year 1970. If the Pacific oyster remains invulnerable to the mysterious disease of 1970—1971, if it reproduces prolifically in the Arcachon waters, and if no other pests were introduced by this "kill or cure" remedy, it is to be expected that the Arcachon oyster industry will sooner or later recover, although its traditional structure, with many hundreds of small farmers, may be over.

D. ECONOMIC ASPECTS

D.1. Rent

During the period under investigation, the annual lease was FFr 1.40 per are, irrespective the quality of the parks. This fee was stepped up to FFr 4.50 per are in 1974.

D.2. Inventory items

As is usual in oyster farming, it is the fleet of boats which is one of the most expensive inventory items. M. Daubric has three motorized wooden boats: one measuring 12.5 m in length, maximum breadth 1.20 m, depth 0.75 m, drawing 0.30 m, keel of oak, frames alternately of oak and boiled acacia, walls of local pinewood, deck and superstructure of mahogany, equipped with a 45 h.p. "Couache" diesel engine; one of 10 × 3 m, made of pinewood and equipped with a 30 h.p. Mercedes diesel engine; one, used in the Gironde, of 10 × 3 m, equipped with a 16 h.p. "Couache" engine, and also with a winch and dredges for fishing on the natural beds. Properly maintained, the ships should last some 30 years. As the boats used in the Bay of Arcachon are for transportation only and not for dredging operations, the useful life of their engines is estimated at 12—15 years. The largest of the boats would now cost, if newly constructed, about FFr 50 000.

In addition to the motor boats, M. Daubric works with four wooden chalands of the usual type, measuring 10 × 3 m, drawing 0.65 m when loaded. Other expensive inventory items are in the spacious packing shed at

Fig. 56. Modern oyster boat, now much in use in the Bay of Arcachon, on the wharf.

Gujan-Mestras: a "David Frères" sorting machine, costing approximately FFr 15 000; the "Package Sealing Ltd." automatic tieing machine for closing large packages with steel bands, costing about FFr 12 000; the "Strapex" automatic tieing machine using nylon cord, of Japanese—Swiss origin, costing about FFr 9 000. The company uses three trucks for transportation, with carrying capacities of 6, 3 and 2.5 tons, all having an estimated life of 3—5 years. Several pumps are in use: those for use on board having 2.5 or 5 h.p. petrol engines; an electric one for pumping salt water up from deeper layers to fill one of the storage basins in periods of low salinity. The company owns four harrows and a 3 h.p. petrol engine to operate them on the parks.

M. Daubric's operation uses 17 000 tiles costing FFr 0.25 each, breakage requiring annual renewal of 1—2% of the stock each year. He has three wooden troughs for liming the tiles, and about 5 000 plastic bags, 0.90 m in length and 0.17 m in diameter, for filling with shells as collectors. He has several hundred iron frames for supporting both these bags and the scrap iron used as collectors. Some of the iron frames are used for carrying the larger plastic bags, costing FFr 5 each, for the further growth of oysters produced using shells as collectors. Finally should be mentioned, some 2 500 metal baskets, costing FFr 12 each, about 8 000 oyster trays, some with wooden frames, some entirely metal, costing FFr 4—5 each and five barrows with pneumatic tyres, costing FFr 300 each.

D.3. Expendable items

To maintain the hedges around his parks — consisting of 7 000 "piniots" — M. Daubric annually buys about 2 000 branches, costing some FFr 1.60 each, of which some of the larger ones serve as sea marks. For liming the tiles, 100 kg of lime is used for every 1 000 tiles. The "ruches", the wooden crates for putting out the tiles, cost, mounted and coal-tarred, FFr 12—13 each. They contain about 100 tiles each, which means that the company uses about 170 "ruches" which last, at the most, 2 years. To support the ruches four short poles, costing FFr 0.35 each and four longer poles, costing FFr

0.70 each, are required per ruche. Other expendable items are the diesel oil (6 l per h for the larger boat), petrol and electricity for the various engines both at sea and ashore, and the very large number of boxes used for packing the oysters for market.

D.4. Personnel

The company operates the year around with a staff of 16, among which are four truck drivers. It should not be forgotten, however, that as well as these, not only do M. Daubric's two sons take part in the operations, but also their wives, and that Mme Daubric acts as the head of the sorting and packing department. This means that some 20 tons of oysters are handled per worker. In comparing this figure with that given for flat oyster production, using shells as collectors, in a Dutch oyster company: 100 000 oysters per worker, it should be remembered that the Portuguese oyster only takes about 3.5 years to grow against 4.5 for flat oysters, and that M. Daubric's company grows less than one-third of its oysters from spat, the remainder being purchased as oysters for re-laying, requiring park space and maintenance for 1 year only. All the oysters, however, have to be fished, transported, washed, graded, stored and packed.

D.5. Purchase of oysters

It is clear from the above, that M. Daubric only grows with the aid of his own collectors 120 tons of the 400—450 tons of oysters for re-laying required for stocking his fattening beds. The remainder is partly purchased, at varying prices, from farmers in the Charente Maritime, partly purchased or fished from the Gironde Estuary, and occasionally supplemented directly from natural beds in Portugal. If all the fattening beds can be adequately stocked, M. Daubric produces enough marketable oysters to serve his clientele, but if the odds go against him, either through poor growth or heavy losses inflicted by some agent or other, he buys marketable oysters from small farmers around the Bay of Arcachon to supplement his stock.

D.6. Sales

Prior to 1966 M. Daubric shipped about 50 tons of flat oysters in addition to a much larger tonnage of Portuguese. Up to 1970, he considered an annual sale of 400—450 tons of marketable Portuguese oysters as a fair quantity, but regrets the present total absence of flat oysters, for which he had a special clientele.

The official prices for Portuguese oysters farmed in the Bassin d'Arcachon were for the season 1970—1971 as follows:

Category	kg per 1 000	Price per 100 in FFr
7 bis	25	8.00
7	30	16.00
6	35	24.00
5	40	28.00
4	50	32.00
3	60	40.00
2	80	56.00
1	100	72.00

For the smaller consignments — containing less than 240 oysters — FFr 3.00 should be added for packaging.

E. GOVERNMENTAL ASSISTANCE

The Arcachon branch laboratory of the Institut Scientifique et Technique des Pêches Maritimes services the local oyster industry by forecasting spatfall on the basis of analysis of plankton samples, and by carrying out bacteriological cleanliness control for which it issues the "étiquettes sanitaires" attached to each package of oysters. In addition to this routine work, the scientists of the laboratory carry out investigations on the hydrographic, chemical, and biological aspects of the Bay of Arcachon, and, in close collaboration with colleagues from other shellfish laboratories, on the diseases and parasites which threaten oysters.

F. GENERAL IMPRESSION

Although the Bay of Arcachon, the cradle of the French oyster industry, started off by farming the flat oyster, *Ostrea edulis*, over the years the production of Portuguese oysters became more and more important. The flat oyster appears to be the more vulnerable of the two species and, due to serious mortality in recent years, its production is now at a very low ebb in this area.

The style of farming is less sophisticated than that employed for the flat oyster in Brittany. Most of the spat is obtained using tile collectors but the farmer does not keep track of the quantities produced. When he does not have enough oysters to cover his fattening parks, he purchases supplementary quantities elsewhere. An advantage of growing Portuguese oysters in Arcachon over the production of flat oysters in Brittany, is that the Portuguese oyster can be marketed 1 year earlier in life; that is, when called "3 ans" (in reality 3.5 years old at the turn of the year) this is in contrast to the flat oyster which needs to be 4.5 years old at the turn of the year it is marketed, the heavier categories being older still. This means 1 year less maintenance work, 1 year less occupancy of park acreage, and a reduced risk of losing oysters before they reach market size.

Events in recent years show that again the oyster farmer has to face greater risks, often completely beyond his control, than a manufacturer of industrial products. Considering these risks it is surprising that none of the larger shippers of oysters confine themselves to shipping marketable oysters, bought from small farmers. The main reason that one does not find this pattern in France is that farmers—shippers fall into the "agriculture" category, for taxation, whereas pure shippers would be in the "commercial" sector, with its considerably heavier taxes. The structure of the French oyster industry, previously based on offering compensation for the "inscrits maritimes", which led to large acreages being split up into very small units, and to oyster farmers, assisted by the members of their household, each producing only a small tonnage, made it very difficult for the industry to keep pace with economic and social evolution. It is hardly possible for a small oyster farmer to mechanize his enterprise, as he lacks the required capital and cannot use expensive equipment all the time. Nevertheless, some technical

Fig. 57. Pinasses, the traditional graceful boats of the Arcachon oystermen are gradually becoming obsolete. (Photo P. Korringa.)

evolution can be observed. Not only is some type of engine or other now used to motorize the numerous boats, but also the traditional "pinasse", the graceful boat so characteristic of Arcachon (Fig. 57), is now gradually giving way to a sturdier type of craft with a large working deck, better suited for work on board and for transporting oysters and other material.

It was a dramatic but wise decision to introduce the Pacific oyster in an effort to safeguard the existence of the local oyster industry when the Portuguese oyster, which had rendered such excellent services for more than a century, practically disappeared under the fatal attack of a disease which, until then, had been unknown in European waters. However, it is too early to forecast the ultimate result but it seems possible that the oyster industry will revive, though the number of oyster farmers will be drastically reduced.

Scientific research should continue to play an important role in the support of the oyster farmer. Not only is more insight into the biological characteristics of the microbial diseases and into the factors which lead to their fatal explosions required, but also, more knowledge of the potential productivity of the area should be obtained, in order to estimate the extent of optimal production. It has been surmised that primary production in the basin itself is of crucial importance to the growth of oysters, but the noteworthy fact that the Arcachon oyster farmers select the parks near the entrance of the bay for fattening their oysters might be interpreted in terms of planktonic food being transported from the open sea. A good quantitative insight into this matter would be very welcome indeed, in which comparison with other shellfish districts might be enlightening.

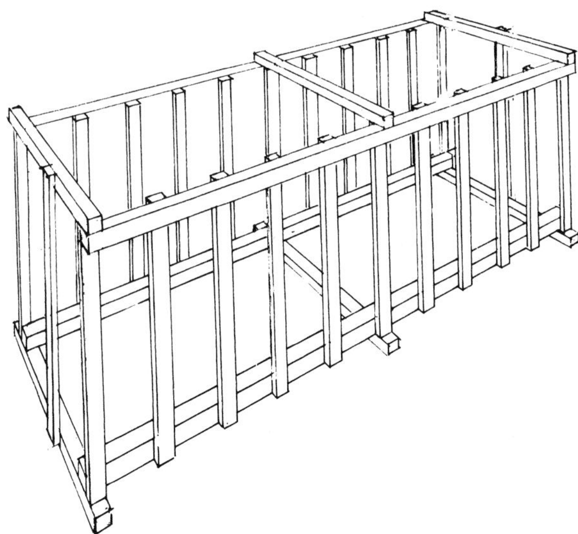

Fig. 58. Construction of a "ruche" for tile collectors. When empty they can be folded up for transportation on a "chaland".

G. TECHNICAL DETAILS

G.1. Ruches (Fig. 58)

The open-work crates for the tiles, or "ruches", consist of a simple rectangular frame-work made of double laths. They measure 210 × 60 cm, are 72 cm high and have extra laths across the middle of the top and bottom frames to give the crate greater strength. Boards, 6.5 × 1.5 cm are nailed vertically: ten on the long sides, two on the short sides. They are nailed onto the outer side of the bottom frame, as far as the long sides are concerned, and to the inner side of the top frame. The crates are fixed onto the heads of the poles by driving a nail through the bottom frame, leaving its head far enough out to facilitate withdrawal at the end of the season.

G.2. Spat detaching table

This table, about 2 m in length, is of simple construction. It is supported by two pairs of sturdy beams connected crosswise and has walls of deal with a slit left open on the under side through which the scrapings fall onto the deck.

G.3. Harrow

The harrows in use on the parks at Arcachon are square in shape and measure 1.50 × 1.50 m. They carry rows of 15-cm long teeth along their length. Two types are in use, one with teeth 20 cm apart, the other with teeth 10 cm apart, their use depending upon the type of oysters to be treated. The harrows are moved over the parks with the aid of a petrol engine, in a way similar to that described for oyster farming in the Marennes—Oléron area.

H. BIBLIOGRAPHY

Borde, J., 1938. Etude du plancton du bassin d'Arcachon, des rivières et du Golfe du Morbihan. Rev. Trav. Off. Pêches Marit., 11: 523—541.

De la Blanchère, H., 1866. Culture des Plages Maritimes. J. Rotschild, Paris, 296 pp.

Guérin-Ganivet, J., 1909. Notes préliminaires sur les gisements de mollusques comestibles des côtes de France. L'estuaire de la Gironde. Bull. Inst. Océanogr. Monaco, 131: 1—12.

Hautreux, A., 1909. Bassin d'Arcachon et région côtière des Landes. Températures et densités. Bull. Stn Biol. Arcachon, 12: 277—290.

Ladouce, R., 1938. Observations sur la reproduction du naissain dans le bassin d'Arcachon. Rev. Trav. Off. Pêches Marit., 11: 207—211, 493—502.

Ladouce, R. and Le Dantec, J., 1954. Importance de l'oxygène dissous dans l'eau des bassins ostréicoles. Sci. Pêche, Bull. Inf. Doc. Inst. Pêches Marit., 14: 1—9.

Lafuste, J., Le Dantec, J., Marteil, L. and Trochon, P., 1957. La reproduction de l'huître portugaise (*G. angulata* Lmk) dans les centres de captage de la côte Atlantique. Rev. Trav. Inst. Pêches Marit., 21: 401—414.

Lambert, L., 1932. L'acclimatation de la portugaise sur les côtes françaises. Rev. Trav. Off. Pêches Marit., 5: 343—365.

Lambert, L., 1938. Les gisements d'huîtres indigènes (*Ostrea edulis*) et d'huîtres portugaises (*Gryphaea angulata*) sur les côtes françaises. Rev. Trav. Off. Pêches Marit., 11: 465—476.

Le Dantec, J., 1955. Note sur les gisements coquilliers de la rive gauche de la Gironde. Rev. Trav. Inst. Pêches Marit., 19: 347—360.

Le Dantec, J., 1957. Le Bassin d'Arcachon: Conditions, de Milieu et Gisements Naturels d'Huîtres. Cons. Int. Explor. Mer, Comm. Mollusques et Crustacés, No. 49, 5 pp.

Le Dantec, J. 1958. Quelques observations relatives à l'action du froid sur les huîtres. Ann. Biol., 13: 126—127.

Le Dantec, J., 1960. Observations Complémentaires sur les Conditions de Milieu du Bassin d'Arcachon. Cons. Int. Explor. Mer, Comm. Mollusques et Crustacés, No. 32, 4 pp.

Le Dantec, J., 1963. L'ostréiculture dans le bassin d'Arcachon et ses rapports avec les variations du milieu. Rev. Trav. Inst. Pêches Marit., 27: 203—210.

Le Dantec, J., 1965. Expérience sur l'élevage dans le bassin d'Arcachon de naissain d'huîtres portugaises capté en Gironde. Sci. Pêche, Bull. Inf. Doc. Inst. Pêches Marit., 141: 1—6.

Le Dantec, J., 1968. Ecologie et reproduction de l'huître portugaise (*Crassostrea angulata* Lamarck) dans le bassin d'Arcachon et sur la rive gauche de la Gironde. Rev. Trav. Inst. Pêches Marit., 32: 239—362.

Le Dantec, J., Marteil, L. and Trochon, P., 1958. Le dragage des huîtres portugaises en Gironde. Rev. Trav. Inst. Pêches Marit., 22: 353—368.

Chapter 6

FARMING THE PACIFIC OYSTER (*CRASSOSTREA GIGAS*) IN HIROSHIMA BAY, JAPAN

Example
Oyster firm of Mr Hisami Kurihara, Ondo-cho, Kita-ku, Yasu-gun, Hiroshima Prefecture.
Period of observation: 1971—1973.

A. BACKGROUND

A.1. General principles

Sea food has always been an important item of Japanese diet. That molluscan shellfish have played an important part in this since time immemorial is witnessed by the prehistoric shell mounds found in many places in the Japanese archipelago. The fact that shells of the oyster *Crassostrea gigas* are found in such mounds in great numbers, demonstrates that this species cannot possibly have been imported from Portugal, as has been surmised by some taxonomists surprised by the great similarity of *Crassostrea gigas* and *Crassostrea angulata*.

Oyster farming in Japan dates back to the first half of the seventeenth century and several legends give cause for belief that this industry had its cradle in Hiroshima Bay. Parallel to what occurred in the case of the red-weed *Porphyra*, it must have been the observation of oysters settling on the bamboo sticks of which the fish weirs were constructed which led to the initiative to place bamboo sticks specially for the purpose in the intertidal area, and also to lay blocks of stone as collectors for oysters.

However that may have been, Hiroshima Bay was, and still is, the main area for oyster farming in Japan. Its high degree of shelter, its rather wide tidal range combined with a not too steeply sloping shoreline, leading to an acreage of intertidal ground of some importance, are certainly factors conducive to oyster farming.

For centuries oyster farming was based on simply planting bamboo hedges as collectors from which the oysters were harvested in due course (Fig. 59). A break-through came in the year 1923 when the biologists H. Seno and J. Hori of the Kanagawa Laboratory of the Tokyo Fisheries College, while experimenting with oysters, came to the conclusion that a system of hanging culture could be advantageous. This was certainly so, and led to the flourishing of the Japanese oyster industry. The main reason why the use of rafts and other floating equipment was so important in this case, should primarily

Fig. 59. Ancient method of oyster culture in Hiroshima Prefecture. (From an old woodblock print.)

be sought in the geomorphological structure of the Japanese islands, where the mountainous character leads to rather steeply sloping coastlines, leaving only narrow strips of intertidal ground. Raft cultivation made it possible to utilize a fairly broad sheet of water beyond the low water line, in addition. It is the food contained in a given volume of water, oscillating with the tide, which determines how many oysters can be grown in a given well-defined area. If an area is flat, with extensive tidal grounds, oysters can be spread over a large number of plots on such grounds; the basis of French-style oyster farming. Where tidal ground is limited, as in Japan, however, optimal use of the potential richness of the area can only be made by growing oysters in a three-dimensional way, so that the oysters can utilize the food available in the whole water column without being overcrowded on narrow strips of tidal land. Additional advantages of raft cultivation are that benthic predators such as crabs, starfish and drills cannot reach the suspended oysters, and deposition of silt and shifting sand cannot harm them. On the other hand, areas which are adequately sheltered are required, and also additional labour for stringing and hanging the oysters from the rafts. The cost of raft building has to be kept low enough to make this style of farming remunerative. Nevertheless, the Japanese oyster industry is nowadays predominantly based on the hanging system of culture and, especially since 1950, has shown high production figures.

Although there are over 15 species of oysters found in Japanese waters, oyster farming is almost exclusively based on the species *Crassostrea gigas*, locally known as "magaki". There are three main oyster farming regions, namely, the Miyagi region on the northeastern coast of the main island of Honshu, the Hiroshima region on the northern coast of the Inland Sea and the Nagasaki area on the west coast of the Isle of Kyushu. Of these, the Hiroshima area is by far the most important for the production of marketable oysters; it takes care of about 60% of the national production. There are 3 600 ha of oyster ground here, compared to about 2 300 ha in the Miyagi region. Some 700 oyster farmers operate in the Hiroshima district, using about 8 000 rafts.

Japanese oyster farming is a semi-culture in which larval development is fully left to nature. The larvae are produced by stocks of mother oysters belonging to the oyster farmers and not to any appreciable extent by wild oysters from natural reefs. The oyster farmer offers the larvae ready for settling, suitable collectors at the right moment. The collectors now predominantly used in the Hiroshima area are *Pecten* shells, bought elsewhere in the country. These are offered to the oyster larvae by hanging strings of them from racks and rafts.

Growth is rapid under the subtropical conditions obtaining in southern Japan, and the required planktonic food is freely provided by nature. Man indirectly stimulates the development of phytoplankton in the coastal waters through the nutrients contained in the run-off from his well-manured arable land.

In the Hiroshima area, only oysters for consumption are produced. This is based on two systems, one leading to the marketing of medium-sized oysters within 1 year of farming, the other to larger oysters grown in 2 years. The former system is preferred by many farmers as it suffers less from summer mortalities.

Well over 99% of these oysters are shucked ashore and shipped to the consumer as raw meat. Some of these oysters are eaten raw with some sauce or other, others are used for a variety of cooked dishes. Oysters are certainly not a luxury product in Japan and thus the price paid for shucked oyster meat is quite modest. A quantity of canned or frozen oysters is exported, particularly to the United States, and since 1925, Japan has exported a fair quantity of seed oysters from the Miyagi Prefecture.

A.2. Biology of the species

Crassostrea gigas Thunberg is the oyster known as the "magaki" in Japan, as the Pacific oyster in the United States, and as the Japanese oyster in Europe. As its biology has been treated in the chapters dealing with oyster farming on the Pacific coast of the United States (Chapter 7), and moreover, comes so close to that of the Portuguese oyster *Crassostrea angulata*, little has to be added to what has already been said about this species, and reference can be made to the respective chapters.

It is interesting to note that the species *Crassostrea gigas* abounds in Japan in several varieties, distinguishable by the size, shape and colour of their shell. The shells of the variety occurring in the Miyagi area are large and rather poorly cupped; those found off the Isle of Hokkaido are still larger; those of the Hiroshima area are smaller, but better cupped and heavier; whereas those from the southern area, usually called Kumamoto oysters, are rather small, strongly pigmented, and of a special flavour preferred by epicurists. Experiments carried out by Imai and Sakai have demonstrated that the differences observed are truly significant, and are of a hereditary nature as they have persisted through generations of in-breeding. The cross-breeding of inbred strains has led to hybrid oysters of intermediate character in several respects. These hybrids show a higher adaptability to environmental conditions than the inbred strains, and no regression of characteristics was observed in the F_2 hybrids. It is interesting to note that while Imai and Sakai could easily produce hybrids of *Crassostrea gigas* and *C. angulata*, cross-breeding of *C. gigas* did not work with *C. virginica*, *C. echinata* or *C. rivularis*.

Crassostrea gigas is, like all members of the genus, of a subtropical nature. Spawning takes place at water temperatures of 20°C and higher, each female oyster producing millions of eggs. The optimal temperature range for larval development is from 23 to 25°C. The species is adapted to a wide range of salinities — from 10 to 36‰ — but for larval development, the optimal range is said to be from 23 to 28‰. Excellent settling has, however, been recorded for Hiroshima Bay at salinities as high as 31—32‰.

Crassostrea gigas is renowned for its rapid growth, surpassing that of all other cultivated oysters. It is, therefore, possible to produce marketable oysters within 7 or 8 months of settling.

A.3. Geographical situation

Hiroshima Bay is situated on the north coast of Seto Naikai (the Inland Sea). It is strewn with islands of different sizes and thus has excellent shelter and a considerable length of tidal flats. The firm under consideration is located on a small peninsula at the northeastern tip of Kurahashi Island. Its headquarters are not far from the town of Ondo, geographical position 34° 10′ 20″ N, 132° 33′ 20″ E, some 24 km south-southeast of the city of Hiroshima.

The racks for oyster farming are built in the immediate vicinity of Mr Kurihara's headquarters, within 10—150 m, and his rafts are moored conveniently close by, 500—1 500 m away.

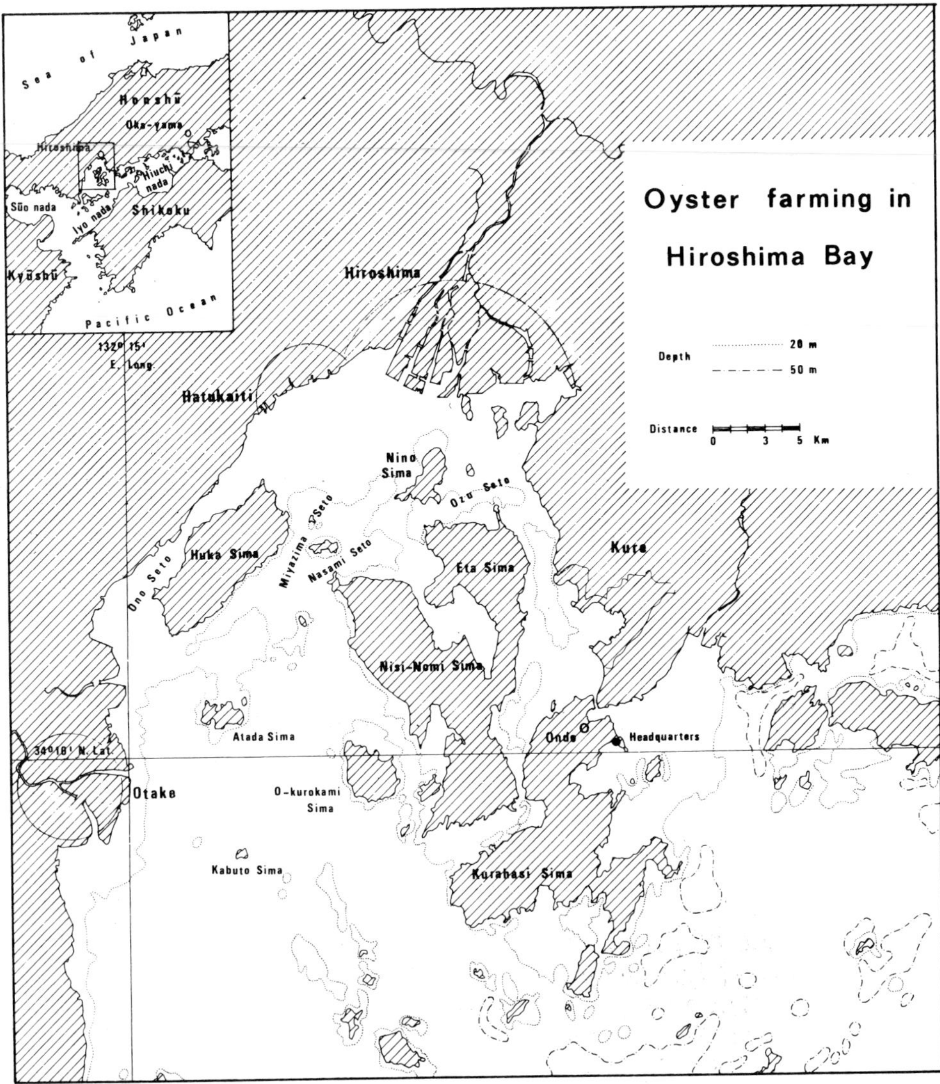

A.4. Hydrographic pattern

The hydrographical pattern of Hiroshima Bay is partly formed by the characteristics of the land bordering it. The bay is sheltered by hills and mountains up to about 800 m high on the mainland and by numerous hilly islands. Although most of the coast is quite steep, so that a depth 10 m is found close inshore, there are locally some more modest gradients which permit the oystermen to build their racks on a fair acreage of intertidal ground. Unfortunately, suitable tidal areas are becoming increasingly scarce here due to coastal landfill and construction, and also due to pollution. Along the peninsula where Mr Kurihara's plant is located, there are intertidal grounds of some importance, suitable for building racks. There is no industrial pollution in this area and discharge of domestic sewage is not a matter of great concern either, as the area is rather thinly populated.

Depth. Mr Kurihara's racks are in the intertidal zone in the immediate vicinity of his headquarters. There are plenty of grounds close by of about 10 m depth, excellent for mooring rafts. The deepest parts of Hiroshima Bay have a depth of 30 m.

Tides. There is a fair tidal range in Hiroshima Bay, about 2.50 m at spring tide and 0.80 m at neaptide. The tidal currents are not very fast and do not endanger the rafts, but are strong enough to prevent much stratification of the water.

Water temperature. Temperatures in the area are of a Mediterranean character. Water temperatures rarely drop below 10°C in the winter (February—March) and rise to a maximum of 24 or 25°C in the summer months. Thus, the oysters can grow and fatten the whole year round. Growth slows down somewhat in the colder months but fattening is usually best towards the end of the year. Water temperatures favourable to the reproduction of the oyster can be expected in July, August and September. Temperatures of over 15°C may be expected from early May until the middle of December.

Salinity. Salinities are quite high and equable in Hiroshima Bay as the Oto River, discharging into it, does not flood to any great extent. Lower salinities may occur during the summer season when more rain can be expected. A series of observations made at a hydrographical station in the immediate vicinity of Mr Kurihara's plant shows that the salinity of the water was fairly constant from April 1971 to March 1972; with a minimum of 31.6‰ in October and a maximum of 32.7‰ in July/August and again in December/January. Stratification is hardly noticeable here up to a depth of 10 m. As a rule, salinities in Hiroshima Bay range from 31 to 33‰ for most of the year, and from 27.5 to 31‰ in June, July and August, covering most of the reproductive season of the oyster.

Chemical composition. The Japanese scientists analyse the chemical composition of water samples collected on a monthly basis from several stations in Hiroshima Bay. A series of samples taken at station 19, where the company under consideration operates, shows that in 1971—1972 the pH fluctuated from 8.0 to 8.4, with high values from January to April; the oxygen content ranges from 4.3 to 7.1 cc/l, the lower values being found from July to November; for COD (chemical oxygen demand) figures from 0.5 to 1.4 ppm were recorded; for total nitrogen compounds from 1 to over 500 μg/l, the peaks being due to remarkably high NH_4 values in April and September, at the 5-m depth and in the surface layer, respectively. Other stations in the bay also showed high NH_4 values in those months. PO_4-P was recorded in values from 0 to 7 μg/l. The transparency of the water varied from 2.7 to 5 m.

Sea bed conditions. The bottom is fairly stable in Hiroshima Bay, consisting of small particles of weathered granite.

A.5. Legal aspects

Mr Hisami Kurihara's oyster firm is a private enterprise. He works together with his brother, who is in charge of the field work, whereas he himself concentrates on the processing and sale of the oysters. The Kurihara brothers are contemplating the conversion of their business into a limited company, as personal liabilities and risks are becoming too great.

According to the Japanese law, the state is the owner of all the grounds up to the high water line. Oyster farmers can, however, lease grounds for placing racks or rafts for periods of 5 years, with the chance of an extension. They are not able to approach the State authorities direct for this, but must accept the mediation of the co-operative association of which they have to be a member. Prefectural or municipal authorities allocate space to the co-operative association which in turn grants the use of specific areas to individual farmers. Usually, the farmers pay the nominal fee indirectly through their membership of the co-operative association, which is officially instrumental in the registration and allocation of space. No selling or sub-leasing is allowed. Raft locations are being leased at Y 5 000—8 000 per 200 m^2 raft.

There is no need for official supervision as a measure against poaching. Since all the oyster farmers are organized in co-operatives and know each other well, there is sufficient safeguard against theft in this intensely used area.

B. SEQUENCE OF OPERATIONS

B.1. Preparing shell strings as collectors

The collectors used in Hiroshima Bay are strings of scallop shells. The shells are purchased from fishery enterprises in the north of the country, from Aomori and Hokkaido. A characteristic of the shells of *Pecten ambicans* is that both valves are saucer-shaped, but flat scallop shells can also be used. The company under consideration uses slightly over one million shells as collectors every year.

The shells are perforated with a sharp pointed hammer, but this has often already been done at the shipping point. The shells are strung on 16 gauge galvanized half-steel wire, cut into 80-cm lengths for "single" strings and into 1.60-m lengths for "double" strings. This wire is specially made for the oyster industry. Mostly double strings are made. Only in years with poor spatfall

Fig. 60. Strings of scallop shells to be hung out as oyster spat collectors. Miyagi Prefecture. (Photo P. Korringa.)

is it better to use single strings. To keep the shells separate from each other use has to be made of spacers. In the past, pieces of bamboo were used for this purpose, but now more durable plastics have taken over. Such spacers consist of short pieces (1.5 cm) of plastic pipe, about 1 cm in diameter. A brightly coloured plastic is used, to facilitate retrieval from waste for repeated use. With spacers of this length it takes about 80 scallop shells to make one 1.60-m string. It takes less than 5 min to make such a string and this work has to be done during the months preceding the spatfall season, that is, in May or June.

B.2. Racks for exposing collectors

The racks used for the various phases of oyster farming are of simple construction. Bamboo poles, about 1.50 m in length, are driven in long rows perpendicular to the coastline into the sea bed; first on the intertidal ground and then as far out as a man can wade, using somewhat longer poles. Next long bamboo poles are fastened on top of the vertical supports. Usually two to four such rows are made close together, cross-bracing them with shorter bamboo poles for greater strength. Generally, the racks are not built precise-

Fig. 61. Making strings of oyster shells, the preferred collector for spat that is to be exported. Miyagi Prefecture. (Photo P. Korringa.)

ly horizontally, but sloping towards the deeper water (Fig. 62). The racks have to be rebuilt every year as the wood deteriorates rapidly in the intertidal zone.

B.3. Rafts for exposing collectors

Although spat collection was formerly confined to the intertidal zone, it has been learnt from experience that spatfall can be profuse on suitable objects permanently washed in sea water. Therefore, large numbers of shell strings are hung from the rafts used for the various phases of oyster farming. In the Hiroshima area, the standard size for a raft is 18.20 × 9.10 m. These rafts are constructed of 10—15-cm diameter bamboo poles. Six supporting rails form the basis of the raft; these are placed lengthwise in three groups of two, the rails in each group being 50 cm apart from each other. Buoys are placed under the supporting rails, usually 10 or 11 along the length, 30 to 33 for the entire raft (Fig. 63). Nowadays, buoys made of styrofoam encased in polyethylene bags are preferred but hollow concrete drums and tarred wooden floats are still widely used. Bamboo crossbars (36 or 37), 9.10 m long, are placed perpendicularly over the supporting rails and at-

Fig. 62. Racks with strings of scallop shell collectors. (Photo P. Businger.)

tached to them with wire. Finally, bamboo holding bars are fastened lengthwise over the structure, 3 m apart from each other. Such structures are fairly cheap to make and last for three or four seasons. Since bamboo rafts are not rigid, but rather flexible, they are not so easily damaged in rough weather. The rafts are tied together lengthwise in groups of five and anchored on both sides by 5-ton concrete dead-weights. A space of up to 20 m is maintained between rafts in the same group. Between the groups of rafts, 100 m of water is kept open. The shell strings or strings with oysters are hung from these rafts.

B.4. Sailing out the collectors

Once the racks and rafts are ready to receive the shell strings the farmer has to wait for the best time at which to sail the strings out. This will usually be some time in July, but occasionally spat may be harvested in August and September. Japanese oyster larvae prefer a clean surface to settle on and therefore sailing out shell strings too early in the season should be avoided. In order to determine the right moment, the experimental station scientists take plankton samples at frequent intervals; they study the appearance of

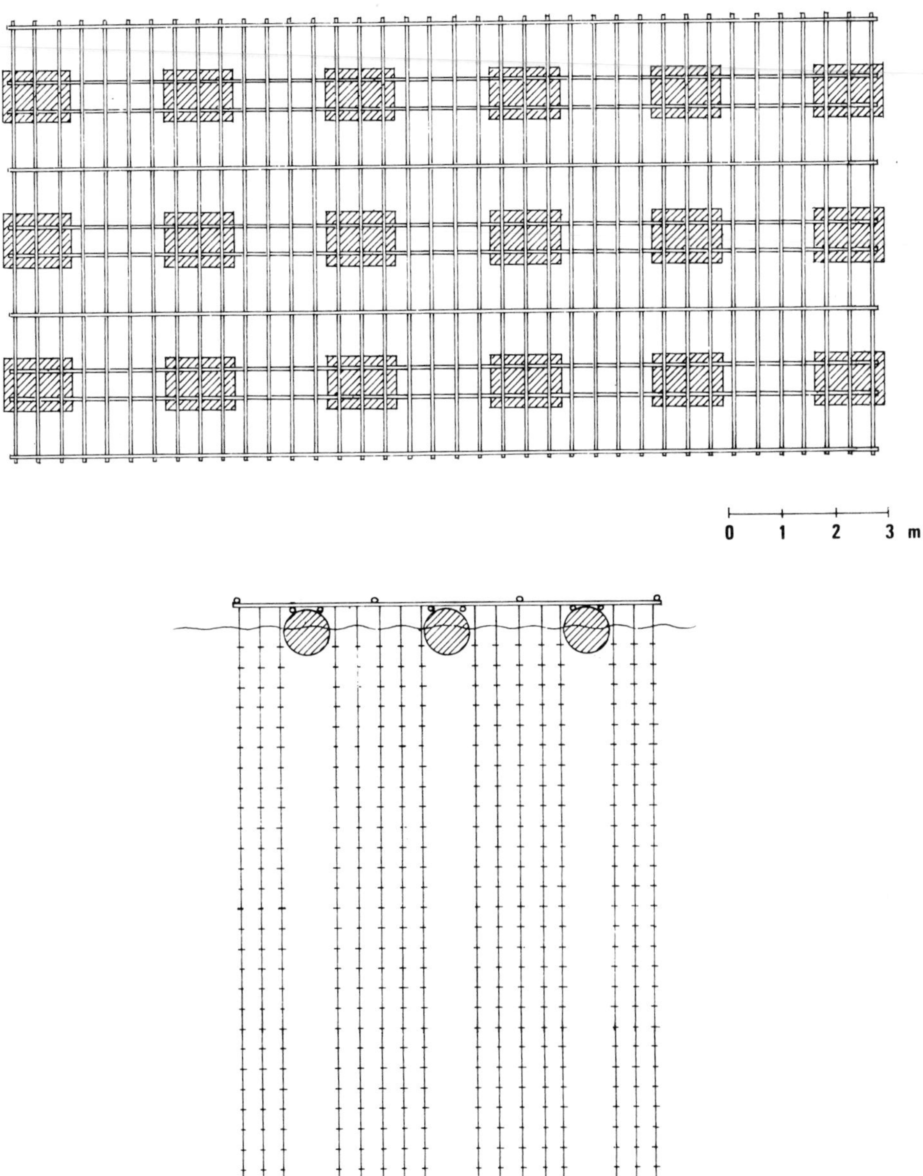

Fig. 63. Construction of oyster rafts for hanging out shell collectors and strings with growing oysters. Instead of drums along the length, 10 or 11 styrofoam floats are usually used nowadays. (After Cahn, 1950.)

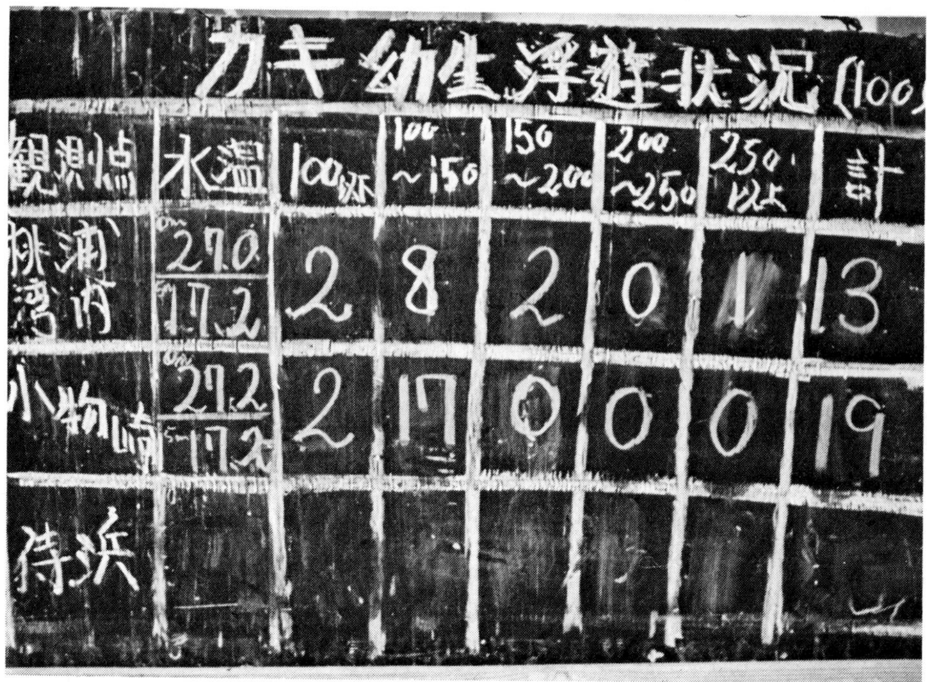

Fig. 64. Scientific information on settling prospects giving hydrographic data and numbers of oyster larvae in different size categories per 100 l of water. Miyagi Prefecture. (Photo P. Korringa.)

the larvae in the water, observe their development and forecast settling time and settling intensity on the basis of their findings, taking water temperature and other hydrographical factors into account. The oyster farmers are kept informed on the settling prospects (Fig. 64).

The shell strings are usually loaded on small wooden boats, equipped with a 3 h.p. diesel engine (Fig. 65), and taken to the racks or rafts. Although the racks offer certain advantages, the trend in Hiroshima Bay is towards using rafts for spat collection. Usually the 1.60-m long shell strings are folded double and hung, using a wire, from the racks or rafts, well above the sea bed. The 0.80-m "single" strings are put out singly without folding. Hanging out the shell strings does not take much time. The company under consideration can easily sail out all its shells (roughly 15 000 strings) within 1 week.

The forecasts regarding the intensity of settling can be used to advantage. If it is expected that large numbers of larvae will settle, the strings are hung close together, always using double strings, occasionally even triple strings. This ensures less trouble from the settling of competitive organisms such as acorn barnacles and mussels, and still catches the appropriate number of oyster spat per shell. When the settling is forecast as light, it is wise to space the shell strings out more, in order to catch enough spat per shell, even though there is a risk of a heavy set of mussels or barnacles.

B.5. Transfer of the newly caught spat

Spat which has settled on the shell strings hung from racks can stay there for months in succession. They live intertidally, which means that feeding is interrupted for varying lengths of time at low tide and thus growth is rather slow. This spat is hardened by the repeated exposure to air and suffers relatively little from fouling organisms.

Spat attached to shells hung from rafts may suffer heavy losses during the first few weeks of their sedentary existence. These losses are partly brought about by the fouling of the shells by a variety of vigorously growing invertebrate organisms. Some farmers take this risk, but Mr Kurihara moves the shell strings from the rafts to the racks about a week after the spat has settled. This extra work pays off, as the chance of survival is much better on the racks and fouling is slighter there.

B.6. "1-year" and "2-year" farming systems (Fig. 66)

In Hiroshima Bay the oyster farmers speak of "1-year" culture and "2-year" culture. In the former, the young oysters are transferred to rafts in the second half of the summer. Growth may be so rapid here that they can be harvested as medium-sized marketable oysters from January onwards. In the 2-year system, the young oysters are transferred from the racks to the rafts

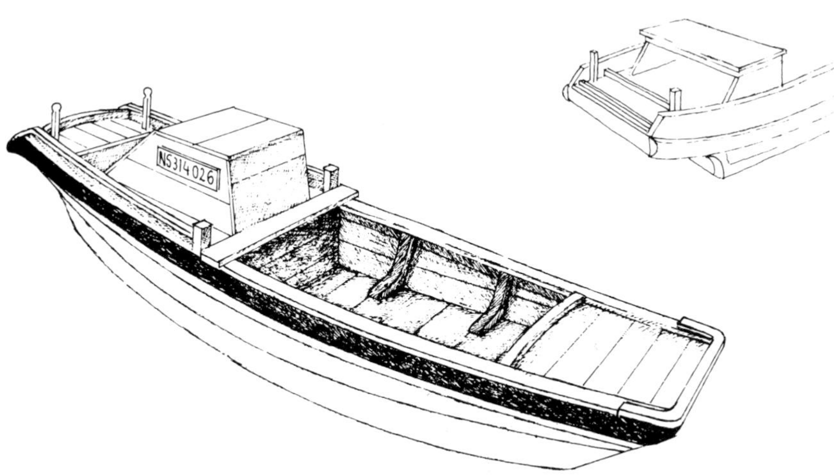

Fig. 65. Working boat for transferring shell strings to rafts and racks.

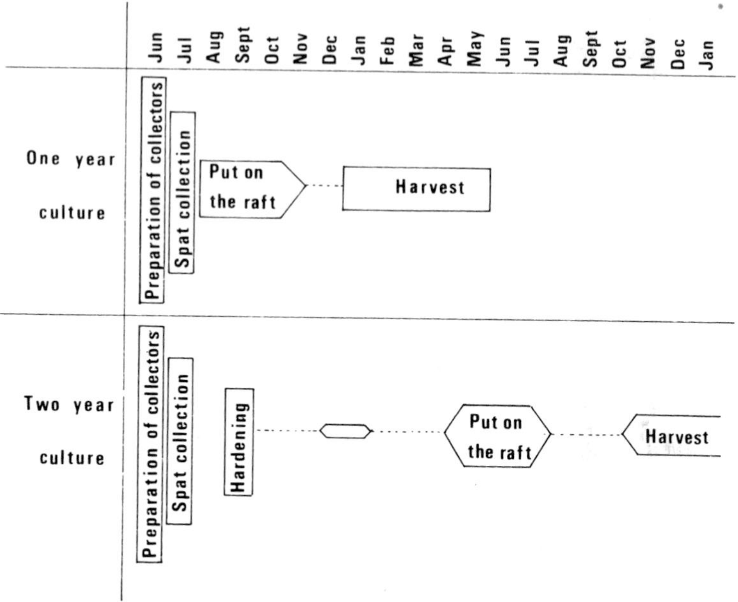

Fig. 66. Scheme of "1-year" and "2-year" farming systems.

in the spring of the following year (April—June) and harvested as fair-sized market oysters from October onwards.

By applying both systems, the farmers can cover the whole marketing season, with peak production in December, tapering off in January and February. Occasionally the oysters suspended from the rafts show heavy mortality in the summer months, particularly the larger oysters under the 2-year system. Thus, many farmers are hesitant to operate on too large a scale with the 2-year system. In general, about 70% of the oysters grown in Hiroshima Bay are "1-year" oysters.

B.7. Transferring the shells to new strings

Before moving the young oysters from the racks to the rafts they are restrung to give them more space to grow. This is done from August to November in "1-year" culture and from April to June under the "2-year" system.

It is considered satisfactory if 15 to 20 young oysters are found on each scallop shell. The collectors are brought ashore for restringing, where shells and spacers are stripped off from the iron wire. The shells are individually cleaned with the aid of a tool resembling a miniature pick, consisting of a sharp piece of steel for removing the fouling organisms, fastened at an angle to a wooden handle (Fig. 67). The shells are next restrung on steel wire of the same type, but now cut into sections about 8 m in length. The

Fig. 67. Tool used to clean shells and oysters and to pry oysters open during the shucking procedure.

exact length is dependent on the depth of the site where the raft to receive them is moored — bearing in mind that the oysters should never touch the bottom, not even at low tide. When restringing, only 40 shells are placed on a string, making use of plastic spacers now 20 cm long. A female worker can clean the shells from two to three "double" strings ("rens") per h, but it takes only 5 min to restring the shells. About 10% of the shells are discarded because they carry too few young oysters. The shells from one "double" settling string are sufficient to make about two long strings for growth and fattening.

B.8. Growth and fattening

The new strings, with the shells kept apart by 20-cm spacers, are transferred to a raft for growth and fattening. About 600 of these long strings are hung from one standard-sized raft. Growth is rapid in this area, the water being quite rich in phytoplankton and detritus, and the water temperature never dropping enough for growth to come to a complete standstill. During the whole period of growth and fattening, 6—9 months in the "1-year" system, 6—12 months for the "2-year" system, no maintenance work is required. Sometimes a whole raft is moved to another site, especially when the experimental station scientists advise it, for instance, if a case of "red tide" threatens the oysters locally. If the weight of the oysters increases so much that the raft tends to sink too low in the water, more buoys are placed beneath it.

B.9. Harvesting the marketable oysters

When the oysters have grown to marketable size the wires with the shells and oysters on them weigh from 30 to 50 kg, occasionally even up to 100 kg. It is not easy to collect these long wires without losing oysters. For harvesting, a large working boat equipped with a 60 h.p. diesel engine on which

Fig. 68. Oyster rafts moored in Kesennuma Bay, Miyagi Prefecture. (Photo P. Korringa.)

Fig. 69. Oyster rafts in Kesennuma Bay, Miyagi Prefecture. (Photo P. Korringa.)

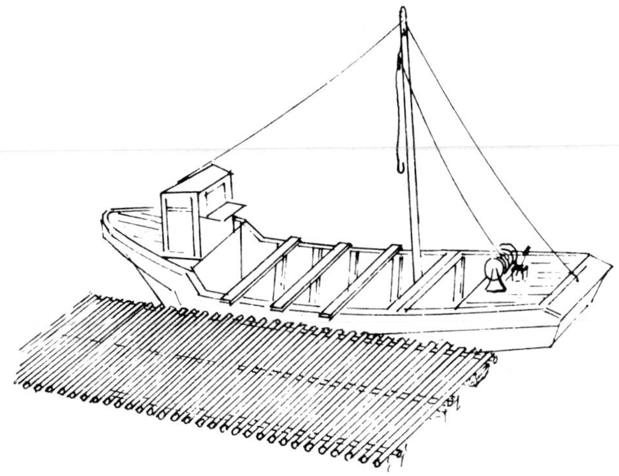

Fig. 70. Large working boat, with 10-m mast and winch, alongside oyster raft. Note distance kept free along the stem.

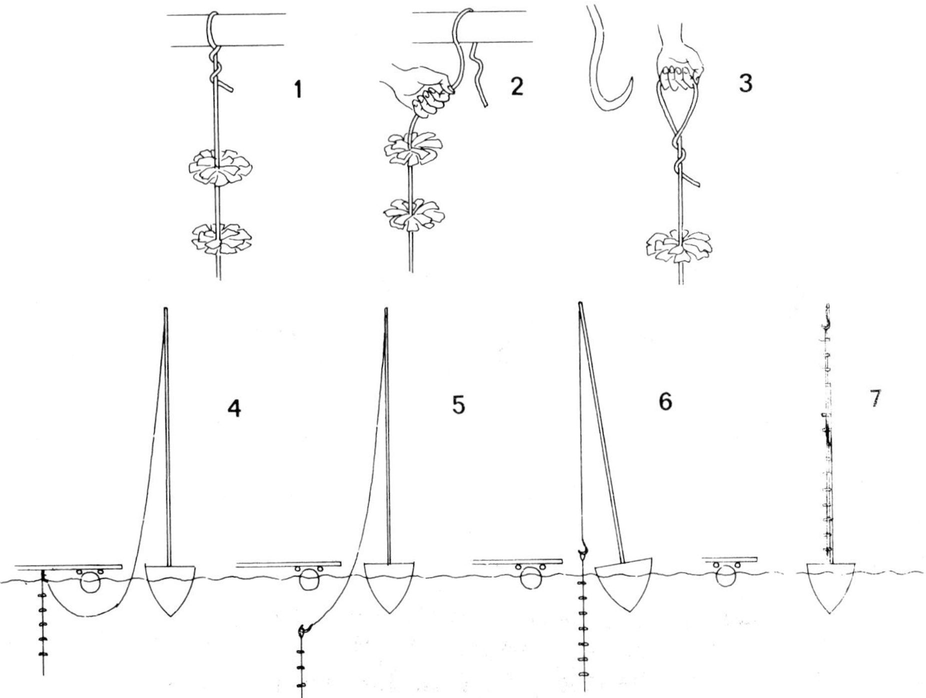

Fig. 71. How to collect strings with oysters from a raft using the large working boat.

a 10-m long loading mast has been erected, is used (Fig. 70). This boat is moored to the raft in a special way, leaving some open water between them along the stem. A line is taken to the raft and slipped by hand beneath the carrying rails to the position of the string. This string is then unfastened from its bamboo support. Because of the bouyancy of the water, it is easy to hold it despite its considerable weight. A loop is made in the top end of the wire and a hook at the end of the ship's line fastened to it. This is then let go so that the string hangs straight under the ship's board and is hoisted up by means of a power winch. Swung inboard, the shells and oysters are collected by simply cutting the lower end off the wire allowing the heavy shells to slip off under gravity. If the whole load were released at once, this would damage the oysters, so the shells on the lower half of the wire are released first, while the upper half are held by a brake attachment on the mast. The second group are lowered afterwards. The shells, together with the oysters and spacers, drop onto the deck. The spacers are collected for further use, and the oysters are collected in wide-meshed square metal baskets (1 × 1 m), which are lifted off the fishing vessel onto a small boat which takes them to a dock.

This method of harvesting strikingly resembles the system formerly used on the mussel rafts in Galicia (Spain). In the latter area they have, in recent years, given up the use of clumsy tall hoisting masts and now install triple-drummed winches in the bows of relatively small ships and collect the strings loaded with mussels coiled in a steel basket which is lowered from the ship. Such coiling is, however, only possible when ropes are used for making the strings, not when the more rigid steel wire is used (see Chapter 4, Volume I).

B.10. Washing and shucking oysters

The Kurihara brothers' processing plant consists of a rather small building in which the main room serves for shucking oysters. Just outside the building, a cleaning installation has been set up. This consists of a rotating cylindrical steel cage equipped with water jets (Fig. 72), not unlike the rotating washers used in The Netherlands for cleaning mussels. A travelling crane takes the oysters from the boat and unloads them in the hopper of the washer. On leaving the washer, the cleaned oysters are dumped onto a conveyor belt which transports them to the baskets of a second travelling crane which carries the oysters to the main room of the building. Here, there are two concrete counters, back to back, with a centrally placed elevated bin having a series of openings. This bin is filled with oysters. All the transportation work is carried out by male staff.

Up to 26 female workers kneel at the counter opening the oysters. They use a hand-pick, consisting of a narrow steel blade, bent and fastened at an angle to a wooden handle (Fig. 67). With this tool, they break the rim of the shell opposite the hinge, inserting the blade between the valves to cut the

Fig. 72. Washing installation at Mr Kurihara's oyster plant with travelling crane, hopper and rotating cylindrical cage. (Photo Y. Akimoto.)

adductor muscle. They next pry the shell open, take the meat out, deposite it in a plastic bucket and throw the empty shells onto the table. The shells drop through special holes onto a conveyor belt which removes them. The whole operation takes less than 5 sec per oyster. Skilled workers can produce up to 20 kg of oyster meat per day, depending on the size and quality of the oysters.

The oyster meat is collected in cans, weighed, and taken to a cleaning installation in an adjacent smaller room. The oyster meat is then carefully washed in a conical vessel which receives a continuous flow of chlorinated sea water. The meat is allowed to overflow from this vessel onto a wire mesh conveyor belt (Fig. 73). During its passage it is drained, hand-graded and fed into plastic-lined shipping cans, holding 20 kg.

B.11. Shipment of oyster meat

The Kuriharas usually pack the oyster meat in plastic-lined cylindrical tins containing 20 kg, but as some local markets traditionally require units of 3, 5 or 7 kg, cans of these sizes are also used. The oyster meat is either shipped

Fig. 73. Washing and draining the shucked oyster meat in Mr Kurihara's plant. (Photo Y. Akimoto.)

directly to the markets of the big cities, usually 100—120 kg per day, or sold via brokers, again some 120 kg per day. Meat which is not immediately shipped is placed in cool storage (10°C) until the next day.

Isothermic trucks, kept at a temperature of 10°C, carry the cans of oyster meat to the various markets. The marketing season for fresh oysters is from November to March. Oysters harvested from April to June are sold to canneries. The peak month for the sale of oysters is December.

Some of the oyster meat is consumed raw, with vinegar or some sauce or other, some is used in preparing various cooked dishes. Industrial processing takes place in a huge plant near Hiroshima, which produces a variety of foodstuffs. Here oysters, bought in the shell, are washed, shucked, cleaned and graded. Then they may be encased in dough, covered with flour and then deep-frozen. These oyster fritters, are in due course, simply fried in hot fat or oil. Other oyster meat is individually packed and deep-frozen at −30°C in the raw state; other again is smoked and packed in oil. The industry under consideration handles some 200—300 tons of oyster meat per year.

C. FARMING RISKS

C.1. Hydrographic factors

Hiroshima Bay is almost perfectly sheltered and moreover situated outside the typhoon area — rough seas are no reason for concern here. Neither need

Fig. 74. Where the use of rafts is too risky, tarred wooden barrels, interconnected with thick nylon ropes, are used to support the strings of oysters. Ojika Peninsula, Miyagi Prefecture. (Photo P. Korringa.)

dangerously low salinities be feared in this area. In less sheltered regions, the use of rafts is often considered too risky. In such areas long-line farming, in which strings with oysters are fastened to heavy ropes supported by big wooden drums and placed in long lines, is preferred (Figs. 74 and 75).

The quality of the water in Hiroshima Bay may sometimes show unfavourable trends. In the spring and autumn, when the currents are more sluggish, there are phytoplankton blooms of diatoms or dinoflagellates. If the poisonous dinoflagellate *Gymnodinium* reaches a density of 2 000 to 3 000 cells per ml it is advisable to move the rafts to safer grounds.

When oysters are grown too densely, overcrowding may lead to poor growth and mortality. This is not only due to scarcity of food, but also because the faeces and pseudofaeces of the oysters themselves and of all the fouling organisms which settled on the shell strings drop to the bottom and require a considerable amount of oxygen for their biodegradation. This may lead to low oxygen values, high NH_4 figures, and even to the development of poisonous hydrogen sulphide (H_2S) where the water is shallow and flushing poor. This may also be one of the reasons why the best growth and fattening of oysters is usually found in the middle section of the strings, rather than close to the bottom or near the surface.

Fig. 75. Numerous lines supported by barrels carry the oyster strings along imperfectly sheltered sections of the coastline of Ojika Peninsula, Miyagi Prefecture. (Photo P. Korringa.)

Industrial pollution has to be feared on all the Japanese coastlines, as the geomorphological structure of the islands has led to industrial development taking place mainly along the coasts. Local industry in Hiroshima is not predominantly in the chemical sector, so the oyster industry can still continue to exist here, close to the city, although occasionally, Hiroshima oysters are found to have a high cadmium content.

C.2. Predators

The most serious oyster predators in Japanese waters are the drills, gasteropods belonging to various species, among which *Tritonalia japonica*, *Rapana thomasiana* and *Thais tumulosa clavigera* are the most notorious oyster enemies. Oysters hanging from rafts have, however, nothing to fear from these types of drill which have no pelagic larvae; oysters hanging from racks little, but those grown on the bottom very much. Starfish are not a major problem either, but predators belonging to the Turbellaria family, on the other hand, are a serious menace. Two which should be mentioned are *Pseudostylochus ostreophagus*, especially dangerous to oyster spat, and *Stylochus ijimai* which kills the adult oysters. In periods of high salinities the losses inflicted by these flatworms may be very serious indeed and the best method of control is to dip the oysters for some time in fresh water.

Occasionally fish such as the Black Sea bream (*Mylio macrocephalus*) are reported destroying oysters grown on rafts.

C.3. Diseases

Japanese biologists claim that they do not know of any disease of an infectious nature among the oysters and their spat. However, occasionally mass mortality takes place the causative agent of which is not known. In some years between 1961 and 1964, 40—60% of the oysters in the Matsushima area, north of Sendai were lost. This was tentatively ascribed to a metabolic disorder caused by too rapid growth and too early maturation. For a country which exports oyster seed, this sounds better than speaking of a mysterious infectious disease.

C.4. Competitors

In the Hiroshima Bay oyster industry, competitors of various description give far greater problems to the oyster farmers than predators or disease. As is always the case in hanging culture, many invertebrate organisms gladly settle on all objects within reach, far from smothering silt or sand, and out of reach of a variety of bottom-dwelling predators. The Hiroshima farmers fear most of all the serpulid worm, *Hydroides norvegica*, which settled profusely in 1969 and 1970 and smothered the oysters so badly that great losses were suffered. Of the rafts in the Hiroshima area, 60% were then badly affected. Methods of control are exposure to air (at least 12 h in sunny weather), repeated brushing, powerful jets of water (29 kg per cm^2) and even fire.

Another competitor is *Mytilus*, the mussel, which often settles in enormous numbers and grows very rapidly, reaching a shell length of 5 cm in a few weeks. Mussels can be killed without injuring the oysters by immersing the shell strings in water at 70°C for 20 sec.

Other competitors are Tunicates (e.g. *Ciona*), acorn barnacles, bryozoa, sponges, saddle oysters (*Anomia*) and the Polychaete worm, *Polydora*, which burrows into the shells of oysters but is not a major headache in the Hiroshima district.

The types of competitor with which the Japanese hanging culture has to cope are exactly the same as elsewhere in the world; for example, those from which the Spanish hanging mussel culture suffers. Eradication is technically a difficult and time-consuming matter. As a general precaution against the ravages of competitors among the spat, the shell strings are hung as closely together as possible, taking the predicted intensity of settling oyster larvae into account. Dense masses of collector shells are rarely invaded by large numbers of invertebrates competing for space and food; but in later phases, shells with oysters cannot be hung too closely together.

D. ECONOMIC ASPECTS

D.1. Rents

Oyster farmers have to lease the ground for building their racks and mooring their rafts. Mediation of the co-operative fisheries associations of which each farmer has to be a member, is compulsory. For the location of a standard 200-m^2 raft he has to pay Y 5 000—8 000 per year. The company under consideration operates with 35 rafts.

D.2. Inventory items

The main inventory item for the production of oysters is the fleet, consisting of a big wooden boat (15—16 tons) with a 60 h.p. diesel engine, equipped with a motor winch and a tall mast for hoisting the strings of oysters from the rafts, and two small motor boats (3—4 tons), equipped with 3 h.p. diesel engines. The boats last 10—15 years if properly maintained. The large fishing boat costs about Y 20×10^6 and the smaller boats Y 300 000.

The 35 company rafts have a life span of 3—4 years. For one raft 70 to 80 bamboo poles, costing Y 500—800 each, are required. In addition, styrofoam floats and enough wire to construct the raft are necessary. One raft costs roughly Y 55 000 in material.

For processing the oysters, the indoor inventory items consist of a building with one large and several smaller rooms, equipped with a shucking counter, bins, conveyor belts, chlorination installation, and a cleaning installation, altogether costing some Y 2×10^6. The outdoor equipment consists of the travelling cranes, costing about Y 1×10^6, and the rotating washer equipped with motorized pumps, purchased at a price of about Y 450 000.

D.3. Expendable items

Every year the company has to purchase scallop shells as collectors. Such shells cost about Y 2 each. The company operates with slightly over 10^6 shells, but as 30% of the shells can be used for a second season the annual purchase amounts to about 700 000 shells. For stringing the shells half-steel galvanized wire, costing Y 15 for one 1.60-m string, has to be bought. The company operates with some 14 000 shell strings. Plastic spacers can be used repeatedly and do not weigh heavily on the budget, though they cost three times as much as bamboo spacers. Every raft can carry 600 strings with oysters. Each string has a length of about 8 m and costs Y 72. The company operates with 35 rafts. The racks for holding the shell strings and for hardening the spat caught on the rafts require renewing each year, so a fair number of bamboo poles, costing Y 500—800 each, have to be bought. Further, fuel is needed for both the smaller and the larger fishing boats. The distance to be covered is very limited as the rafts are moored in sight of the headquarters.

D.4. Personnel and wages

The two Kurihara brothers operate with a staff of 30; four male workers and 26 female hands. They are all employed full-time, on a 6-day working week basis. Seasonal workers are difficult to find in this highly industrialized area. The average wage is Y 1 500 per day, rising in the height of the season to Y 2 000 per day.

D.5. Production

Production figures are given in the form of meat yield per raft. Oysters produced by the "1-year" farming system contain about 10 g of meat, whereas those from the "2-year" system contain 20—30 g. Each scallop shell carries about 15 young oysters at the time of restringing and about ten at harvest time. One raft carries about 600 strings of marketable oysters, each string holding 40 collector shells. One raft, therefore, carries an average of 250 000 oysters. For the conversion of oysters into oyster meat the ratio 6 : 1 is usually used, although 7 or 8 : 1 would often be more realistic. The average meat production per raft is 2.6 tons, but occasionally yields of 3—4 tons are recorded in the "2-year" culture. From their 35 rafts, the Kurihara brothers expect to harvest about 90 tons of oyster meat per year. The enterprise is larger than average, as 700 farmers operate with 8 000 rafts in the area.

D.6. Sales

The average price for shucked oyster meat is Y 350—370 per kg, but in December the price can soar to Y 600. On the market in Tokyo, however, a price of Y 800—1 200 is paid per kg. Oysters in the shell are sold at prices varying from Y 60 to 250 per kg. About 40% of the oysters produced by the Kurihara brothers are sold in the shell to local canning industries. The gross revenue from these amounts to Y 5.5×10^6 per year. The remaining 60% is shucked and sold, partly via brokers, partly packed and shipped direct to the big city markets. The gross revenue from these oysters amounts to Y 19×10^6. The total gross income of the company thus amounts to Y 24.5×10^6 per year.

D.7. Liabilities

The fees paid to the co-operative association depend on the gross production of the enterprise. The co-operative association, charged with the allocation of the ground and co-operative purchase of various materials, charges 5% of gross income. The sales co-operation likewise charges 5% of each farmer's gross income.

E. GOVERNMENTAL ASSISTANCE

As will be clear from the foregoing, Japanese oyster farmers are favoured by governmental assistance in various phases of their operations. The rents required to be paid for the intertidal grounds, where racks can be built, and for the deeper water areas, where rafts can be moored, are low, and the mediation of the co-operative associations (controlled by the government) prevents dangerous financial transactions being made in efforts to obtain such grounds.

The co-operative associations instrumental in the purchase of materials and those intervening when the marketable product is sold assist the farmers in obtaining a fair price and in avoiding mutual competition.

Scientific advice is offered free of charge by government agencies. The prefectural experimental stations survey the quality of the water, forecast the time and intensity of the settling of oyster larvae, give the oystermen advice on the control of predators and competitors, and give early warnings against red tide. The public health authorities control the hygienic condi-

Fig. 76. Mohne Inlet at Kesennuma, Miyagi Prefecture is so perfectly sheltered and well-flushed that it is an almost ideal site for experimenting with the rearing of molluscan shellfish of various descriptions from eggs. It was the late Japanese pioneer, Dr Takeo Imai, who selected this site for his numerous experiments. (Photo P. Korringa.)

tions of shellfish farming and processing, which ensures public faith in the safety of the product. The research department laboratories of the Japanese fisheries agency are charged with research and experimentation to frame the future of the oyster industry and to assist the farmers in keeping their ventures up to date. University laboratories contribute to the study of the more fundamental aspects of the biology of the oyster. Their findings are sometimes of paramount importance to the future of the whole industry. As the various laboratories engaged in research on shellfish concentrate nowadays on molluscs other than oysters, the total number of scientists working full time on oysters is more limited than the figures on the total number of scientific employees of all the institutes combined, at first glance suggest.

F. GENERAL IMPRESSION

Japanese oyster culture, based on age-long experience, is certainly an industry of considerable importance. The total production of some 40 000 tons of oyster meat per year, equal to some 245 000 tons of oysters in the shell, is certainly impressive. Favourable climatic conditions, leading to almost continuous growth, and the biological characteristics of *Crassostrea gigas*, the fastest growing cultivated oyster, are the basis for this. The tonnage of meat produced by the oyster industry accounts for an appreciable percentage of the food-stuffs rich in protein available to the Japanese population, and is of the same order of magnitude as all the oyster meat produced in the United States, or as all the mussel meat produced in Spain and The Netherlands together. When the financial aspects are taken into consideration, however, it can immediately be seen that oysters in Japan occupy a very different place in the market than they do in Europe. A kilogram of shucked oyster meat yields about Y 350 to the farmer; 1 kg of oysters in the shell only about Y 100. Oysters account for about 3% of the tonnage of all Japanese fishery products, but only for 1% of its proceeds. In France, on the other hand, oysters account for 11% of the tonnage and 25% of the value of all fisheries products landed.

The Japanese population is truly sea-food minded, perhaps more so than any other people in the world. This makes it all the more surprising that the oyster is virtually the only mollusc which is cultivated on a large scale in Japan. Of all the other molluscs on the Japenese market, often far more valuable per unit weight, it is only scallops which are the subject of cultivation on any scale, and even then, they so far have only a rather modest production. Peculiarly enough, the mussel (*Mytilus*) is not farmed in Japan, though it occurs profusely and would be easy to farm. It seems that mussels are considered repugnant in Japan, and it certainly is not an easy matter to break through such traditional prejudices.

The hanging culture system is certainly interesting and many biologists have been impressed by it. If production figures are expressed per hectare, high values result if a Japanese oyster raft or a Spanish mussel raft is taken as the basis. It is, however, somewhat misleading to calculate on this basis, for it is not the limited raft area which produces the food for the oysters, but a far greater area, and it is the tides which bring food to the oysters. Calculated per acreage of bay, the figures have the same order of magnitude for oyster farming on the sea bed in France, The Netherlands and the United States, as for farming with rafts in Japan, and also for mussel farming — hanging culture in Spain compared to bottom culture in The Netherlands. It would be better to state that the system of hanging culture is practical for Japan, as it is adapted to the local geomorphological situation: steep coastlines with narrow strips of intertidal ground. The views of Bardach et al. (1972) that "per-

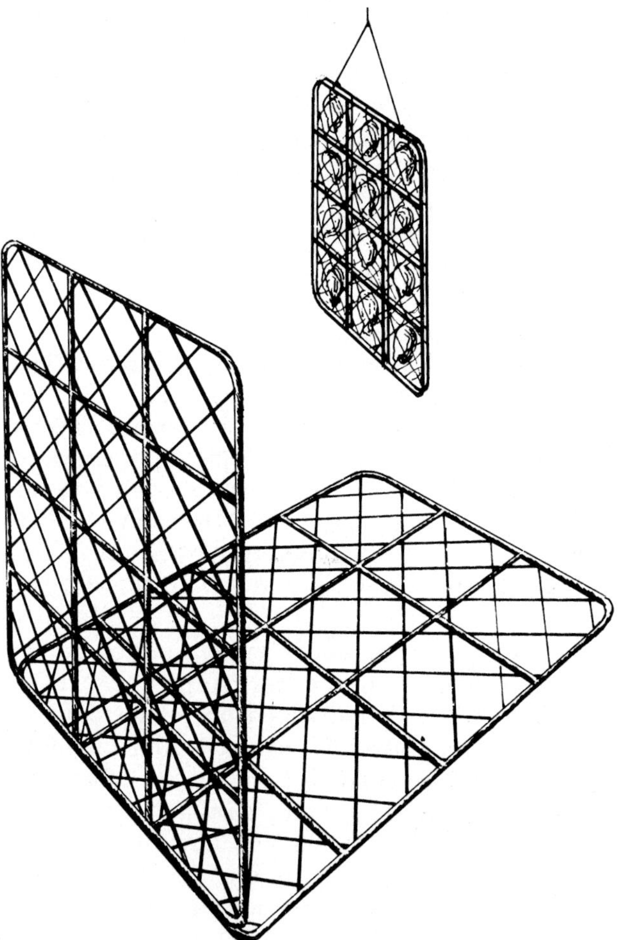

Fig. 77. Vertical frame to produce well-shaped single oysters.

haps the most sophisticated and productive oyster culture in the world is that practised in Japan" and of Fujiya (1970), who, referring to the three-dimensional way of farming, concludes "certainly future marine oyster farming should be done along these lines", are not shared by the author of this book. The very same species is farmed in Willapa Bay using bottom culture with considerable success, a method adapted to the local situation. Where tidal currents reign two-dimensional farming can be just as productive as three-dimensional farming elsewhere, and mechanization is certainly more practicable in the two-dimensional system.

The Japanese style of oyster farming is certainly not the most sophisticated in the world. Very little is done to produce oysters of equal shape and size to serve the discriminating oyster eater. As the Japanese public is satisfied buying shucked oyster meat, there is no need to produce single oysters of perfect shape, so they can be kept on the collector shells from settling until harvesting. A certain degree of clustering can be accepted. It should be noted that a small percentage of oysters is now being served on the half shell, predominantly in western-style restaurants. Such oysters can also be farmed using hanging culture, but they should then be detached from the collector and placed individually in a kind of vertical frame ("book-net") hung from a raft (Fig. 77). The company under consideration operates in this way on a small scale.

The oyster industry in Japan is by no means the most profitable example of farming the sea. The proceeds from nori farming are about eight times as high. Since nori farming is more profitable and requires a lesser degree of manual labour in the field, there is a tendency for a levelling-off and even a decline in the oyster industry, and for an increase in nori farming.

Lack of suitable ground is another factor endangering the future of the oyster industry. Engineering works and pollution have already expelled farms from many erstwhile good spots. The government evidently gives priority to the needs of industry. Recreation has not yet ousted the oyster farms from the water close to densely populated areas, but the day will surely come when pressure is put on the government to reserve important areas of water for recreational purposes.

G. BIBLIOGRAPHY

Amemiya, I., 1928. Ecological studies of Japanese oysters, with special reference to the salinity of their habitat. J. Coll. Agric. Tokyo Imp. Univ., 9: 337—379.

Anonymous, 1966. Method of Oyster Culture. Agric. Econ. Dep., Hiroshima Prefect., Mar. Prod. Sect., Hiroshima, October, 52 pp (in Japanese).

Anonymous, 1970. Marketing of Oysters. Hiroshima Prefect., Hiroshima, 70 pp (in Japanese).

Anonymous, 1972. Annual Report 1971. Hiroshima Prefect. Mar. Prod. Exp. Stn, Hiroshima, March, 71 pp (in Japanese).

Arakawa, K.Y., 1970. Notes on damage to cultured oysters caused by predation of a species of Turbellarian, *Stylochus ijimai* Yeri et Kaburaki. Venus, Jap. J. Malacol. (Kairuigaku Zasshi), 29: 65—74 (in Japanese with English summary).

Bardach, J.E., Ryther, J.H. and McLarney, W.O., 1972. Aquaculture, the Farming and Husbandry of Freshwater and Marine Organisms. Wiley-Interscience, New York, N.Y., 868 pp.

Cahn, A.R., 1950. Oyster Culture in Japan. U.S. Fish Wildl. Serv., Leafl. 383, 80 pp.

Fujiya, M., 1970. Oyster farming in Japan. Helgol. Wiss. Meeresunters., 20: 464—479.

Furukawa, A., 1967. The raft method of oyster culture in Japan. In: Proceedings of the Oyster Culture Workshop, Georgia. Ga. Game Fish Comm., pp. 49—62.

Furukawa, A., 1971. Outline of the Japanese Marine Aquaculture. Jap. Fish. Resour. Conserv. Assoc., Tokyo, 39 pp.

Imai, T. and Sakai, S., 1961. Study of breeding of Japanese oyster, *Crassostrea gigas*. Tohoku J. Agric. Res., 12: 125—171.

Koganezawa, A., 1964. Oyster Culture. Miyagi Prefect. Exp. Stn. Leafl. No. 2, 22 pp. (in Japanese).

Marteil, L. and Barran, W., 1972. L'ostréiculture Japonaise. Sci. Pêche, 215, 23 pp.

Sato, T., 1967. Oyster Culture, Aquaculture. Koseisha-Koseikaku, Tokyo, Fish. Sci., No. 23, pp. 571—620 (in Japanese).

Seno, H., 1937. Oyster culture in Japan. Bot. Zool. Tokyo, 5 (1): 77—104 (in Japanese).

Seno, H., 1938. Review of the development of oyster culture in Japan. Kagaku (Science), Tokyo, 8: 214—256 (in Japanese).

Seno, H. and Hori, J., 1927. A new method of fattening oysters. J. Imp. Fish. Inst. (Jap.), 22 (4): 69—72 (in Japanese with English summary).

Seno, H., Hori, J. and Kusakake, D., 1926. Effect of temperature and salinity on the development of the eggs of the common Japanese oyster, *Ostrea gigas* Thunberg. J. Imp. Fish. Inst. (Jap.), 22 (3): 41—47.

Chapter 7

FARMING THE PACIFIC OYSTER (*CRASSOSTREA GIGAS*) IN WILLAPA BAY, WASHINGTON, U.S.A.

Example
Wiegardt and Sons, Incorporated, Oyster farming enterprise: Director Lee J. Wiegardt.
Wiegardt Brothers Incorporated, Oyster processing company: Directors, Lee J. Wiegardt and Gustav Adolf Wiegardt.
Box 298 Ocean Park, Washington 98640, U.S.A.
Period of observation: 1970—1972.

A. BACKGROUND

A.1. General principles

Ostrea lurida, the small native oyster found off the Pacific Coast of the United States and Canada, was once extremely abundant on the flats of Willapa Bay, situated at the extreme southwest of the State of Washington. In the middle of the nineteenth century man began to exploit this natural resource, and great quantities of these oysters were shipped in sailing vessels to booming California. The supply of these oysters seemed to be inexhaustible and no attention was paid to framing conservation measures. Over-exploitation led to depletion and by 1888 the stock had already dwindled to insignificance, so that it was no longer profitable to collect these oysters from the natural beds. A section of Willapa Bay is still designated as the "State Oyster Reserve" and some native oysters can still be found there, though not yet in sufficient quantities for commercial exploitation.

Towards the turn of the century, an effort was made to revive the oyster industry in Willapa Bay by introducing *Crassostrea virginica*, a larger oyster from the Atlantic Coast of the United States. The first consignment came in 1894 and they continued to be brought in until 1917. It was a venture which did not lead to commercial success. Reproduction was very poor and mortality was repeatedly extremely high for reasons then poorly understood. A few oysters of this species eked out their existence until 1939.

The introduction of *Crassostrea gigas*, an oyster native to Japanese waters was a daring venture. Taking certain precautions, it appeared to be possible to transport juvenile specimens of this oyster alive all the way from Japan. Some small-scale trials were first made, from which it was soon found that the Japanese oyster grew extremely well under the local environmental conditions. Importation of Japanese spat on a commercial scale started in 1928 and has since then only been interrupted by World War II.

It appeared to be possible to grow these oysters on the mud flats of Willapa Bay, where they could reach a large size in 2—3 years of cultivation. These oysters are not held in high esteem as oysters for eating in the raw state from the half shell, but are readily appreciated after preparation in the kitchen, and lend themselves admirably to canning.

It soon transpired that a spatfall of commercial size could not be relied on every year, not even when large numbers of these oysters were grown on the parks of Willapa Bay. Water temperatures were sometimes not even high enough to trigger off spawning, and when the larvae did appear in the water they often disappeared again before reasonable numbers had settled on the cultch offered. Thus, the oyster industry on the Pacific coast, based on this species, cannot achieve consistent results unless the importation of spat from Japan is organized, especially during years of scarcity.

Farming the Pacific oyster is another typical example of a semi-culture, as growth and fattening depend completely on the natural food supply. Spat, either introduced from Japan, or produced in the States using shell collectors (the latter either locally (Willapa Bay) or in bays with more favourable hydrographic conditions, such as Dabob Bay and Pendrell Sound) is planted on intertidal beds with a rather soft bottom. About 22 months later the half-grown oysters are thinned out and transferred to somewhat deeper beds. Having attained marketable size, the oysters are harvested and taken to the oyster canneries from where they often find their way to the Middle West.

A.2. Biology of the species

The Pacific oyster, *Crassostrea gigas*, is closely related to the Portuguese oyster *Crassostrea angulata*, described and discussed in the chapter on oyster farming in the Charente Maritime (France). Some taxonomists feel that these two species come so close together that it is questionable whether they should not be considered as one and the same species, despite the enormous geographical gap between their ranges. Hybridization experiments carried out by Imai and Sakai (1961) seem to give some support to this view, but there are, on the other hand, so many differences in exterior appearance, in growth rate and in flavour, that no experienced oyster farmer has any difficulty in telling them apart.

Crassostrea oysters differ from flat oysters (*Ostrea*) in their shell shape, anatomy and reproduction: their shells are more elongated and more deeply cupped; they possess a promyal chamber, leading to greater efficiency in filtering water, which makes it possible for them to live in rather turbid water; and their eggs are freely spawned into water, unlike flat oysters, which practise incubation and eject the veliger larvae only when these have reached a fair size, and can reasonably take care of themselves.

The Pacific oyster, *Crassostrea gigas*, bears its name with honour, for its shells attain a length of at least 30 cm. The shape of the shell may be quite irregular, depending on the features of the site where the oyster grows and on the degree of crowding. Externally, the shell varies from smooth to fluted and often shows deep radial grooves; the colour is grey with streaks of brown or purple externally, white inside with a mauve hue at the scar of the adductor muscle. In Japan, the country of origin, the different forms or races of this oyster are distinguished. The type commonly introduced to Willapa Bay is the "Miyagi" oyster, grown in the bays of the Miyagi prefecture north of the city of Sendai.

Crassostrea oysters differ from flat oysters not only because they spawn their eggs freely into the surrounding water, so that both fertilization and development of the eggs into veliger larvae must take place without any form of maternal protection, but also in their temperature requirements for larval development. The planktonic larvae of flat oysters, characteristic for the temperate zone, develop normally at rather modest water temperatures: some species from 13°C upwards, some at 15—16°C, and others require a minimum temperature of 17.5°C for larval development. All *Crassostrea* oysters need higher temperatures — they are of a more subtropical nature. They do not spawn at water temperatures below 19.5°C and although the larvae can survive at somewhat lower temperatures, 20°C and higher is required for their normal growth leading to settlement within 3 weeks of spawning. *Crassostrea* larvae require very clean cultch for settling.

Maturation of the gonads begins at a much lower temperature than spawning does so it can happen that, although the gonads are filled with eggs or spawn ready for spawning, the water temperature does not rise sufficiently high enough in a particular year to trigger off spawning. In such a case, the oysters may proceed to reabsorb the gametes, but such reabsorption takes some time and may leave the oysters in a rather poor condition. Oysters that have spawned recuperate much more quickly by feeding vigorously and storing glycogen in their connective tissues. If the Portuguese oyster fails to spawn because the water temperature remains too low in the area where they are grown, the discriminating consumer may complain about their oily tang, which makes it virtually impossible to sell them. Such complaints are not heard in the Willapa oyster district, but as these oysters invariably pass the kitchen before being served, it is not so easy to notice a slight difference in flavour. The oyster canners do, however, complain when the oyster meat is too soft, as often happens after failure to spawn, and will not buy such consignments.

A.3. Geographical situation

Willapa Bay is situated at the southwestern tip of the State of Washington, U.S.A., due north of the mouth of the Columbia River. It measures 109 square miles and is separated from the sea over most its length by an 18-mile long low-lying spit, the Long Beach Peninsula. At its northern end, there is a wide, open entrance to the Pacific Ocean. Several rivers and rivulets debouch into it. Ocean Park, the headquarters of the company under consideration, is to be found in the middle of the peninsula at a geographical position of 46° 28′ N, 124° 03′ W.

A.4. Hydrographic pattern

Depth. Willapa Bay is predominantly quite shallow. Its total acreage is 109 square miles (almost 70 000 acres) but most of this becomes exposed at low tide. In the Bay 42 000 acres can be considered as tidal land.

The mouth of Willapa Bay, the entrance to the ocean, is about 5 miles wide at high tide. It is quite shallow and has a rather unstable character. Shoreline erosion is a normal phenomenon here. The bar at Cape Shoalwater, on the northern side of the entrance, is liable to substantial shifting which affects the flushing of the bay. The greater the flushing rate, the poorer the retention of oyster larvae within the bay. This led to unfavourable settling conditions around the year 1960, but at present the bar is longer, so that the oyster larvae have a better chance of staying and settling in the bay.

Tides. The tidal range is approximately 12 feet at spring tide and 6 feet at neap tide. At low water spring tide, a level of —4 feet can be observed and at high water spring tide, the water may rise to +10 or +12 feet. About two-thirds of the water filling the bay at high tide leaves on the ebb tide. Current velocities show a maximum of 2.5 knots. Usually the plume of the Columbia River heads due north, stemming the ebb current coming out of Willapa Bay and driving most of that water into the bay again. Sometimes, however, the plume points in a more offshore direction, which affects the flushing of the bay in a way unfavourable for larval retention.

During the period that oyster larvae are developing in the bay, the thing that is feared is the springing up of strong northwesterly winds which affect the flushing pattern. Huge cold water masses suddenly penetrate into the bay, leading to both a steep drop in water temperature and to poor larval retention.

Waves. Willapa Bay offers little shelter. The surrounding land is rather flat. On the eastern side, the Willapa Hills offer some protection, but unfortunately, strong winds often come from the south and southwest, especially during April. This may locally lead to the silting over of the oysters and to their rolling away to deeper places, in which case the oyster farmer has to try to salvage them by picking them up at low tide. The limited degree of shelter necessitates the use of quite sturdy material for farming the oysters.

Water temperature. A long series of observations with a thermograph at the Nahcotta landing stage has given good insight into the water temperatures obtaining in Willapa Bay throughout the season, and especially into the

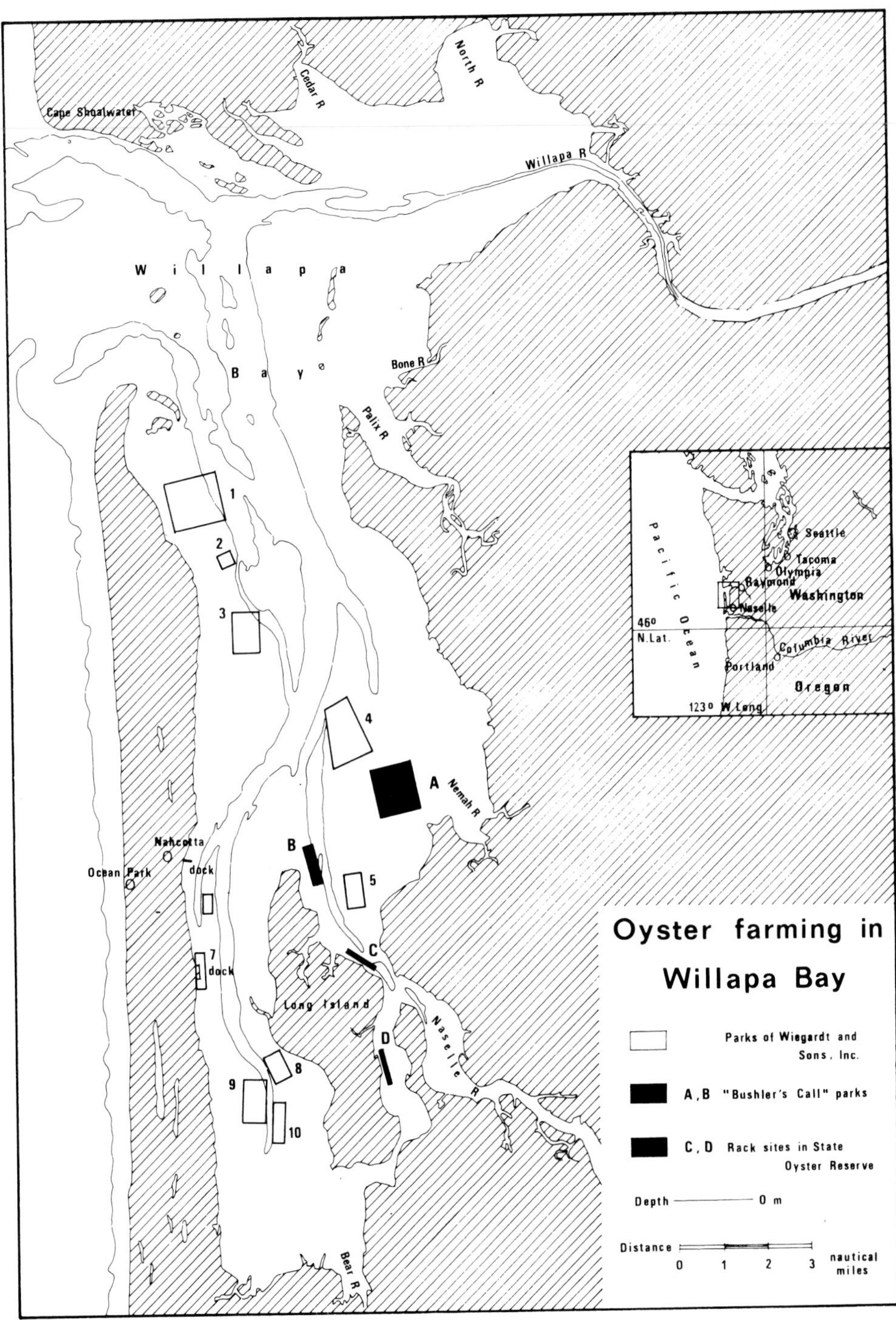
Cape Shoalwater
Cedar R
North R
Willapa R
W i l l a p a
B a y
Bone R
Palix R
1
2
3
4
A
Nemah R
B
5
Nahcotta
Ocean Park
dock
C
7
dock
Long Island
D
Naselle R
8
9
10
Bear R
Pacific Ocean
Seattle
Tacoma
Olympia
Raymond
Washington
Naselle
46°
N.Lat.
Columbia River
Portland
Oregon
123° W.Long.
Oyster farming in Willapa Bay
Parks of Wiegardt and Sons, Inc.
A, B "Bushler's Call" parks
C, D Rack sites in State Oyster Reserve
Depth — 0 m
Distance
0 1 2 3 nautical miles

sudden changes arising under the influence of the wind.

In winter, the water temperature is as a rule 5—6° C, occasionally somewhat lower; it begins to rise in March and reaches the 15° C level on about June 1st. Then comes the critical period for the reproduction of Pacific oysters, which require a temperature of 19—19.5° C for triggering off spawning. Such temperatures do occur in most years, but often northwest winds drive in cold water masses before the oyster larvae have had enough time to develop and to settle. A prolonged spell of temperatures of 20° C and higher is of rare occurrence here, and yet a subtropical species such as the Pacific oyster requires this if consistent results in procuring spat are to be obtained.

The water masses bathing the Pacific coast of the United States and Canada are greatly influenced by the Kuroshio. This sea current is somewhat capricious in nature. As a result of this, the period 1957—1959 was characterized here by water temperatures which were several degrees above the average and which not only led to good spatfall years in the area under cultivation, but also to spontaneous outbursts of settling of Pacific oyster spat over a large area, including the Strait of Georgia and its tributaries in British Columbia. In many bays the summer temperature of the water rose to over 20° C in those years. It was then that Pendrell Sound (50° 15′ N, 124° 43′ W) received its tremendous set of Pacific oysters on natural collectors. Similar events must have taken place around the year 1936, leading to the good settling of Pacific oysters in many bays, but far fewer hydrographic observations were made at that time.

Salinity. The salinities measured at the Nahcotta dock range from 16 to 30‰; in the middle of the bay they may rise to 32‰. The streams and tributaries debouching into the bay (for example, the Willapa, Naselle, Bear, Nemah, Palix, Cedar and North Rivers) are not very long, but the bay receives drainage from some 900 square miles and about 60 inches of rain may be expected each year. During the last decade, even more than this has fallen: up to 110 inches. The forests surrounding the bay do not retain the water so well as they did previously, due to increased lumbering. The primary run-off period is from November to April, whereas low stream flows occur from June to September or October.

Sea bed conditions. The bottom of Willapa Bay consists of sand, muddy sand, and mud. The sand is found where strong currents prevail. The southern half of the bay has a predominantly muddy bottom, consisting of fine clay deposits. There, a pole 4 inches in diameter can easily be pushed some 8 feet into the mud. On many oyster parks in the bay a human foot can sink 8 inches (Fig. 78), and higher in the bay the bottom is too soft to even walk on.

The quality of the bottom of many parks gives reason for concern. Dredging is the easiest and cheapest way to harvest oysters, but where dredging away the top layer of sediment risks turning the bottom into shifting sand, the oysters have to be harvested by laborious hand-picking.

Fig. 78. The bottom of the oyster plots in Willapa Bay is in many places so soft that the human foot sinks 8 inches or more into the mud. (Photo P. Korringa, October 1948.)

A.5. Legal aspects

According to the American law, a corporation has to include three directors. For this reason, the oyster farming company of Wiegardt and Sons, Incorporated, set up by his father in 1962, now has Mr Lee J. Wiegardt as president, his wife, Mrs Wiegardt as vice-president, and his cousin, Gustav Adolf Wiegardt as secretary-treasurer. Since his father died in 1971, Mr Lee J. Wiegardt, his only son, owns all the shares.

The oyster processing company, Wiegardt Brothers, initiated in 1921 as a formal partnership of three brothers, became incorporated in 1962. Mr Lee J. Wiegardt and Mr Gustav Adolf Wiegardt each own half of the shares.

Some of the parks Mr Wiegardt exploits are his own property, whereas others are leased from the State of Washington or from other owners. Here too, tide land can be bought down to the low water spring tide mark (—3.5 feet). The upland owner, however, has preferential rights to the buying of tide land. This option holds good up to 50 feet from the meander line. If, therefore, a piece of tide land further away from the high water line and not touching the 50-feet zone is selected, these preferential rights do not obtain and there is no need to notify the upland owner.

The oyster farming company exploits the following parks:

Number indicated on chart	Number of acres	Owner
1	200	133 acres of own property 50 acres leased from other owners 17 acres leased from the State
2	15	Own property
3	70	Private lease: US $0.05 for every bushel of oysters planted, with a guaranteed minimum of US $2 000 per year
4	130	Predominantly own property, small section in the north leased
5	39	Own property
6	12	Own property
7	20	Own property with landing stage, hopper and causeway
8	59	Own property
9	50	Own property
10	37	Own property

In addition, there is a contract which states that all the oysters produced on parks A and B, belonging to the owner from whom park no. 3 is leased, will be purchased by Wiegardt and Sons for US $0.56 per bushel-on-the-ground. This is a so-called "bushler's call". In fact it is a transition measure. In a later phase, Wiegardt and Sons plan to exploit these parks. Good oyster ground has become very scarce in Willapa Bay and is virtually unavailable.

The sites indicated on the chart as C and D are situated in the State Oyster Reserve. The company received permission to place racks there for collecting spat, but is not required to pay any rent. In Dabob Bay (47° 50′ N, 122° 50′ W), outside Willapa Bay, the company has rented 12 acres of deep sea lease for mooring spat-collecting rafts.

Surveillance is carried out by the "State Fisheries Patrol", keeping an eye on the State Oyster Reserve, originally set up to protect the local stock of the native oyster, *Ostrea lurida.* In addition, Mr Wiegardt inspects his beds repeatedly with his speedboat. Theft of oysters, however, very rarely occurs here.

B. SEQUENCE OF OPERATIONS

B.1. Purchase of Japanese spat

As the subtropical *Crassostrea gigas* does not really belong in the temperate waters of Willapa Bay, consistent spatfalls of commercial importance cannot be relied on. Introduction of spat from elsewhere is, therefore, a necessity. The original and most reliable source of spat is Japan, where Japanese oyster farmers specialize in producing spat hardened for export. The company under consideration buys its Japanese spat exclusively from the Miyagi prefecture, where it is grown in Matsushima Bay and in various inlets around the Ojika Peninsula (38° 23′ N, 141° 28′ E), some 60 km east-northeast of the city of Sendai. To be sure of obtaining the best quality spat, Mr Wiegardt takes the trouble to go to Japan himself, usually twice a year, to buy stock for his own company and for five colleagues, who pay their share of the travelling costs. There are always Washington state officials in Japan during the season spat is packed, to survey and inspect the material for the presence of unwanted predators, such as the drills *Tritonalia japonica, Thais haemastoma* and *Rapana thomasiana,* and of their egg capsules. A tax of about US $0.25 per case is levied to pay for these services. In the Miyagi prefecture, the spat is collected on strings of oyster shells which, at the end of summer, are transferred to hardening racks. The young oysters are exposed to air for several hours every day. It is thought that this provides them with training against desiccation, so that they can survive a prolonged sea journey. Packing begins in February and March, when it is still quite cool in the Miyagi area. The shells are taken from the strings, thoroughly washed, and packed in wooden boxes measuring 36 × 18 × 12 inches. Either whole shell or "broken" shell (shells cut into two or three pieces) are packed. In the first case, each box should contain 10 000 spat; in the second, 14 000, the spat measuring 6—18 mm in shell diameter. The boxes with spat are then placed on racks in the intertidal zone. They are not hermetically closed, so that the spat receives a fair supply of sea water at high tide. It takes several weeks to assemble enough cases to form a cargo. The sea journey itself, as deck cargo, takes about 10—14 days, use generally being made of logging ships returning from taking lumber to Japan.

The cases are kept slightly separated from each other by means of dunnage, and are covered with rice straw matting to ensure that they will all receive their share of moisture when the deck cargo is sprayed each morning and evening.

Mr Wiegardt usually buys 3 000 to 4 000 cases of Japanese spat per year.

B.2. Arrival of Japanese spat

The ships arrive at Raymond (only smaller ships; 46° 42′ N, 123° 44′ W) and at Olympia (47° 03′ N, 122° 53′ W). The cases are transported, in a hired trailer and truck, to a section of park no. 7, which is thoroughly hardened with oyster shells so that the truck can drive out on it. The boxes are then placed unopened at a level where they are exposed for about 60% of the time. There is enough leakage in every box to provide the spat with sea water at high tide.

When they arrive, sometime late in March, the water is still too cold for growth, and April gales from the southwest can still be expected. Silt swirled up by the gales would easily smother the tiny spat if they were planted on the parks.

B.3. Planting Japanese spat

In the second half of April, the spat is loaded onto a scow[1] which is tugged to a park by the company motor boat[2]. On arrival at the park, which is delimited and subdivided by sea marks, the scow is carefully sailed in lanes in order to scatter the shells with spat evenly over the park at 75 up to 100 boxes per acre. They are only planted as thickly as this on a well-sheltered park, such as no. 1. If less-sheltered parks, such as nos 4, 6 or 9, are to receive some of the spat, this is not done before May 1st, and no more than 50 boxes are scattered per acre.

B.4. Spat collectors used in Willapa Bay

Although Pacific oyster spat does not settle in commercial quantities in most years, the Willapa Bay farmers always prepare a sufficient quantity of collectors ready for action in case the oyster biologists indicate that a good wave of larvae ready to settle is likely to be forthcoming.

The usual collectors here are strings of Pacific oyster shells, which are

Fig. 79. Hammer for perforating oyster shells to be used as clutch.

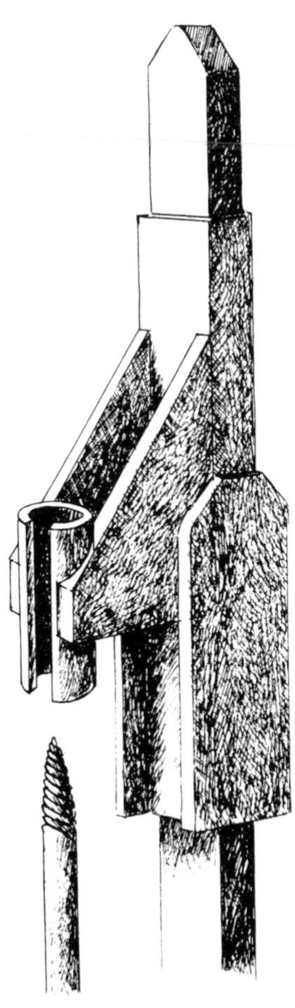

Fig. 80. Apparatus used for mechanical stringing of oyster shells. The shells are placed on the "easy-out".

abundantly available at the canneries. To string the shells it is first necessary to punch a hole in them. This can be done with a hammer, to the head of which a cut-off valve stem from a petrol engine has been welded (Fig. 79). This piece of high quality steel, a pointed spike 5 mm in diameter, serves the purpose very well. The perforated shells are strung on 12 gauge galvanized wire (1/8 inch in diameter) cut off in lengths of 2 m. The shells are placed alternately cupped side up or down, and it takes 80 to 100 shells to make one string. To allow for breakage, 1.25 bushels of shells should be allowed for every string. In an 8-h day, one worker can make about 60 strings if a hammer is used for perforating the shells.

Making shell strings has, however, been to some extent mechanized. For this, use is made of a vertically placed round steel bar, about 90 cm long,

Fig. 81. Mechanized stringing of oyster shells in the shed of the Coast Oyster Company. (Photo P. Korringa.)

held in position with a clamp, on top of which a so-called "easy-out", a tapering spirally-grooved piece of high quality steel has been welded (Fig. 80). A shell is placed by hand on the point of the "easy-out" and, every second, an iron arm fitting over the easy-out comes down with sufficient force to punch a hole in the shell. The motor-driven iron arm slides up and down over a square vertical bar. The perforated shell slides down the round bar (Fig. 81). When the latter is filled to the top, it is lifted up in order to slide the shells onto the attached piece of galvanized wire. With this con-

Fig. 82. A slightly different apparatus for stringing shells is used at Nahcotta. (Photo P. Korringa.)

traption, several of which are placed in a row and kept in motion by the same motor, one worker can make 100 strings a day.

Mr Wiegardt aims at a production of some 50 000 strings per year, partly for use in Willapa Bay itself, partly for hanging from the rafts in Dabob Bay. Shell strings can easily become entangled. They are, therefore, placed lengthwise in special wooden bins which taper at the bottom (Fig. 83). The strings are put in such a bin or "pallet", 50 at a time, then strapped at both ends with 2.75-inch galvanized bands. A strapping machine is used for this pur-

Fig. 83. In Mr Wiegardt's plant the shell strings are placed in bins to be strapped to avoid their becoming entangled. (Photo P. Korringa.)

pose. The shell strings can then be easily transported using a scoop-loader, and put on piles without running the risk of their becoming entangled.

B.5. Sailing out the shell strings

Pacific oysters require very clean cultch for settling. Sailing out of collectors therefore has to be carefully timed. Moreover, it quite often happens that the local hydrographic conditions are not conducive to larval development and larval retention. Sailing out collectors serves no purpose at all in such years, so the farmer usually refrains from offering cultch in years with poor spatfall prospects. In the year 1969, no shell strings were put out in Willapa Bay, and in 1970, when Mr Wiegardt took shell strings to the racks in spite of the poor settling prospects, it resulted in complete failure. In 1968, on the other hand, his company hung out 35 000 strings, although the spatfall prospect was not too good. In this instance each shell caught two to four spat, which allowed the replanting of 75 000 bushels of oysters on the fattening beds in the year 1970.

It is very difficult for the oystermen themselves to decide when to sail out the collectors, so the Willapa Bay Shellfish Laboratory at Nahcotta gives assistance. In the appropriate season, plankton samples from 60 gallons of water are collected every day at six stations in Willapa Bay. On every station one sample is taken from close to the surface and one from deeper layers. Analysis of these plankton samples, combined with temperature data produced by the Nahcotta thermograph, forms the basis of the weekly bulletins issued by the laboratory. In these bulletins, the oystermen are informed of the appearance of oyster larvae and their development, and forecasts are given on settling. The bulletins are mailed to the oystermen around the bay, but in addition there is frequent personal contact during this critical period.

B.6. Hanging shell strings on racks

The preferred spat collecting system for the conditions prevailing in Willapa Bay, with its muddy bottom, is that of hanging shell strings from racks[3]. These racks can be assembled fairly quickly, as they are made of prefabricated frames. A rack structure for 10 000 strings can be put up by ten men in 2 days. The scow containing the rack material arrives at the chosen spot (sites C and D in the State Reserve), the rack frames are pushed into the mud, and stepped on and wobbled until the mudsills touch the bottom. On top of the frames, placed 8 feet apart, five "stringers", of 2 × 3 inch creosoted wood, are nailed to support the shell strings. Such racks, made of creosoted wood, have a life span of some 10 years, but sometimes mud tends to accumulate under them, which can reduce the current velocity so much that settling is adversely affected. The shell strings are simply hung over the stringers, dangling down on both sides. As the shell strings are 2 m long and, as the distance between the stringers and the sea bed is 52 inches (1.32 m), their lower ends are always kept well off the muddy bottom. It is up to the farmer to decide how many strings he puts on his racks. A larger number will reduce the cost of the racks per shell string but may at the same time reduce water circulation to such an extent that he will harvest fewer oysters per shell. Usually, Mr Wiegardt hangs 15 strings per section of stringer, which means 75 strings in each bint between two rack frames. Mr Wiegardt is considering putting only four stringers on any new racks and reducing the number of strings to 12 per section of stringer. He is also thinking of making his racks somewhat higher; 60 inches (1.52 m) from stringer to bottom.

Once the settling prospects appear promising, the shell strings are loaded onto a scow with the aid of the loader. As good settling may last for only a short time, it is necessary to sail the collectors out as quickly as possible. It is possible to transfer 6 000 shell strings to the racks in one tide by loading 500 strings on each of the nine scows and an additional 1 500 strings onto the big power scow[4]. This takes eight or nine men 4 h to load. At low tide, the racks are for the greater part exposed, but at high tide they are covered by 3—4 feet of water.

Of the 50 000 shell strings made by Mr Wiegardt, he sails out 30 000 to the racks in Willapa Bay, which can be done in five tides, and he reserves 20 000 strings for the rafts in Dabob Bay.

In September the racks are inspected to obtain an estimate of the quantity of spat collected during the summer. The shell strings are then left on the racks until the following April.

B.7. Collecting spat in Dabob Bay

There are two bays on the Pacific Coast of North America where settling is consistently better, both in respect of the number of spat per shell, and the frequency of years when settling reaches a commercial level. These are Dabob Bay (47° 50′ N, 122° 50′ W) * and Pendrell Sound (50° 15′ N, 124° 43′ W). Both these bays resemble each other in many respects. They are both quite long, rather narrow, quite deep and almost perfectly sheltered. High water temperatures and excellent larval retention are the factors which make these bays so conducive to the settling of Pacific oyster larvae. Hydrographic observations made in these bays show that the water is layered in the summer season with a warmer layer, up to 7 m deep, lying on top of colder water. The former layer carries oyster larvae. Strong northerly winds blowing lengthwise in the bays may, however, destroy this pattern and lead to failure in settling. Fortunately, this does not happen very often during the settling season and thus most years' spatfall is good or even excellent here. From the observations made, it is not very clear just why the water temperature regularly rises above the 20°C level here, and not in the upper parts of other bays with the same tidal range. If it were due to heat from solar radiation, reaching the water either directly, or indirectly via tidal flats heated at low tide, this marked difference to the other bays could hardly be understood. It is possible that the answer lies in conditions similar to those obtaining in the Norwegian polls, where a thin layer of fresh water on top acts similarly to the glass of a green-house, preventing nightly back radiation, leading, in early summer, to the rapid warming up of the saline layers beneath. The fact that fresh water from melting ice debouches into both bays (for example, from the Dosewallips River into Dabob Bay) may be a factor to be taken into account.

However, for the oystermen, there is no need to explain the very special hydrographic conditions prevailing in both Dabob Bay and Pendrell Sound when no strong winds disturb the layering; for them, it is sufficient to know that these are the only areas where consistently good results can be expected from spat collecting operations. Thus, they do not hesitate to take their collectors there, even from a considerable distance away. Mr Wiegardt operates

---

* See chart in chapter dealing with farming of the Olympia oyster, *Ostrea lurida*, in the volume (III) dealing with farming flat oysters.

in Dabob Bay, whereas several of his colleagues take their collectors to as far away as Pendrell Sound.

The some 20 000 shell strings, destined for Dabob Bay, are taken there by a truck which can carry 2 000 strings at a time. For operations in Dabob Bay Mr Wiegardt works with a Japanese partner, Mr Jerry Yamashita, the raft owner, who also assists with the hanging out and collection of the shell strings. For his services, Mr Yamashita keeps one third of the strings, and in the future his proportion may be raised to a half.

The rafts[5] are moored in 30 feet of water, fairly close to the shore at a well-sheltered site some distance away from the head of Dabob Bay. About 20 shell strings are hung from each of the round poles put across the raft, some 18 inches apart from each other. Here the strings are not slung over the poles, but their whole length (2 m) is hung vertically from an extra piece of wire attached to the pole. Mr Yamashita operates with some 150 rafts in Dabob Bay.

The shells with spat are kept in Dabob Bay until the next spring. If it can be arranged that new shell strings can be brought to Dabob Bay by the same truck which takes the shells with spat from the previous summer back, there

Fig. 84. Spat of the Japanese oyster born in 1947 and imported in the spring of 1948 looked like this in October 1948. The hole in the original collector shell shows up in the centre. Declustering with an iron tool was then a necessity if one wished to produce fair-shaped oysters. (Photo P. Korringa.)

is a saving on transportation expenses. For this, however, it is necessary to store the new shell strings temporarily ashore.

B.8. Transferring the spat to the parks

Taking shell strings off the racks in Willapa Bay takes about the same amount of time and labour as sailing them out. On board the scow, the wire is cut and the shells with spat are shaken loose. The shells are scattered over parks 4 and 8 using a shovel. This work is done in April and May. On these parks the spat will grow well, but in due course, about 22 months after planting, the oysters have to be taken to deeper water for fattening.

As a rule, several young oysters will have settled on every shell. This leads to the formation of clusters of oysters, as the original shell is often not brittle enough to fall apart. If there are five to ten oysters per shell, this clustering does not adversely affect their final shape and size, but where there are more than ten, it is preferable to decluster them in the course of the farming process. Formerly, the farmer visited the beds at low tide to break the old shells carrying the half-grown oysters using a tire iron or similar tool, although this inevitably led to some losses. Nowadays, however, this procedure is considered to be too costly and harrowing is used as a substitute for declustering by hand.

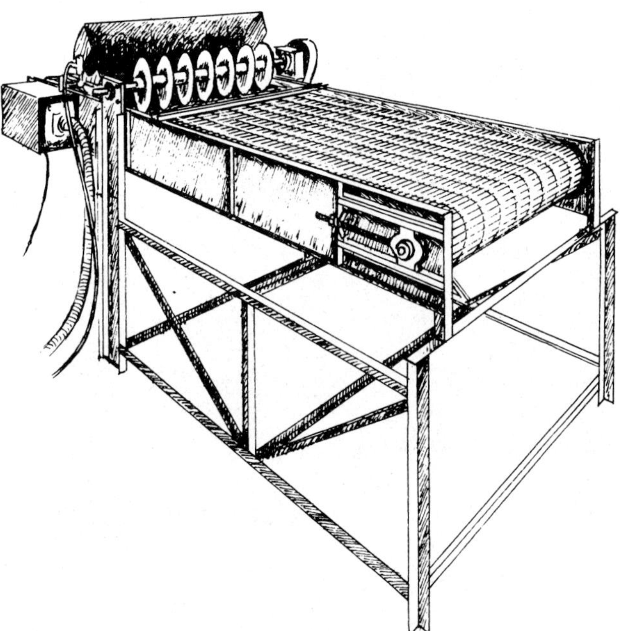

Fig. 85. Gang saw to cut oyster shells with a great number of spat. The lid has been lifted up to show the saw blades.

The shells hung from the rafts in Dabob Bay usually carry a far greater number of spat than those hung from rafts in Willapa Bay. Thus these shells cannot immediately be planted, they have first to be cut into pieces. This procedure is imperative when 30 or more young oysters are counted on each shell. Mr Wiegardt uses a gang saw mounted over a conveyor belt (Fig. 85) for cutting shells carrying a large number of spat. The saw blades, nine of them in series, are made of the same type of carborundum blades as those stone cutters use. Experiments with more expensive diamond blades showed them to be less satisfactory. The oyster shells are passed through this apparatus, cutting them into 2.5-inch pieces, under a constant spray of sea water. In 8 h 2 000 strings can be handled.

Mr Wiegardt found that nine strings of shells from Dabob Bay produce about the same number of young oysters as is contained in one case of Japanese seed. The broken shells from Dabob Bay are planted either on park 1 or park 6, by being scattered from a scow with a shovel. As soon afterwards as possible, two men go there at low tide to spread the material somewhat better, just as is done with the spat imported from Japan. At low tide, one man can spread the shell fragments planted over about 1.5 acres, i.e. the material contained in 100 to 150 cases of Japanese spat or material from 900 to 1 400 Dabob Bay strings planted on the same area. Somewhat less is planted when use is made of park no. 6. Mr Wiegardt frequently inspects his parks containing the young oysters using his speedboat [6]. Since suitable low tides occur between 9 and 10 o'clock in the evening, he takes along a flashlight and a Coleman lantern for the purpose.

B.9. Transferring the oysters to the fattening grounds

After a sojourn of about 22 months the oysters should be transferred to deeper grounds for fattening, in other words, to the deeper parts of parks 1 and 2. For this, special 25-bushel tubs[7], which are first spread over the park at high tide, are used. At the following low tide, a crew of 13 men walk out onto the park to pick up the oysters by hand. They wear heavy rubber gloves and collect the oysters in metal baskets, the contents of which are dumped into the larger tubs previously distributed over the park. When the tide comes in again, the workers leave the park and some time later the big power scow[4] hoists the tubs on board. As the tubs are each equipped with a plastic float on a strong 1-inch line made of synthetic fibre, they are easily found at high tide and the winch can be used to lift the filled tubs, each weighing 1 ton. The boom carrying the tubs is swung inboard, a line hooked onto a ring on the underside of the tub being used to dump its cargo onto the deck. It takes three men on board the power scow about 1.5 h to pick up 60 tubs and dump their contents on the deck. The oysters are then taken to the fattening parks to be planted. If the oysters have been hand-picked into the tubs and then transferred to the deck of the power scow, they are washed

Fig. 86. Some oyster farmers use this sort of harrow for maintenance of their oysters on the parks. (Photo P. Korringa.)

off with the aid of a powerful water jet. If the oysters are hand-picked onto a standard non-motorized 10 × 10 foot scow, they are shoveled off onto the fattening beds by hand.

The Wiegardt company usually hand-picks the oysters into the round tubs. It may happen, however, that the crew is either busy transplanting oysters elsewhere, or that the low tides are poor; in this case a dredge is used to harvest the oysters.

B.10. Harvesting marketable oysters

Exactly the same procedure as described earlier is used for harvesting the oysters from the fattening beds. This operation begins in October and can continue for several months. Fattening takes one summer season. After the turn of the year, when the oysters are in a dormant stage, usually a gradual decline of the meat yield is observed. Moreover, the weather may begin to worsen. It is therefore advisable to harvest most of the oysters before the end of December. Autumn is the best time of the year for a good meat yield.

Hand-picking oysters and dumping them into the large cylindrical tubs is a rather laborious job, and therefore quite expensive (US $ 0.30 per bush-

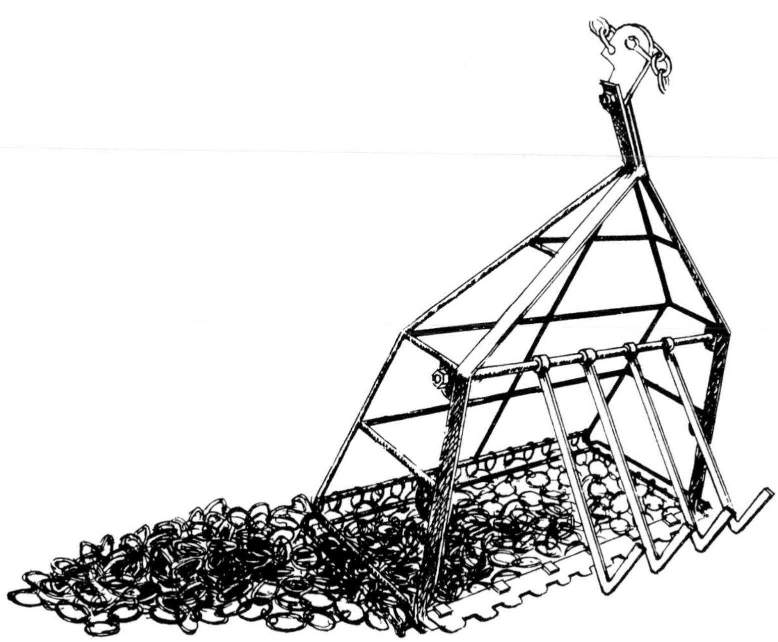

Fig. 87. The 250-pound dredge with articulated iron hooks used on Mr Wiegardt's boat.

Fig. 88. Oyster biologist Clyde Sayce shows the 350-pound oyster dredge of the rigid type in use in Willapa Bay. (Photo P. Korringa.)

el). Dredging is much cheaper (US $0.10 per bushel) but only possible on grounds which are so stable that the dredge does not remove the topsoil, which would otherwise transform the park into shifting sand on which no oysters can be grown. If it is possible to dredge, two dredges, preferably with metal frames, are used simultaneously.. Under excellent conditions 600 bushels of oysters can be dredged per h, in poorer weather this can be reduced to 400 bushels per h. There are two types of dredge in use in Willapa Bay: a 250-pound dredge with metal rings on the top and bottom, equipped with a series of articulated iron hooks for digging the oysters out of the soft bottom (Fig. 87), and a 350-pound dredge with an inclined row of teeth in front for digging the oysters out of the mud and a rectangular steel cage with walls of wire netting to receive the oysters, a door aft serving to dump them out (Fig. 88). Although the Wiegardt company prefers to hand-pick marketable oysters, they do make use of a 250-pound dredge when harvesting from the parks nos 2, 8, 9, and 10, rarely on parks 3 and 4, and never on parks 1, 5, 6 and 7.

B.11. Unloading the oysters

The ship loaded with marketable oysters harvested from the beds has to make a 6-mile run to the dock. Unloading takes place either at Mr Wiegardt's

Fig. 89. Hand-picking marketable oysters on one of Mr Wiegardt's parks. (Photo D. Tufts.)

Fig. 90. Lamps are placed on the park to allow continuation of harvesting after sunset. (Photo D. Tufts.)

own dock, facing his park no. 7, or at the Nahcotta port dock. The former dock can only be used when the tide is fairly high, the latter permanently, but here the farmer has to pay US $ 0.025 per bushel unloaded. The boat carrying the oysters on deck, surrounded with baffles, is unloaded with the aid of a powerful jet of water (Fig. 92) which drives the oysters onto the beginning of a conveyor belt that carries them up to an elevated holding bin. A truck is driven under this hopper to receive a load of oysters for transportation to the Wiegardt cannery, 1 mile away. This system can handle 800—1 200 bushels of oysters a day and, at the height of the season, is used for 5 or 6 days per week.

B.12. Processing the oysters

The oysters, already thoroughly washed during unloading by the powerful jet of water used, are, on arrival at the Wiegardt Bros, Inc. cannery, led through a steam compartment which steams them open without making use of overpressure. They are then led onto a shucking table where female workers pry the valves further open using a knife to take out the meat (Fig. 94). The meat is carefully washed making use of a blower, an apparatus in

Fig. 91. Willapa Bay barge with a load of oysters collected with tubs, showing booms and rigging of wires. (Photo P. Korringa.)

which the meat is agitated with air to remove any silt or sand particles, and then led onto a stainless steel washing table where it is thoroughly doused. From there it goes to the grading table where it is packed in 10-ounce and 8-ounce cans (Fig. 95). Good quality oysters total 120 to 150 to the gallon. The cans with the oyster meat are filled up with 5% brine, sealed and sterilized by cooking for 30 min at 115°C.

Steam-canned oysters form the most important product of the Wiegardt Bros cannery, consuming 50 000—70 000 gallons of oyster meat per year,

Fig. 92. The "Tidepoint", the motor scow of the Wiegardt Company, unloads oysters with a jet of water driving them to the conveyor belt at the dock of park 7. (Photo P. Korringa.)

Fig. 93. The Wiegardt Oyster cannery at Ocean Park. (Photo P. Korringa.)

Fig. 94. Shucking the steamed-open oysters in Mr Wiegardt's plant. (Photo P. Korringa.)

Fig. 95. Packing oyster meat in tins in Wiegardt's processing plant at Ocean Park. (Photo P. Korringa.)

predominantly from Mr Wiegardt's own parks: 60% in 1970—1971 up to 80% in 1971—1972. Another product of the company is oyster stew. For this, the oysters are opened raw with the aid of an oyster knife, sliced by a battery of revolving circular sharp-edged blades and pre-cooked in a little water. The liquid ("nectar") is drained off and rapidly cooled using a heat-exchanger. The cut-up oyster meat is then put in a can, which is filled with a mixture of milk and oyster nectar, some butter and salt, and a little mono-sodium glutamate and disodium phosphate added. After sealing the cans, the contents are heat sterilized.

B.13. Marketing the oysters

The end products of the Wiegardt Bros cannery find their way by truck and rail to the Middle West, particularly to Missouri, Oklahoma, Texas, Nebraska and Colorado. They are sold there in supermarkets and through wholesale outlets. The price paid for canned oysters is higher than that for low-grade meat. There is a kind of gentleman's agreement among the canners of Willapa Bay, giving every cannery a sort of monopoly to develop a market in a given district.

C. FARMING RISKS

C.1. Hydrographic and biological conditions

The effects of gales are feared in Willapa Bay with its limited amount of shelter. Sands may shift, smothering the oysters, and silt may locally be deposited on the oysters in dangerous quantities. Silt menaces oysters of all sizes. It is occasionally observed that growth and fattening are poor, although it is not usually clear which hydrographic or biological factor is to blame for this. The primary production and the total quantity of phytoplankton seem to be high enough in the area, but the possibility remains that there are fluctuations in the quality of the phytoplankton which could lead to differences in growth and fattening.

C.2. Predators

The starfishes, *Asterias forbesi* and *Pisaster ochraceus*, do occur in Willapa Bay but nowadays give little reason for concern. Formerly *Pisaster* was much more numerous on the local oyster beds. It is thought that intensive dredging may have brought down its numbers. The crab *Cancer magister* is found here, but does little damage on the oyster beds. The Japanese drill *Tritonalia japonica*, introduced with Japanese stock, occurs locally, for example, on Mr Wiegardt's no. 6 park. However, as it has no pelagic larvae it cannot reach the oyster spat on the shell strings hung from the racks and larger oysters do not have to fear much from this predator.

Pseudostylochus ostreophagus, a flatworm introduced from Japan, can destroy oyster spat, but does not attack older oysters. So far, Mr Wiegardt has not observed serious damage by this predator.

As in all oyster areas, the larvae have to fear a multitude of predators during their pelagic life. In Willapa Bay it is probably the large schools of anchovies which filter the water almost continuously, which are responsible for the destruction of countless oyster larvae.

C.3. Diseases and parasites

Though in recent years no losses due to unknown causes have been suffered, diseases included, the oyster farmers of Willapa Bay, like their colleagues elsewhere in the world, live in constant fear of a sudden mass mortality among their oysters.

C.4. Competitors

The most serious competitors are the mud shrimp *Upogebia pugettensis* and the ghost shrimp *Callianassa californiensis*. These are a serious menace, digging burrows in the ground and smothering the oysters. On many grounds it would have been impossible to grow oysters because of the presence of countless burrowing shrimps, if steps had not been taken to overcome them. In Willapa Bay dikes in which sheets of lumber or plastic are installed at a depth to make the area uninhabitable for burrowing shrimps have not been constructed, as the size of the parks makes this economically impossible. There is, however, a good method of chemical control for fighting these shrimps. This is the product sold under the trade name of "Sevin", a non-persistent carbamate methylnaphthol. It is not officially certified for use and should never be used on grounds stocked with marketable oysters. It is, however, permitted to "experiment" with "Sevin" on barren grounds to make them suitable for oyster farming and also to some extent on grounds carrying only juvenile oysters. The product is mixed with a wettable powder and sprayed as a liquid from a helicopter, at low tide while the bed is exposed. An application requires 10 pounds of the 10% dispersible powder per acre. This kills 100% of the mud shrimps and keeps the grounds free of this serious oyster pest for a long time.

Another competitor is "the cup", *Crepidula fornicata*, originally introduced along with American Atlantic oysters. It competes for space and food with the oysters, but is not a major pest in Willapa Bay, as it cannot thrive where it does not find sufficient solid objects to settle on.

D. ECONOMIC ASPECTS OF OYSTER FARMING

D.1. Rents

Mr Wiegardt owns most of the grounds he uses. There is a system of valuation per acre in the State of Washington, according to the use made of the ground, on the basis of which taxes are levied: for instance, US $300 per acre for first class ground and US $10 per acre for fourth class ground. The tax basis is then 50% of the valuation and the tax levied 30‰, which comes, for instance, for a valuation of US $300 per acre to US $4.50 tax per acre. Most of Mr Wiegardt's grounds are second class tide lands. In addition to the taxes on his own grounds, Mr Wiegardt's company has to pay rent for the leased grounds, for example, US $2 000 for park 3, or US $0.05 for every bushel of oysters planted there if this surpasses US $2 000. For the 12 acres of deeper water in use in Dabob Bay US $150 has to be paid per year.

D.2. Inventory items

The company fleet of Wiegardt and Sons Inc. forms the most expensive items on their inventory. First the power scow "Tidepoint", equipped with two four-cylinder diesel engines of 120 h.p. each, serving the twin screws, and a single-cylinder diesel auxiliary of 27 h.p. for running the winches for the dredges and the booms. This boat was built in 1956 for US $32 000, but would now presumably cost about US $80 000. The boat has a life span of at least 50 years and the engines of, at the most, 20 years. The two dredges have a life span of 4—5 years and the dredge cables of 1 year only. The maintenance costs amount to about US $5 000 per year. It is intensively used, about 8 h per day, for up to 280 days per year. It uses 50 gallons of diesel oil per day now costing US $0.18 per gallon. In the period 1956—1971 it used a total of 65 000 gallons of diesel oil.

The second ship is the tow-boat, a converted Columbia River gill-netter, equipped with an eight-cylinder "Royal" Chrysler marine engine of 140 h.p. The boat itself should have a long life span, the engine a life of 4—5 years. The boat was purchased for US $3 000 in 1955, while a navy surplus engine to replace the original engine was purchased for US $875.

Mr Wiegardt's company makes use of nine non-powered flat scows. They have a life span, when properly maintained, of over 50 years. Twice a year they require a coat of copper paint. Each treatment requires 1.5—2 gallons of paint per scow. The paint costs US $14.50 per gallon. 40 years ago a scow could be bought for US $100, whereas in 1953 Mr Wiegardt paid US $1 450 for a scow. Today one would cost US $3 000, assuming the proper vertical-grained wood could be found.

The last vessel in the fleet is the fibreglass speedboat Mr Wiegardt uses to inspect his parks. It is equipped with an 150 h.p. gasoline engine and was purchased for US $4 300 4 years ago. The engine requires overhauling every year.

For use for various transport purposes on the peninsula there are four 2-ton trucks with a life span of 4—5 years. The most recent of these was purchased second-hand for US $2 700.

For carrying shell strings and other equipment, use is made of a "loader" with pneumatic tires, purchased second-hand for US $1 500. This vehicle should also have a long life span.

Among the smaller equipment are the stringing machine and the strapping machine, both used for making shell strings.

Other inventory items are the steel tubs for collecting oysters on the parks. Mr Wiegardt has 73 such tubs, which cost US $100 each, and 20 steel baskets, costing US $7 each, used for collecting oysters in the field.

The dock at the end of the causeway opposite park 7 with its hopper and conveyor belt also belongs to the list of inventory items.

As this section deals with oyster farming only, the cannery inventory items need not be listed.

D.3. Expendable items

If new racks for hanging out shell strings have to be constructed, the racks having a life span of 10 years, US $200 per 1 000 board feet has to be paid for creosoted lumber. For putting out 10 000 strings, US $2 300 is needed for wood when the racks are built according to the new system described above. For the old system, in which the strings are hung closer together, considerably less outlay is required.

The shells for the strings come from the Wiegardt Bros Co., but as they could be sold for US $0.10 per bushel and since 1.25 bushels are required per string, the shells used for 50 000 strings should be evaluated as costing US $6 250.

For every string a 2-m length of 12 gauge galvanized wire, costing US $0.06 is needed. For 50 000 strings this amounts to US $3 000 per year. Saw blades for cutting the Dabob Bay shells have a short life span. Two sets, i.e. 18 blades, per day, are required costing US $4 per blade.

For boat maintenance copper paint costing US $14.50 per gallon is required. A scow requires two coats a year, at 1.5—2 gallons per coat. The company has nine scows plus two motorized wooden ships.

For treating shrimp-ridden ground with "Sevin", US $7 per acre is required for the "Sevin" itself and spraying it by helicopter costs US $70 per acre. The power scow uses 50 gallons of diesel oil per day, at US $0.18 per gallon, and is used up to 280 days per year. The motor boat, the speedboat and the trucks also consume a certain quantity of fuel.

For transport beyond the peninsula, the company makes use of professional carriers. This is always cheaper as these companies can usually arrange a return freight. The transport of cases of Japanese spat from the ship (docked at Olympia or Raymond) to the company headquarters usually costs US $0.50 per case. To take a load of 2 000 shell strings to Dabob Bay costs about US $170.

D.4. Purchase of stock

In 1970 cases of Japanese spat each cost, freight and charges included, US $20, whereas in 1971 they cost US $25. Mr Wiegardt has often purchased 3 000 to 4 000 cases per year. To this should be added the costs of two trips a year to Japan, amounting to about US $2 500 per year. However, as Mr Wiegardt also buys for five colleagues, these costs are shared.

Shell strings with spat from Willapa Bay cost the company about US $0.50 each. Those from Dabob Bay cost US $0.80 each. The latter carry more spat, but as the partner keeps between a third and a half of the quantity originally hung out, the costs for material and transportation are higher. Mr Wiegardt does not buy or sell garnished shell strings, but knows that the prices for Dabob shell strings with spat would be US $1.75 f.o.b.

Wiegardt Brothers work predominantly with marketable oysters produced by Wiegardt and Sons, but need to buy supplementary quantities to the extent of from 20 to 40% of their total output. The "bushler's call", for parks A and B, which obliges Mr Wiegardt to pay US $0.56 per bushel of oysters on the ground also has to be taken into account.

D.5. Personnel

The oyster farm works with an average staff of 12, varying between eight and 14 depending on the season. The company annually produces about half a million oysters per worker, which is considerably more than European farmers working with flat oysters. However, there are a few points that should be taken into consideration: the Pacific oysters are marketed from Willapa Bay 3.5 years after settling as spat; only part of the spat is produced in Willapa Bay itself, the remainder being imported from Japan or obtained from shell strings hung out in Dabob Bay, and the oysters do not need to receive the individual treatment required by flat oysters. In fact, they are only once transferred to deeper beds, and without culling, during their sojourn in Willapa Bay.

Most of the operations are carried out as piece-work. For instance, Mr Wiegardt pays US $0.224 for making a shell string for which he has supplied the shells and wire and the use of a stringing and strapping machine. Some 50 000 strings are produced per year and one hand can make up to 100 strings per day using a stringing machine. For fishing oysters with the dredge Mr Wiegardt pays US $0.10 per bushel, and for hand-picking oysters US $0.30 per bushel. Other types of worker are often paid by the hour. A good worker can make US $9 700 gross per year, to which 17% should be added for social security contributions. Three men are required to man the power scow, one in the wheel-house and two on deck. In the Wiegardt Brother's cannery there is a staff of 40, predominantly female, hands.

D.6. Sales

From the parks of Wiegardt and Sons 50 000—70 000 gallons of oyster meat are harvested per year. It is usual to measure the gallons of oyster meat after opening the oyster (gallon of meat bulk) but prior to processing. If the company sells oysters for canning, the buyer has to pay US $3.25 per gallon meat yield for oysters in the shell f.o.b. the plant. If oysters are purchased after shucking, but prior to processing, they cost US $6.00 per gallon for canning oysters, and US $4.40 for stewing oysters. If steamed oysters are sold in 10-ounce tins the actual price is US $7.50 per 12 tins, transportation costs included. This is the price the producer receives, with a 1.5% reduction for cash payment. The supermarket prices of canned oysters in the Midwest are US $0.95 for a 10-ounce can and US $0.75 for an 8-ounce can.

E. GOVERNMENTAL ASSISTANCE

The oyster growers of Willapa Bay are assisted by the scientists and technicians of the State of Washington. The scientists are in Japan at the time of packing the cases with seed in order to inspect them for the presence of unwanted pests, and do not hesitate to refuse consignments which fail to meet the requirements. They also carry out routine observations of the hydrographic and biological conditions in Willapa Bay, which includes intensive work on the appearance and development of the oyster larvae, on the basis of which they issue weekly forecasts on the intensity of settling. The laboratory at Nahcotta carries out an extensive programme on the control of oyster pests and diseases. They check their findings and forecasts by practical experimentation in the field and give a great deal of valuable advice to the oyster farmers, both verbally and in a processed or printed form. They also discuss new techniques with the oystermen and are always ready to try these out experimentally.

F. GENERAL IMPRESSION

Nearly every conceivable mistake has been made in the Willapa Bay oyster district. When people were willing to pay US $20 for a plate of oysters in San Francisco during the gold-rush days, Shoalwater Bay, as it was then called, was the scene of unprecedented prosperity for the local oystermen. No at-

Fig. 96. For many years in succession, Dr Trevor Kincaid carried out research on oyster biology and oyster farming in Willapa Bay. Here he is shown on a barge carrying the type of collecting tubs then in use, at the age of 76 years. (Photo P. Korringa, October 1948.)

tempts were made to prevent over-exploitation of the natural beds of the native oyster, *Ostrea lurida*, and no efforts were made to switch over from oyster fishing to oyster farming. This led to the complete destruction of this natural resource, of which only very scanty remains can now be found. When attempts were made to revive the oyster industry by introducing the American Atlantic oyster, *Crassostrea virginica*, it was soon discovered that this species did not reproduce in these cool waters and the venture met with disastrous mortalities. What unfortunately remained were imported pests such as "the cup", *Crepidula fornicata*, and the eastern drill, *Urosalpinx cinerea.*

The next stage, importation of Japanese stock, was at first carried out without the vitally necessary scientific supervision, with the result that pests such as the Japanese drill *Tritonalia japonica*, the devastating flatworm *Pseudostylochus ostreophagus*, and the parasitic copepod *Mytilicola orientalis*, were introduced. In more recent years, however, intensive inspection on the packing site has been organised to prevent recurrence of such disasters.

Despite all these past mistakes, the Willapa Bay oyster industry is now thriving. Although the Pacific oyster, *Crassostrea gigas*, requires higher water temperatures in summer than Willapa Bay can offer for a regular settling of commercial size, the oyster farmers have learned to get round the problem of inconsistent spatfall by introducing spat from Japan and by hanging collectors in Dabob Bay and Pendrell Sound, where settling is much better.

The Pacific oyster is not a luxury item to be served on the half shell, but rather a nutritious raw material well suited for processing and then using as the basic material for a variety of dishes. It is particularly popular in the Mid-west of the United States where fresh molluscan shellfish are never seen.

The canneries surrounding the bay appear to flourish and experience no difficulties in selling their products. The demand is often greater than the supply. The spat comes from three different sources, so the parks are never empty; nevertheless, it is not possible to substantially increase production in Willapa Bay because the availability of suitable oyster ground is a serious bottle-neck.

G. TECHNICAL DETAILS

G.1. The scow

Scows are sturdy rectangular flat-decked boats, measuring 30 × 10 feet, rounded off at stern and stem. They are made of 2-inch Douglas fir (*Pseudotsuga taxifolia*), preferably vertically grained wood. The scows are equipped with gunwales. They should receive a coat of copper paint twice a year and are periodically submerged in sea water to prevent dry-rot.

G.2. The motor boat

The company motor boat is a converted Columbia River gill-netter, 30 feet long by 10 feet broad. She is made of 1-inch Port Orford cedar from the Oregon coast, a very durable wood. The motor boat is equipped with a 140 h.p. eight-cylinder "Royal" Chrysler marine engine. The motor boat is used to tug the scows.

G.3. Racks

Racks are used for hanging out the shell strings in Willapa Bay. The rack frames are constructed ashore, in which a "jig" is used to ensure a uniform size and shape. The rack frame consists of three vertical beams, 2 × 4 inch rough cut, 8 feet long, pointed at their lower extremity. They are kept 4 feet apart from each other by a 2 × 4 inch cross-beam, 6 inches below the top, a 2 × 4 inch mudsill, 3 feet above the lower extremity, and a 2 × 4 inch beam placed diagonally. Galvanized 3/8-inch carriage bolts, 5 inches long, are used to fasten the top cross-beam. The prefabricated rack frames are transported to the spatfall site and pushed into the soft bottom until the mudsill touches it. Then the five 2 × 4 inch stringers are nailed to the top cross-bars, making use of galvanized nails. The stringers are 16 feet long, serving two "bints" (spaces between two rack frames).

The new-style rack frames differ in so far that 10-foot pieces are used instead of 8-foot beams and four instead of five stringers are nailed onto the top beams. This keeps the shell strings further from the bottom, and since 12 instead of 15 are put on each section of four instead of five stringers, the shell strings are less densely hung from the racks, ensuring better water circulation and thereby promising a greater number of spat per shell.

G.4. The power scow

The power scow is 56 feet in length and 18 feet broad. It is a sturdy rectangular flat-decked wooden boat with a wheel-house in front. It is equipped with two four-cylinder diesel engines of 120 h.p. each to serve the twin pro-

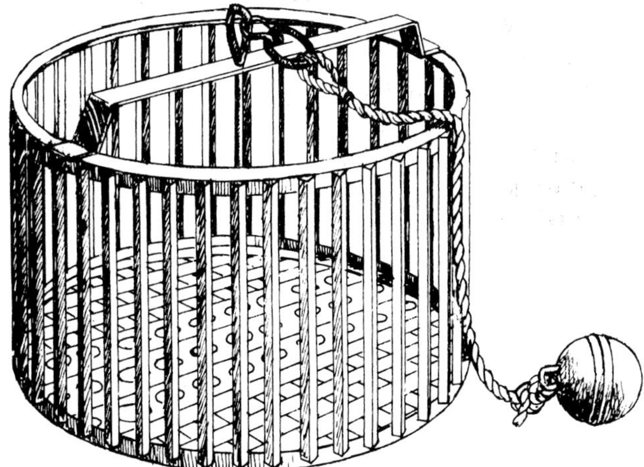

Fig. 97. These metal tubs for collecting hand-picked oysters can contain 25 bushels. The float makes it possible to locate and pick up the tub at high tide.

pulsion screws, and a 27 h.p. diesel engine for the winches to operate the dredges, the booms, and the pump for planting and unloading the oysters.

G.5. Rafts

Rafts are used for hanging out shell strings in Dabob Bay. The rafts used in Dabob Bay measure 30 × 12 feet and float on "styrofoam" (polyurethane), obtainable in blocks 16 × 10 inches in cross section and 9 feet long. 2 × 12 inch lumber planks are fastened on top of the rectangular frame to serve as a catwalk and also on the underside of the frame, fastened to the top one with bolts. Across the raft a series of round poles, about 3 inches in diameter, are nailed to the top planking 18 inches apart from each other. The shell strings are hung from these round poles.

Dead-weights fore and aft, attached to a polypropylene rope, serve as anchors.

G.6. The speedboat

Mr Wiegardt uses a speedboat for inspecting his parks which is made of fibre-glass, measures 18 feet in length and is equipped with an 150 h.p. gasoline engine.

G.7. Tubs for collecting hand-picked oysters (Fig. 97)

The cylindrical tubs for collecting hand-picked oysters (Fig. 97) can contain 25 bushels of oysters. They are 4 feet in diameter and 32 inches high. They are made of 1-inch steel angle-iron strips with the top circular rim of 1 1/4-inch angle iron and the bottom of 1/8 × 3 inch flat iron strips. They are sand-blasted after construction and then galvanized. They require regalvanizing every 5 years. On the cross-bar at the top there is a ring to which is attached a 1-inch propylene rope carrying a 10-inch plastic trawler float at its end. This facilitates the picking-up of the filled tubs at high tide by simply lassoing a thin chain around the float and hoisting up the tubs with a boom and winch. A ring on the underside serves to empty the tubs onto the deck by hooking a line from the winch to the ring.

H. BIBLIOGRAPHY

Galtsoff, P.S., 1929. Oyster industry of the Pacific Coast of the United States. Doc. 1066, Append. VIII Rep. U.S. Comm. Fish. 1929, pp. 367–400.

Imai, T. and Sakai, S., 1961. Study of breeding of Japanese oyster, *Crassostrea gigas*. Tohoku J. Agric. Res., 12 (2): 125–171.

Kincaid, T., 1951. The Oyster Industry of Willapa Bay, Washington. Calliostoma Company, Seattle, Wash., printed by The Tribune, Ilwaco, Wash., 45 pp.

McKee, L.G. and Nelson, R.W., 1960. Culture, Handling and Processing of Pacific Coast Oysters. Fish. Leafl. 498, U.S. Dep. Inter. Bur. Commer. Fish., Washington, D.C., 21 pp.

Quayle, D.B., 1969. Pacific Oyster Culture in British Columbia. Bull. Fish. Res. Board Can., 169, 192 pp.

Sayce, C.S. and Larson, C.C., 1966. Willapa oyster studies. Use of the pasture harrow for the cultivation of oysters. Commer. Fish. Rev., 28 (10): 21—26.

Westley, R.E., 1956. Retention of Pacific oyster larvae in an inlet with stratified waters. Fish. Res. Pap. Wash. State Dep. Fish., I (4): 1—7.

Westley, R.E., 1968. Relation of hydrography and *Crassostrea gigas* settling in Dabob Bay, Washington. 1967 Proc. Nat. Shellfish. Assoc., 58: 42—45.

INDEX